Let It Simmer

Making Project, Portfolio and Program
Management Practices Stick
in a Skeptical Organization

Douglas M. Brown

Published by Caltrop Press
Alexandria, Virginia

Copyright © 2015, Douglas M. Brown. All rights reserved.

First Edition

ISBN: 978-1522797531

The name and product, **The Simmer System**[SM] is owned by the author. At the time of publication, it is undergoing registration with the U.S. Patent and Trademark Office.

This book contains material protected under International and Federal Copyright Laws and Treaties. Any unauthorized reprint or use of this material is prohibited.

No part of this book may be reproduced or transmitted in any form or by any means, electronic or mechanical, including photocopying, recording, scanning or by any information storage and retrieval system without express written permission from the author.

Published by
Caltrop Press
Alexandria, Virginia
www.Simmer-System.com

Editor:
Mary Jo Stresky
The Write MoJo Literary and Research Services
www.thewritemojo.com
thewritemojo@gmail.com

Cover Designer:
Joni McPherson
McPherson Graphics
http://mcphersongraphics.com
joni@mcphersongraphics.com

What People Are Saying About Douglas Brown and The Simmer System...

"Doug's the Chef! This book is full of proven recipes for management success. Management excellence is more than a set of executed processes and procedures – it's the delivery of mission and corporate results. To those who read and apply the truths of Let It Simmer, a finer plate of management successes will be had by none."
Emory Miller, former U.S. federal government executive and industry vice president

"I was drawn into the book from the outset. It puts into plain language many things that I too have seen in several companies while teaching my staff how to manage effectively. Trying to force-fit full-scale best practices is a recipe for disaster. Let It Simmer provides the opposite recipe: how to change the culture and build the skills in a way that may seem gradual but achieves results and permanent effects."
Lynn Padgett, Vice President, Medical Education Association

"I loved this book. Everything made so much sense and was easy to implement within existing programmes in incremental steps that will deliver real value while allowing work to go on and deadlines to be met. I'd like my boss – and their bosses too! – to read this as it would make my life so much easier and my programs so much more successful."
Dade Bridgeman, Group Programme Manager, British Telecom

"How do you get started managing a project? You can't just turn it on and expect it to get under control! Let it Simmer is really helpful to guide you through ramping up the management of the projects, particularly where there is some resistance (like when will there be no resistance?). The principles – and as important – the tone, will apply whether the environment is private sector or government projects."
Jim Walsh, former Enterprise Architect, Rural Development Agency, U.S. Department of Agriculture

Contents

Acknowledgements

Overview 1

Why Let It Simmer is Different from Other Books 1
What You'll Learn 3
Who Needs This Book? 5
What The Simmer System Is and Isn't 6
How Can You Be Sure This System Will Work?........................... 6

Chapter 1: Why Are You Here? 9

Why Another Book on Project, Portfolio and Program 11
   Management?
What's Different About The Simmer System? 12
   And Why Should You Trust It?
What Exactly Will The Simmer System Accomplish 13
   for You?
Don't Forget Who Does the Real Work 14
It's Not All That Easy 15
Why Not Best Practices? 16
Right Medicine, Wrong Treatment 20
Welcome to The Simmer System! 22
   Simmering for Success 23
   What "Ingredients" Are in The Simmer System? 24
Next Steps 25
Exercise 1: Envisioning the Future PPFMO 27

Chapter 2: How the Simmer System 29
Bubbled Up From Real Life

Case Study 1: Unexpected Success 30
Case Study 2: Violent Insurgency 32
   Setting Up the Struggle 32
   Damage Control 33
   The Path Upward 35
   Stability for the Long-Term 36

Case Study 3: Building From the Grassroots 37
    Setting Up the Struggle 37
    Damage Control 38
    The Path Upward 39
    Stability for the Long-Term 39
Finding and Using The Simmer System 42
Building Theory with Experience................................44
Case Study 4: Waking Rip Van Winkle.........................45
What's in it for You? 46
Next Steps 48
Exercise 2: Setting the Feel-O-Meter 49

Chapter 3: There Be Dragons Here 51
(How to Deal with Seven Common Monsters
That Can Swallow Your Initiative)

Change is Always Hard 53
Seven Causes of Failure 54
Taming the Dragons: More Case Studies 59
Case Study 5: Killing Your Own Initiative With Kindness 59
    Symptoms and Causes 59
    Solution and Cause Overcome 60
    Outcome 61
Case Study 4 Revisited: Benign Neglect 62
    Symptoms and Causes 62
    Solution and Cause Overcome 63
    Outcome 64
Taming the "Dragons" in Your World 65
Next Steps 67
Exercise 3: Assessing the Voyage 68

Chapter 4: The Four Core Bedrock Principles 69

Red Pill, Blue Pill? Just Give Us the Magic Pill! 71
Guiding Compromise 72
The Peril of a Restart 75

The Four Core PPFM Principles: 76

1. Integration: The Pasta Principle 76
    Bypass the Swamps – Take the Trail 77
    The "Pasta" in the Principle 78
    Any Noodle Will Do 79
    The Slippery Slope 81

   2. Zero-Sum 81
      Exactly What is Zero-Sum? 83
      An Alternative to Zero-Sum 84
      Don't Worry About Being a Big Zero 85
      Zero-Sum Doesn't Eliminate Managerial Flexibility 86
      Zero-Sum in Practice 88

   3. Integrity (and Compromise) 89
      Basic Integrity Issues 90
      We've Got Pictures 91
      Handling the Heat 92
      Make Sure It's Not About You 93
      Provide a Safety Valve 93
      Know Your Material 94
      Know What the Best Practices Are 95
      Agree With Enthusiasm 95

   4. Purposeful Humility 96
      Doing Jobs Nobody Wants to Do 96
      Assuming Tasks Program Managers Won't Do 97
      Limitations of Humility 98

When Does Compromise Become Surrender? 99
Next Steps 100
Exercise 4: Define Your Red Lines 101

Chapter 5: Top Cover - The Executive Support ... 103
You Need (But May Not Get)

What is "Top Cover"? 103
Why Top Cover is Needed 104
Socked In: No Top Cover Today 106
   Why Top Cover Could Be Missing 107
   What if You Don't Get the Cover? 109
The Sky's Clear 112
Confirm Your Support 112
The Battle Rages On 113
The Real Reasons for Resistance: Autonomy and Disbelief 114
Get a Charter 116
   Sample Charter 117
   Making the Charter Mean Something 118

Many Charters Are Better Than One	119
Project-Type Charter	119
PPFM Initiative Charter	120
Charter of the Governance Board	120
Program Charter	120
Sweeping Away Obstacles	121
Keeping Managers Accountable	123
Keeping the Troops Motivated	124
Next Steps	125
Exercise 5: Setting the Stage	126

Chapter 6: Ready, Set, Govern! 127

Setting Up the Board	127
Board Principles and Roles	127
A Key Sponsor Role: Assure Attendance	127
Make It Live and in Person	129
How Many Meetings?	131
How the Sausage Got Made	133
Setting Up a Program Structure	136
Determine the Language	136
Consider Capacity: Don't Bite Off What You Can't Chew	139
Respect the Existing Structure	140
Adopt a Business Lifecycle	142
General Frameworks for Project-Type Lifecycles	143
Tailoring for Risk and Complexity	147
Preparing and Supporting the Board	150
A Bolster for the Chair	150
PPFMO Support for the Governance Board	152
Board Training	154
What About Automation?	155
Accountability	156
Next Steps	159
Exercise 6: PPFMO Plan	160

Chapter 7: Seven Things You Need to Know 163
to Get the PPFMO Started

It's Your First Step, So Take it Easy	163
Things You Need to Know to Get Started	166
1. Organizational Chart, Missions and Functions	168
Why Do You Need It?	169
What Will You Do With It?	170
Why Wouldn't People Want to Provide It?	171
What if You Don't Get It?	172

2. Strategic Plans 173
   What Will You Do With It? 173
   Why Wouldn't People Want to Provide It? 174
   What if You Don't Get It? 175

3. Personnel Rosters and Skill Sets 175
   What Will You Do With It? 175
   Why Wouldn't People Want to Provide It? 176
   What if You Don't Get It? 176

4. Budgets 177
   What Will You Do With It? 178
   Why Wouldn't People Want to Provide It? 178
   What if You Don't Get It? 180

Next Steps 181
Exercise 7: Building Data Tables 182
   Organizational Table (Exercise A) 182
   Missions and Functions Table (Exercise B) 183
   Strategic Plan Assignment (Exercise C) 184
   Budget Allocation (Exercise D) 185
   Personnel Capacity (Exercise E) 186

Chapter 8: The Meaty Part of the Lists 187

Getting Down to Work 187
5. Contracts 188
   What Will You Do With It? 188
   Why Wouldn't People Want to Provide It? 189
   What if You Don't Get It? 191

6. Priorities 191
   What Will You Do With It? 192
   Why Wouldn't People Want to Provide It? 193
   What If You Don't Get It? 193

7. Projects and Activities 194
   What Will You Do With It? 194
   Why Wouldn't People Want to Provide It? 196
   What If You Don't Get It? 197

What to Do With the Lists 197
Next Steps 198
Exercise 8: Advanced Data Analysis 200

Chapter 9: See You in the Boardroom – Governance in Action 203

The List Phase 203
Get a Facilitator 204
Early Questions 205
Is it Really on the List? 205
Case Study 6: The Amazing Disappearing Priorities 206
Slicing the Pie: Allocating Funds 208
    How Should it Be Sliced? 208
    How Many Slices? 212
    How Big Does the Slice Need to Be? 213
    Making the Slices 213
Next Steps 216
Exercise 9: Decision Board Records 217

Chapter 10: Let's Make a Deal – Eight Collaborative Agreements 219

All Managers Become Project Managers 219
Stepping Outside the Cubicle 220
The Eight Collaborative Agreements 223
Dependencies First 223
    Agreement 1: How is the Work Broken Up? 223
    Agreement 2: When is the Next Handoff? 225
Don't Worry – You're Gonna Love It! 227
    Agreement 3: Launch Date 228
    Agreement 4: Watizzit? 231
The Balancing Act Begins 234
Getting it Together 234
    Agreement 5: The Resource Pool 235
    Agreement 6: Are We There Yet? Committing to Dates 238
    Agreement 7: Standards of Done 241
    Agreement 8: Stop Whining and Start Winning – Dealing with Issues 242
Make it Worth Doing 244
Next Steps and Summary 246
Exercise 10: Building the Baselines 248

Chapter 11: Waivers – Recognizing the Practical Limits of a Process 251

Aww, Do We Hafta? 251
Waivers That Work 253
The Principal's Office 253

Make Them Get a Signature 254
Total Transparency 255
Next Steps 256
Exercise 11: Build a Waiver Form and Process 257
    Request for Emergency Waiver [template] 257

Chapter 12: Taste Before Serving – Oversight 259

Sample Frequently 261
Calling the Pass: Reviews and Approvals 262
    Approvals 262
    Getting the Governance Board to the Front of the House 263
Milestones and Reviews 264
    Periodic Reviews 264
    Event-Based Reviews 266
    Point to Success Rather than Pointing Fingers 267
Some Meat With That Sauce? Meaningful Oversight............... 267
    High-Level Tracking 269
    Dependencies 271
Red is Good, But Orange is Better 273
Clearing Away the Clutter: Issues Management..................... 275
Seeing Red 276
Reporting Tools: Dashboards or Yellow Pads 277
Next Steps 279
Exercise 12: Measuring Your Progress 282

Conclusion 285
Resources 289
References 290

About the Author

Acknowledgements

The Simmer System[SM] wouldn't have been possible without the efforts of many people who contributed to it out of the goodness of their hearts.

First and foremost my wife, Lynn, who put up with a semi-absent ghostly figure hovering over the computer at all hours for months on end, typing and retyping multiple versions of the manuscript as I came to better understand the mechanics of planning and writing in the publishing industry. She had very good reasons to be wondering where this was all going. Okay honey, I'm done now... with this one anyway. Want to meet me in the kitchen over a plate of manicotti to hear about the next one?

A group of colleagues and friends were kind enough to review a pre-edit version of this book and provided extraordinarily detailed and useful suggestions. So great thanks to:

- Robert Hutchinson, former director of IT at the Logistics Management Institute, now partner at Nex-Lev Consulting in Reston, Virginia.

- Ricardo Lavalle, CEO, Stratexecutives, Rio de Janeiro.

- Emory Miller, former Federal Senior Executive in the General Services Administration, now currently a vice-president of government consulting companies.

- Jim Walsh, former Enterprise Architect in the U.S. Department of Agriculture.

- Dade Bridgeman-Williams, a senior program director at British Telecom (now BT).

Naturally the book is my responsibility. If it flows well and sounds good, credit my editor, Mary Jo Stresky. In any places where it doesn't, then that was probably because I chose to override her very sound advice.

The fact that you decided to acquire this book in the first place is a testament to Joni McPherson, who created a cover that would stand out in a crowded marketplace. Not only is she a wonderful illustrator, her creative suggestions sparked some of the themes in this and other books in the planning phases.

It would only be appropriate to acknowledge the contributions of some of the most insidious opponents of governance, because without them I wouldn't have learned as much as I did about why these best practices are important, and in some cases why they aren't. It would be great fun to name them, but I'm over that now. Really. My doctor said so.

Many of the ideas and activities that eventually became *The Simmer System* were contributed by my colleagues in the PMOs I've worked with over the past 20 years and from whom I learned a great deal. During the storming phases, I felt worse for them than myself since they often took the blunt force of the cultural resistance to introducing PPFMO practices.

There are far too many people on those teams to name each individually. But I'm sure everyone who worked on those projects would agree that all of us were uplifted during the darkest days by the skill, stamina, tenacity and integrity of these astounding people: Scott Pierson, Libby Scott and Brenda Kersh. On behalf of all of us, we salute you!

Over the years I've benefited from collegial advice and sounding boards from people like Joanie Newhart, Ken Lavoie, Richard Gordon, Jonathon Watts, Kent French, and Scott Fass. And some 20 of the Fellows of the Logistics Management Institute where I enjoyed a dozen professionally and personally rewarding years. I feel it's fair to single out a few of my closest colleagues such as Chris Werle, Sonny Oh, Locke Hassrick and the late Steve Stone.

I've probably gotten to this point in my career as a result of the "top cover" provided by my managers over the years: Steve Furman, Corey Booth, Mario Vizcarra, Ty Harmon and Randy Luten. I've always tried to be a supportive troop member. But I probably would have been even more appreciative if I'd have figured out just how much top cover I was getting, even when I couldn't see it.

I saved this acknowledgement for the last to single out a man who set an example for integrity, curiosity, client service and collegiality, as well as being a great guiding manager, a true mentor and a good friend: Paul Dienemann, the former Program Director at the Logistics Management Institute.

Overview

Why *Let it Simmer* is Different from Other Books

What makes this book on project, portfolio and program management ("governance" going forward) different from others on the market?

The Simmer System[SM] will show you how to shift the culture within your organization, even if just enough to make basic governance practices stick.

*Please note the system does **not reject best practices**. Quite the contrary, as it allows you to advance from having basically no practices to a point where actual best practices become possible.*

Many how-to books covering governance discuss planning and carrying out the best practices of those disciplines. Very few show how organizations got to that point, because they assume the values of accountability and efficiency have already been internalized. However, organizations typically don't begin that way.

I wrote **Let It Simmer** for people who've been asked to put governance practices in place in organizations that don't have them.

Or more likely, have already tried to do it but abandoned the effort. Not because the managers of those organizations were bad people, but because they were trying to do something that didn't make sense for that organization at that time.

The problem is many authors and standards-setting bodies assume an organization is fired up to make changes, and all that's needed is someone who knows what they're doing. The fact is if it were that easy, someone would have already done it.

Instituting best practices means you're talking about a major culture shift. It means incorporating processes far beyond anything the organization has done or has been willing to do.

So you have to start at the very beginning.

Learning is a progressive process. You don't get to decide where to start on the expertise curve. You start at the bottom, then move up by learning new techniques and overcoming increasingly complex challenges.

You either push past the obstacles, or stay where you are. But you can't start at the top or even in the middle. In other words, you don't start out with best practices – you aspire to get there.

When you first started learning to cook, you didn't begin with Veal Saltimbocca or Osso Buco (you'll notice an Italian theme throughout the book). You didn't make your own tortellini by thinly rolling out the dough to make the tiny pasta shells, then filling them with veal and pork you had ground together. You also didn't make gelato from cream and fruit in a hand-beaten churn.

Why not? Aren't these "best practices" in the cooking world? Yes, they are. Even so, dishes like those are challenges even for professional chefs. So it was wise that you began with the basics.

As a first-time learner, the all-or-nothing approach can lead to consistent failure. You would become so frustrated that for the rest of your life you'd be intimidated at the thought of microwaving a TV dinner.

In reality, you may well have begun your culinary lessons by opening a can of Chef Boyardee ravioli, your first "technological step" up from peanut butter and jelly sandwiches.

Then you moved from sandwiches and pre-cooked food to experimenting with actual recipes. With every step you gained expertise. Your PB&J sandwiches became *panini*, and you switched from using store-bought crusts for homemade pizza to making the crust yourself.

Dish after dish you got better and more adventurous. Today, perhaps you disdain pasta-making machines, and no longer buy sausage at the store. You make your own dough and sausages by hand, and are now in a league of serious chefs.

Whether or not you realize it, you are doing best practices

Advanced cooking is definitely complicated. But the food doesn't get up and walk away, talk back or fight back. People do. And wow, do they ever!

So if people are reluctant to dive into best practices when dealing with inanimate objects (such as pasta), why would it work when it comes to the more difficult problem of dealing with other people?

Once the organization gets the hang of this governance business and discovers it's not all that scary, you can start thinking about best practices. Then you can line your shelves with all those other books. Until then, *Let It Simmer* gives you a path to get to that point.

As I mentioned earlier, adopting governance practices isn't a simple transition – it's a culture shift. Until this new-fangled idea of yours goes mainstream in your organization, you're not going to have many allies.

For instance, if you're starting or restarting a project, portfolio or program management office, you might be in a situation where you're not sure how much money the organization has to work with.

Or how much the various managers have or what they're doing with it, as they might prefer you don't have access to that kind of information.

I can tell you from the initial reaction to this book that many fellow professionals are dealing with the same problem. Since they probably won't be in your workplace, the best place to find them is in online communities interested in governance (like the one at *The Simmer System* resource website – www.Simmer-System.com – where you'll have access to additional resources such as editable, reusable workbooks and templates).

What You'll Learn

The Simmer System provides small steps to collaborate with line managers to help them work together effectively without raising too many hackles. Change won't occur dramatically, but it will happen steadily. And that's the whole point behind the "simmer."

Within a few months you'll have...

- identified threats to the governance effort, and devised a risk management strategy (Chapter 3).

- established the core principles your governance initiative rests upon (Chapter 4).

- established a viable level of top-down support for the governance effort (Chapter 5).

- established a decision authority or governance board (Chapter 6).

- identified the most important work, and the human and financial resources available to get it done (Chapter 7).

- begun using the governance board to allocate resources to programs, and approve continuations of work through key milestones (Chapter 8).

- identified tiered priorities throughout the organization (Chapter 9).

- integrated resources, budgets, contracts, operations and projects into a coherent unified picture of how the prioritized work is getting done (Chapter 9).

- established cooperative coordination of the work being done with realistic launch schedules and capability expectations; and scheduling of the resources needed to get the work done as promised (Chapter 10).

- provided a safety valve process to obtain rapid approvals in emergencies (Chapter 11).

- conducted oversight of the ongoing work to ensure timely delivery of products, resolve obstacles promptly, and communicate effectively to affected stakeholders (Chapter 12).

The truth is, many "mature" organizations never get that far, so these won't be trivial accomplishments!

Because *The Simmer System* brings an organization along voluntarily, you'll have set workable practices in place, which is much better than publishing a best practice nobody follows. So now you can begin upgrading workable practices to best practices.

NOTE: Throughout the book I'll be referring to the disciplines that contribute to governance activities as **PPFM** - **P**roject, **P**rogram and **P**ort**f**olio **M**anagement.

The staff entity responsible for supporting these practices is called the **PPFM O**ffice (**PPFMO**), rather than the more commonly used "PMO," which is often used to mean any or all of the above.

More importantly, it may serve as a reminder that everything here is an integrated solution of all three disciplines.

Who Needs This Book?

You need this book if...

- you're an executive who thinks your organization could do things better, faster or less expensively, and you want to address that problem by bringing PPFM (governance) into the organization. Once *The Simmer System* seeps in, those results will follow.

- you're an executive or business line manager concerned that an initiative to impose governance is going to create unacceptable levels of disruption and paperwork. *The Simmer System* provides an alternate path.

- you're a project manager, portfolio manager or program manager who has the challenge of leading your organization's efforts to reinstitute governance. *The Simmer System* can help you successfully get through that challenge.

- you're a teacher or student of governance disciplines and management in general. *The Simmer System* shows you how many organizations operate before you have to work in one.

You probably don't need this book if...

- you're cramming for a certification test. Most tests are about the details of a certain set of best practices. This book endorses any and all best practices. It doesn't teach how to do best practices; it's about creating the conditions where they become possible.

- you're trying to learn the basics of formal PPFM. There are many books that summarize or repackage the basic practice standards for better instructional value. They're all similar since they all draw from the same sources.

    (*If your organization is expecting you to change the existing culture by the simple act of mandating these kinds of practices, it might be unintentional, but in fact they are tossing you to the wolves.*)

And you don't need it if you already work in a company committed to process excellence.

If you work for an organization that talks a good game about governance, or already has published the processes, but you know darn well they don't practice them – then *The Simmer System* is perhaps more for you than anyone else!

What *The Simmer System* Is and Isn't

There are basically two kinds of books currently available on the topic of governance: Serious textbooks, or short info-type eBooks containing hastily-Googled pages pilfered from the Internet. *Let It Simmer* certainly isn't the latter. It offers over 200 pages of serious (if occasionally facetious) discussion of practical, tricky issues.

I'm a professional governance manager, not a wannabe Internet marketer. Throughout the book you'll find many examples drawn from over 20 years of actual experience, including my sometimes quirky take on events. You'll also get a full-featured solution for dealing with a substantial problem.

Because the solution differs from what's in other books, *Let It Simmer* is definitely not a rehash of best practices or free white papers. While it's a serious book, it isn't a one-size-fits-all solution. It doesn't apply in organizations that already embrace the necessary mindset. (I will say a sizeable number of organizations claim to be doing robust governance when they aren't. Some have a policy nobody follows, while others are going through the motions without any comprehension, appropriate execution, or follow-through. This book applies to them.)

The Simmer System is a proven method of getting to a point where it becomes reasonable to think about taking on those best practices.

How Can You Be Sure This System Will Work?

The approaches described in *Let It Simmer* evolved after noticing similar patterns had occurred in three different organizations. After identifying the elements of this system, I was astonished at how often the starting situation and solution pattern repeated themselves in other organizations.

This book provides a solution framework of certain steps and advice on how to achieve them when it isn't immediately obvious. Sometimes part of the solution is already in place, whereas some aspects of the solution may not be relevant to the situation. The collaborative efforts I suggest include activities critical to bringing the organization forward.

Considering the framework has proven applicable in numerous situations, there's no reason why *The Simmer System* won't work if you use common sense. However, there's no guarantee in anything that involves human behavior and self-interest.

Results will vary based on the needs of your organization, its executives, your sponsors, staff (if any) and peer managers. And also your ability to build relationships, a critical skill for any governance manager, and even more so with the collaborative aspects of *The Simmer System*.

I'll admit I'm not the world's leading expert on relationship-building and organizational politics. So if these approaches have worked for me, they will certainly work for you.

Now, let's dive in and see what's simmering inside your "pot."

Douglas Brown

8 · DOUGLAS M. BROWN

Chapter One

Why Are You Here?

President Truman was nicknamed "Give 'Em Hell Harry." When asked why, he said, "I don't set out to give them hell. I just tell them the truth. They are the ones who think it is hell."

You go, Harry!

I like to begin any important activity with a constructive thought. You can call it a "happy path" thought if you like. Visualizing the intended outcome, and referring back to it regularly throughout the effort pretty much every day, keeps it top-of-mind as something I want to achieve. After all, if the end point isn't very appealing, why bother with the effort of trying to get there?

Take the next few moments to indulge yourself. Close your eyes and imagine your favorite place where you'd like to retire to when you've collected enough 'cheese' from the rat race.

Mine's easy: The Cane Garden Bay in the Virgin Islands where it never snows and it's not that hot. It's nice and quiet because there's no traffic.

Photo Credit: http://www.ambientreallife.com

The best way to get there is by sailboat, which allows me to be in my "home" on the sea when I want, and on land when I want. Talk about a win/win!

Aside from all the standard tropical bliss, it's a handy refuge to duck into and escape the squalls that regularly sweep down the channel. They're usually not dangerous. But who needs "not really dangerous" when you're paying a lot of money to relax?

(Is your favorite place coming into focus yet? Give this a minute or so to "simmer" just for fun!

After several days afloat on the boat, you can't do much better than a fresh water shower ashore. Then sitting comfortably on a covered patio listening to the steady rhythm of the rain while enjoying a leisurely Red Stripe and a sumptuous seafood chowder. *Aaahhh*, now that's what I call living!

Okay, back to reality. You've got another trip to take.

Unfortunately, telecommuting hasn't advanced to the point where you can do your work in many remote locations. So take another minute to imagine your work environment looking like your favorite place. Not in a physical way, of course. But in an *everything's fine* kind of way.

Picture this: How would your day be if everyone was cooperating and working towards common goals? What if key people were working on the most important tasks so they're not holding everyone up?

You'd probably get a lot more done with little or no extra effort. Support would swoop in from throughout the organization if something turned out to be trickier than it seemed. Frustrations of always having to deal with fixing things that weren't done right would be reduced. A proper work-life balance would be restored, and all would be well.

Gosh, isn't that about as close to nirvana as you can get in a work situation? Go ahead, take a few moments to embellish and enjoy the visualization.

But that's not where you are today. If that were the case, you wouldn't be reading this book about how to change it.

So try not to dwell on the present, because tomorrow it will be in the past. As you continue reading, take a minute every day to think about where you want to be tomorrow.

Why Another Book on Project, Portfolio and Program Management?

"The manager who comes up with the right solution to the wrong problem is more dangerous than the manager who comes up with the wrong solution to the right problem."
~Peter Drucker

If you skipped over the Overview, you missed out on the summary answer to this question. You also missed finding out about the supplementary materials (writeable templates, etc.) available at www.Simmer-System.com. So now you know about that!

Trying to round free-range mustangs back into a corral can result in many kicks and bites. After doing this a few times, I worked out ways to progress with a minimum of bumps and bruises for everyone concerned.

If I had not written this book, I'd feel partly responsible every time I read about yet another PPFMO failure. My objective in sharing valuable lessons I learned the hard way was to help you get to where you want to go in less time and with less hassle.

The Simmer System is for executives and managers planning to implement one or more of these practices in an organization that doesn't yet do that sort of thing. Or that has tried it before and eliminated it; but now they're going to try again. With that track record, you realize that you have a difficult trip ahead of you.

A governance professional finds it hard to imagine why an organization would get rid of something as fundamental as PPFM practices, which is about as ridiculous as getting rid of the entire accounting department. It may not be core to the sales process, but it's imperative to keeping the company operating effectively.

Why would the organization do this? Managers (and not just governance professionals) have been trained on the benefits of properly functioning governance processes that make the organization more effective and more efficient at delivering critical results and outcomes.

The PPFM Trinity:

- **P**roject management helps deliver better quality products and services on-cost and on-schedule.

- **P**rogram management takes a multi-year look at how to deliver an ongoing capability efficiently, while spinning innovation and enhancement efforts to make sure your capability remains industry-leading well into the future.

- Port**F**olio **M**anagement focuses efforts on the most important things.

Once the organization is ready, these three practice disciplines form a unified governance practice. But only once it's ready.

You can't simply direct an organization to behave in a way that's different from what it's been doing for a long time. You'll be ignored – at least at first. If you persist, the change initiative will be put back into its box, or perhaps be thrown out altogether and you with it, neither of which would be the first time for the organization.

It has to be brought to the point where it can accept the basic premises and processes of these governance practices before they can be applied. *The Simmer System* will get you to that point.

What's Different About *The Simmer System*? And Why Should You Trust It?

The Simmer System isn't a "best practice," nor does it reject best practices. The system provides steps to walk the organization willingly down the path towards readiness for those best practices.

I've been down this path in over a dozen organizations in both the public and private sectors. Initially armed with best practices and process blueprints while in the trenches, I learned about how "obvious" improvements can antagonize people.

I made plenty of mistakes before figuring out this way of leveraging cooperation to get people to change instead of trying to drag them through the change.

I'll be sharing how I accomplished that, and a few mishaps that occurred along the way, to help you recognize them when something similar occurs. Some, but probably not all, of the traps can be avoided. But when you do fall into one (as you most likely will), it'll be less stressful because you'll know how to climb out of the hole and back onto the path.

The reason why this book isn't called "Three simple steps to turning your organization into a lean, mean machine in 30 days or less without breaking a sweat" is because it doesn't offer any such magic pill.

A massive culture change can't be achieved just by saying "make it so." You're going to have to influence people to do things contrary to what got them this high in the chain of command.

Don't expect their outlook to change overnight. It's going to take time and hard work, and on occasion some difficult conversations and decisions.

What Exactly Will *The Simmer System* Accomplish for You?

The Simmer System will show you how to move from the point of having very few working processes, and very little interest in having them, to a point where your organization's managers are cooperating to integrate and coordinate their work, and to devise processes they actually do follow.

You'll be instituting processes that from a "best practices" perspective are often so fundamental that they don't make it into "Level One." But they're essential in setting in place the foundation you need to move forward.

The lack of that foundation is the main reason the organization has failed in its previous governance initiatives. Once you've completed the system, you won't be finished with your governance initiative by any means.

However, you *will* have done the hardest part of shifting the culture enough to move it toward best practices. Rest assured, *The Simmer System* will safely help you get down that road.

Even at that point, some of the data you're using will have holes in it, and most of the processes and artifacts are a bit rudimentary. But fortunately you won't be floundering. In fact, what you put in place will place you ahead of many of your contemporaries in other "more mature" organizations.

The other thing you will have done is to make the processes durable, because it will be what your peer managers want to do, not just something you can make them do.

Your fledgling governance initiative won't fail because you don't have the right templates. It will fail because managers will fight to shake off constraints on their ability to do whatever they please.

They want nothing to do with any nasty governance process, and all the paperwork and pointless overhead they understand governance to entail.

The Simmer System is designed to bring along those same managers to work with you on things they've wanted to improve as part of the normal course of business. In doing so you can help them move towards their goals, and in turn you'll move *towards* (not *to*) your own goals.

During the first stages you aren't going to get to best practices as yet. A good-enough practice people follow is better than a best practice they don't follow.

Now that you've demonstrated the ability to add some value without doing the feared damage, your colleagues will allow you to add upgrades to achieve actual published best practices, and become certified against various maturity models, if that's your objective. It will take some work, but it won't be impossible (whereas a year earlier that most certainly was impossible).

For all of those reasons, for the first time in years the PPFMO remains in place, and isn't teetering towards yet another termination.

So that's what The Simmer System will do for you!

Don't Forget Who Does the Real Work

This book speaks to executives and managers of programs, portfolios and projects (the "governance professionals") who combine their perspectives to produce outcomes their organization desires. There are many books, including this one, written about them.

Amidst all this self-inspection and improvement, you must never lose sight of the fact that actual work teams usually think up the solutions, and you depend on them to deliver the actual results.

Those teams also have to prepare and deliver all the information and work products governance managers consider necessary.

You can think up templates and reports faster than everyone else in the organization can fill them out. However, the fact that you can doesn't mean you should. It also doesn't mean these products are essential, or that the teams are derelict if they can't get your reports and their work done.

Given a choice, they *should* do their work in preference to filling out your forms. A lot of resistance to governance is the result of worries that such a choice will be forced on them, and they don't want to have to deal with it.

The fact is, policies, processes and reports can't *make* a work team successful. What you can do is to create an environment in which they *can* be successful, which often means getting out of their way as much as possible.

It's Not All That Easy

The subtitle of this book is "How to Make Project, Portfolio and Program Management Practices Stick in a Skeptical Organization."

"Skeptical"? Well, yes. As a governance professional, you know the topics included in PPFM have been around for hundreds, if not thousands, of years. Unless you're in a very new, very small organization, it's been tried before.

Since you're looking at doing it again, it must have failed before. It's not just a matter of finally deciding to do it – it's not that simple. However, people are counting on you to get it right this time. Well, some are, while others would be just as happy to see you fail.

Setting up a PPFMO would seem to be an easy enough task. There are hundreds of books on the topic, and all of the disciplines in the PPFM family have been common knowledge for a long time.

Despite all this knowledge being readily available, your organization and many others have not managed to pull it off. Maybe it's not so easy after all.

Organizations don't fail at governance because nobody knew about it. They don't do it because their culture doesn't want it. Changing simple organizational processes can be hard enough. Changing the way an entire organization thinks can be very tough to accomplish.

The Simmer System provides a proven path for getting to where you're going. I said it was proven. I didn't say that it's simple, well-marked, and free of dangers. Quite apart from the challenges of doing anything complex, if the organization has been down this road before, people might be skeptical and won't extend themselves until it appears you've achieved some traction. Some people will covertly or overtly undermine you just to prevent you from getting that traction.

Am I saying that this is all too difficult? Maybe the best thing to do is to sit down, shut up, and collect a paycheck as long as you can? Of course not. I survived the experience — several times.

Apparently you're not happy with things the way they are, which is why you're reading this book. Wanting things to be more like that vision of the happy workplace you came up with earlier, you're sure as heck not going back to the place you're coming from. Are you?

No, you're not. Especially not with *The Simmer System* to smooth your way a little!

Why Not Best Practices?

Once again, *The Simmer System* doesn't reject best practices – it endorses them. Just not at the moment. Its purpose is to bring the organization to the point where best practices can be effective.

Over the years I've seen many months and hundreds of thousands of dollars spent as organizations laboriously reinvented the wheel.

As mentioned earlier, there are hundreds of textbooks on these subjects, and probably millions of references online.

If everybody's doing it, why wouldn't it work for you as well? Just run to the library, or go online to find best practices and implement them.

All done. What's next?

If it was that simple, it would have been successful the first time the organization tried it. But it wasn't. So now they need you to implement it for them.

Before ascribing sinister motives to people who disagree with you, let's take a look at this "obvious" thing from an external perspective.

The Best Practices Promise

Do you remember the first time you were exposed to the magical potential of project management?

Early in my career, I was hired with the majestic title of "consultant." My colleagues and I were bright young folks, but didn't have the experience typically associated with what you might imagine an actual consultant to be. Beyond a lack of actual domain knowledge, we weren't too structured about our own processes.

We managed our engagements well enough, and kept track of commitments, contractual requirements and so on. But we considered project management utilizing formal tools as something that only happened on monster defense projects.

One day I was on a team with Paul Koshetar (a fan of desktop project management software) who had a list of things we were going to do and when we were going to do them.

He'd remind us what was coming up, and if we didn't do it he reminded us again until we did. If we needed something from a customer, he reminded them as well.

That project zoomed along because Paul kept us on task. We rolled our eyes when he said he was going to do this, but we actually enjoyed doing it. It's surprising how often you need a bit of structure to leverage common sense.

Impressed with the organization and progress this "project management" stuff brought to the engagement, I climbed on the project management bandwagon, got more training, and became certified.

A vast number of management professionals took a similar route. There are now over 10,000 certified project managers in my metropolitan area alone, and it's not even one of the ten largest cities in the country.

I guess one could say it works. Or at least a lot of people believe it does.

In the new global information economy, governments as well as corporations believe they need to be effective, efficient, and nimble in order to compete or deliver Internet-class service. They also believe that governance will help them get there.

Companies and government agencies have begun levying PPFM-related requirements, such as:

- People must have certifications.

- Contractors must follow industry best practices.

- Engineers must stop reinventing existing capabilities, and begin reusing proven components (enterprise architecture).

- Projects must have sound business cases (portfolio management) and be run effectively (project management).

- Managers of all types must run efficient operations while steadily innovating (program management).

The best practitioners in the world in each of those various disciplines did a lot of research and collaboration to produce dozens of official practice standards. Today, hundreds of books supplement those somewhat general standards with detailed how-to instructions.

Nobody had any doubt those disciplines – which in partnership with some other more specific skills such as operations management, enterprise architecture and security make up the concept of "governance" – were going to turn our businesses and agencies into lean, mean, service-delivering machines. Some organizations have experienced that reality. But only some.

The Best Practices Reality

When things aren't clicking at work, you can become so buried that you don't notice what's going on around you. With all the promises that PPFM disciplines would make your organization more effective, you might be tempted to think the continuing ineffectiveness is somehow your fault.

You might become so consumed with trying to keep things afloat that you don't have time to attend professional association meetings. And now you think you're the only one in this situation.

Trust me, you are not alone!

So here's what really happened to that bright new world.

Traditional project management practices were developed to steer traditional undertakings: construction, engineering, weapons systems, manufacturing, product roll-outs and the like.

I live in the Washington, DC area where we've had some successful major road and bridge projects such as the Wilson Bridge over the Potomac River, the resolution of the infamous I-95 "mixing bowl," and the "Lexus Lanes" variable-toll roads. On the government side, for the most part NASA has had some notable triumphs.

Since we're still here to read and write about these rather ordinary challenges, I have to assume that the legions of the intelligence community are also having their successes. Who knows?

Since daily life is in fact proceeding without noticeable incident (my biggest concern being the morons texting while driving), there must be thousands of projects that by professional standards succeed well but aren't making it into the limelight.

When used in the right context, traditional project management has proven itself over the past few thousand years. The method isn't infallible, and a scanning of any week's worth of news can turn up plenty of examples. Those large enough to remember include the Boston Harbor Tunnel and the Joint Strike Fighter, both billions of dollars over-budget and years behind schedule.

It's not just the government that can make hash out of a project: New Coke, Windows Vista, and some of the case studies we'll discuss in Chapter Two, featured commercial projects and products launched at massive expense with very poor execution and customer validation, to speak only of the parts we know about.

Evidently, the existence of a proven management method is no guarantee of success, even for the type of project that has traditionally been successfully delivered using that method. Launching an initiative without forethought, and executing it without oversight, can overcome a wealth of professional knowledge.

In any case, our data on successes and failures is heavily skewed. In every organization, and especially at the large end of the scale (the very place where heavy duty best practices would be most appropriate), successes are over-dramatized and failures are hidden. Projects "too big to fail" get enough money thrown at them that eventually some sort of product emerges. Whatever it is, and whatever it does, will be hailed as a momentous achievement by the politicians or executives involved.

Politics happens all the time in organizations great and small. Very few leaders or managers are truly altruistic. Most just want to look good and make money now. If that happens to coincide with the long-term consequences to the organization, so much the better. Governance simply harnesses those personal ambitions to the organization's best interests.

In a process-averse organization, that runs you and your PPFMO smack into the power structure and its values. No bonus prize for guessing who wins that contest. That is why organizations may have best practices enshrined in their polices, and may have highly-qualified practitioners on their staffs. Yet they still can and do fail miserably.
Best practices are best only when actually practiced.

Right Medicine, Wrong Treatment

For some years I'd been thinking about writing about program and portfolio management because things on the ground weren't turning out the way many books said they would. For instance, from the eight years as an enterprise PPFMO director, and twice that amount of time as a consultant, I knew that:

- Very few organizations implement portfolio management the way it's described in most books. Though I knew why that was, it didn't seem worth writing a relatively short book on that topic alone.

- Too many organizations are still muddling along, despite having some form of those practices in place. In fact, sincere members of the clients' staffs firmly believe their organization's progress is being impeded by the overhead of those practices.

- When I worked at Gartner, many of their 10,000 client organizations had undergone multiple cycles of trying to institute the governance disciplines, getting rid of them, and then bringing them back.

- The hundreds of project managers I meet every year in the course of regular engagements, as well as professional society meetings, tend to be optimistic, forward-looking people. But nearly all of them shake their head at the degree to which their organizations refuse to take the steps everyone agrees should be taken.

Repeatedly hearing all that, I knew something wasn't adding up. But there's not much point in writing a book that just says "things aren't working." You need to offer a plan to fix them.

I couldn't put my finger on why nobody wanted to do common sense things, nor (more importantly) what to do about it. So the book remained in my thoughts as I and my thousands of colleagues continued to soldier on.

Then one day Jeff Sutherland, a founder of the Scrum methodology that's the leading method of executing the Agile framework, gave a talk on Agile Trends and Developments.

The waterfall approach had just the year before proven the inadvisability of a "big bang rollout" in the form of Healthcare.gov, which for over a half-billion dollars had a website that didn't work. The federal government was now all-in on Agile, and for the most part that meant all-in on Scrum as well.

Because the sun was shining on Agile and Scrum, it seemed obvious his talk would be along the lines of "I told you so" along with a victory dance, and perhaps some refinements in the processes he was using. Much to my surprise, it was quite the opposite (the URL to his speech is in the References annex).

Many of the PPFM professionals in the DC area had heard rumors of numerous problems with the government Agile projects. Perhaps we've been led to expect that any IT project run by the government is quite likely to fail. But it turned out the government wasn't alone.

Jeff revealed that the most recent data, which now included projects in which Agile had been applied to large-scale IT systems, showed results little better than those of the waterfall method.

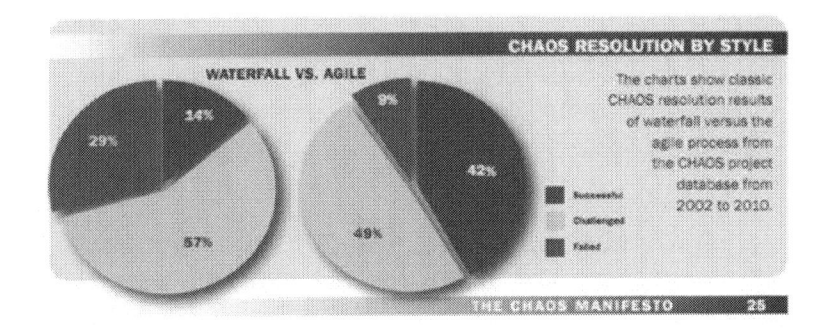

CHAOS RESOLUTION BY STYLE
WATERFALL VS. AGILE

The charts show classic CHAOS resolution results of waterfall versus the agile process from the CHAOS project database from 2002 to 2010.

Waterfall: 14% Successful, 57% Challenged, 29% Failed
Agile: 42% Successful, 49% Challenged, 9% Failed

THE CHAOS MANIFESTO

58% of Agile is "Bad Agile"
More recent data as Scrum is scaling in large companies indicates this is getting worse, not better!

Source: SOFTWARE IN 30 DAYS

scruminc.

It occurred to me that if neither method was working, perhaps the issue wasn't the specific remedy. After all, both have been proven to work, at least under the right circumstances. Instead, I realized the patient's "body" (the organization's culture) was rejecting the "medicine" before it had time to work. Therefore, we needed to find a new way to get the body to tolerate the medicine long enough for it to be healed.

I began to see that the "simmering" approach I'd been using to institute governance was working because it took an alternative way of delivering the same medicine. It seemed to overcome the rejection mechanisms that more aggressive treatment was experiencing, and give the medicine enough time to do its job.

Which was when I realized what this book needed to be about.

Welcome to *The Simmer System*^{SM}!

I like using cooking metaphors because I like to eat. I like the way good food tastes when I eat it. I like the way it smells when it's cooking. I even like the smell and taste of the ingredients that go into it. And in return for all that, I clean up afterwards without much grumbling.

The Simmer System is a "recipe." It has steps to get you where you're trying to go if you follow them. You still have to adjust to the situation and your own level of expertise.

Because my wife loves to cook, she'd rather whip up something in the kitchen than go out to dinner. Sometimes I feel guilty about that, because there are times when we really should get away from it all.

However, I quickly get over my guilt when the aroma of garlic and olive oil wafts across the room. She's a terrific, happy cook. So what the heck, let's stay in. Manicotti tonight? My mouth is already watering. *Mangia! Mangia!*

I could draw on my experience with high-maturity PPFM. I could watch over her shoulder to see if she's following the recipe, and offer criticisms if there are any deviations. That approach would result in me becoming covered in half-cooked pasta and boiling water.

As long as great smells are coming out of the pot, I'm perfectly content to be a bystander and provide support and encouragement as needed. However, if I smell something burning, I am authorized to intervene to save the meal.

Schlubs like me need to follow the recipe, while experts like her use it as a memory-jogger. Great cooks check the recipe for ingredients someone said are supposed to be in that dish, then adjust them to what works. No shallots on hand? Toss in a few leeks instead.

Yumm. Who knew?

With *The Simmer System*, you're going to become comfortable with the "ingredients" and the basic methods. Once you've reviewed the initial recipe, if you're a good cook you'll modify it to suit your needs and the situation. If you're not an expert, you'll follow the steps and they'll get you there. If you're overseeing the process, stand far enough back to allow people to do their work. But close enough that if a flare-up occurs you're on hand to help deal with it.

Simmering for Success

Simmer: intransitive verb. (1): to stew gently below or just at the boiling point; (2)(a) to be in a state of incipient development; (2)(b) to be in inward turmoil (Merriam-Webster).

So to 'simmer' means to make it hot enough to cook, but not so hot as to cause a boil-over.

The Simmer System might seem like an odd name for the, well, button-down environment our governance disciplines tend to operate in. But it really does illustrate exactly what it is. Besides, I'd rather think about a tasty Osso Buco Milanese than Gantt charts, wouldn't you?

Simmering cooks food gently and slowly. Delicate items such as fish are poached at or below a simmer to prevent them from breaking apart. Simmered meat becomes and remains moist and fork-tender, while boiled meat can become dry because the heat from the liquid caused their proteins to toughen.

Cooking Light magazine explains that stocks are simmered so that the fat and proteins released by the meat or bones float to the top. They can be skimmed off instead of being churned back in, which can make the stock cloudy and greasy.

Whoa! That doesn't do much for the appetite when it's said like that.

Sometimes a picture is worth a thousand words.

The Simmer System achieves progress by avoiding boil-over, while slowly dissolving the obstacles that might overcome other faster approaches.

In organizational terms, it allows you to adopt substantial changes over time under circumstances where faster, more structured approaches would only result in hardening the opposition. But not so slowly that the change never really occurs.

During the course of this process, you'll find that people will occasionally make you "simmer" while you're doing the same to them. My system emphasizes pushing hard enough to get a reaction, which is how change happens. But not so much as to create actual conflict.

So simmer ... don't boil!

What "Ingredients" Are in *The Simmer System*?

The Simmer System consists of interrelated actions that will help you get governance practices into place and make them stick.

Most of the books in the governance professional areas describe "best practices." Setting aside the fact that it's hard to find organizations that practice all or even most of them – which might lead you to question whether they really **are** best practices – you can't get there overnight.

It takes a lot of work; in fact, most of those standards point this out. But what they don't tell you is how to make it happen.

The Simmer System will help you get from where you are to a place where you can operate effectively. From there, you can decide to reach for even higher levels of proficiency, levels represented by "best practices."

The Simmer System is a set of five integrated components that include:

1. **Four guiding principles** that will help you stay oriented when things get confusing:

    a. **The Pasta Principle**: In governance, everything is connected to everything else. If you get a good grip on any part, sooner or later the rest must come along.

    b. **Zero-Sum**: Set up a process in which tradeoffs are forced and explicit.

    c. **Integrity**: Once the PPFMO loses that, the game is over.

    d. **Purposeful Humility**: Take on tasks nobody else wants if they lead to your objectives.

2. **Seven sets of data** you'll need to place PPFMO operations in context, and get managers and governance board members asking key questions.

3. **Eight collaborative agreements** that will build your processes to a respectable level of maturity without even trying to do so.

4. **Build high-level support**.

5. **Operate a governance board**, positioning it to provide oversight without too much resistance.

Once you've completed *The Simmer System*, you'll have established effective, if somewhat limited, processes that include the essentials of project, portfolio and program management. You will have done this much quicker, and with much less pain and conflict, than you imagined possible.

Best of all, the system will keep on working once you're done, and you can take that well-earned vacation!

There are people who claim their magic pill will fix whatever ails an organization. *The Simmer System* doesn't offer a different pill or any magic properties – just a new way of getting it into the patient.

The next chapter will explain how the system came about, and why it works.

Next Steps

You're reading this book because you've been asked to make this round of governance work. Or you haven't been asked, but you know it's needed.

You've probably figured out that it won't be a piece of cake, so you're looking for ideas that will help to make it work. That is great news, because it means you're aware that there can be challenges when trying to institute a major change. You may have also observed that going after best practices hasn't worked very well.

I can tell you there's no magic pill to painlessly get you where you want to go and without effort (I'll speak to that in the next chapter). I can also tell you not to overanalyze the situation, because that's just an excuse for not getting started.

The Simmer System provides a framework you'll adapt to the facts, and will keep you moving forward.

> ***"Do. Or do not. There is no 'try'."***
> **~Yoda, The Empire Strikes Back (Star Wars V)**

I'm not asking you to give it the 'old college try.' If the organization detects that you can be persuaded to roll back the clock, it will redouble its efforts to get you to do just that.

Surrendering to pressure means going back to the most unsatisfying place from which you started.

There is no 'try.' You'll either do it or you won't. So to make sure things go well this time you'll need a plan, a system or a method for getting it done. Commit to success, then move forward with *The Simmer System*.

Let's do it together!

EXERCISE 1: ENVISIONING THE FUTURE PPFMO

The next chapter explains how the system emerged from and applies to real situations. If nothing else, it should make you feel more optimistic about your ability to get your organization working better!

If these approaches can fix those organizations, you can fix anything.

Before moving into that chapter, let's review what you think a successful implementation of PPFM would look like.

Take a few minutes to fill in the blanks in the following table. (If you don't like writing in books, copy the page first).

At this point, don't worry about parsing the difference between project, program and portfolio management. Just use your current understanding of those topics.

Where are we? And where do we want to end up?

(*P.S.: If you don't want to write in your nice new book, or if you're reading this in an electronic or audio version, all of the exercise pages are available as free printable downloads at www.simmer-system.com.*)

We need to improve **project** management practices because (*describe the symptoms you're experiencing*):

_____
_____
_____
_____

When we have improved our **project** management practices, (*describe how the improved organization will behave*):

_____
_____
_____
_____

We need to improve **program** management practices because (*describe the symptoms you're experiencing*):

_____
_____
_____
_____

When we have improved our **program** management practices (*describe how the improved organization will behave*):

_____
_____
_____
_____

We need to improve **portfolio** management practices because (*describe the symptoms you're experiencing*):

_____
_____
_____
_____

When we have improved our **portfolio** management practices, (*describe how the improved organization will behave*):

_____
_____
_____
_____

Great job! Now you know where you are and where you want to be.

Just for fun, recall that happy working environment you envisioned earlier and go there.

Chapter Two

How the Simmer System Bubbled Up from Real Life

"Experience is the teacher of all things."
~Julius Caesar, Commentaries on the Civil War

This chapter explains how *The Simmer System*^{SM} grew out of real-life experiences and examples of where the approach has worked. You can determine whether I've walked the walk.

In the upcoming chapters I'll give you specific actions to get things started, then see how they work. If you try them and they don't work for you, let's use our Simmer Community (www.Simmer-System.com) to see if there's something you might have missed or misunderstood.

As previously mentioned, *Let It Simmer* isn't another how-to book slammed together in a few hours by skimming whatever I found on the Internet.

Nor is it another recycling of the standards published by organizations such as the Project Management Institute (those are valuable resources, but they're not fully applicable to your situation yet.) *The Simmer System* is your means of getting to the point where those standards begin to become reasonable objectives.

It's taken me years and a great deal of aggravation to learn these lessons. I'm sharing them with you because it annoys me that people have to take a lot of abuse when all they're doing is trying to make their work environment a better place. Reducing the casualty count by the number of people who read this book will be a fairly good contribution to the professions of project and program management.

You may be wondering if this system really does work. I know it works because I've done it several times. Not by choice! This isn't a system devised by academic introspection, then offered as a solution. It emerged after realizing the ad-hoc solutions in several situations had shown similar patterns.

Because each organization is different, sometimes the same solution looks different until you've had opportunities to look at the same thing. Sometimes a bit of distance helps gain the perspective to see the entire landscape.

During my 20 years of consulting engagements, I've assisted many organizations in setting up a PPFMO. (I use that acronym rather than "PMO" because I want you to remember the solution depends on all of those things working together.)

In the following case studies based on true stories, I'm not going to give the names of the organizations for obvious reasons. Their identities don't matter, because many of the individuals have moved on to wreak their havoc at other organizations.

I'm fairly confident that after you finish reading them you'll think, *Thank goodness I didn't have to deal with that! Things aren't that bad where I am.* At least I hope you will. Otherwise, things are worse than I thought, and the Standish Group will be in business for many decades to come.

However, if you did have that reaction, your road may not be so difficult. If we were able to get *The Simmer System* steps implemented in the organizations I'm describing, you can surely get them done in yours.

Case Study 1: Unexpected Success

Probably the most successful PPFMO I ever worked on was for a small company transitioning from being a team of inventors to producing an actual manufactured product ... and a heavily regulated one at that.

You think your PPFMO support contract is expensive? This one cost about a third of the client's total operating expense, yet they were pleased as punch. Actually, the price tag was as low as we could make it.

Because they didn't have a lot of operating money, to keep the price down we started as light as we thought PPFM could go with part-time help to get it going and keep it on track for a few months.

Taking to it like ducks to water, they had the strong external motivator to become more process-oriented. But in many cases, while such a motivator is necessary to begin a change, it's not sufficient to produce the change.

What was different about this one was that everybody had recently graduated from being a research engineer to being part of a process-based manufacturing company. They were still working out exactly what that meant.

We didn't realize it at the time, but the implementation worked because nobody had any turf to protect or any bad habits to unlearn.

* * * * * * *

The next two case studies have many similarities, which is how I stumbled onto *The Pasta Principle*. (The overall *Simmer System* didn't take shape until later when I had the perspective to compare and contrast the experiences.)

If you took the trouble to look it up, you could deduce from my resume that I've spent time as an employee of governmental organizations, and as a consultant serving both public and private sector organizations.

Don't draw any conclusions from that as to which organizations the case studies apply to. You'd be surprised how wrong you might be!

Perhaps the striking thing is that it might be hard to pick out from these case studies (and all the other "war stories" in the book) which ones apply to federal agencies and which do not.

I didn't have to fuzz them up to anonymize them, because at the root all mid- to large-size organizations have the same back-office functions and the same political dynamics. Which ones have accountability as part of their culture and which ones don't is pretty much random.

That's one of the key points. The various attitudes towards PPFM in general and accountability in particular can be found in any size or type of organization, and it doesn't matter at all whether the organization is in the public, private or non-profit sectors.

Even small local charities and organizations can and will display these behaviors. I've seen these variations, good and bad, in every one of those settings. Human behavior is not about the business model; it's about the people.

* * * * * * *

The two cases described below weren't such a delight. But the silver lining is that it was through those experiences that *The Simmer System* took shape.

In both cases, I was brought on board specifically to start a PPFMO and do it quickly. I began with assurances from the relevant executives that this was very important; that they would get behind it personally and visibly; and that the necessary resources would be provided.

These organizations were under external pressure to get their acts together, or lose tens of millions of dollars of revenue (whether earned or appropriated, it's still "revenue" and a "loss" from the managers' perspective). They had every incentive to want to make this work.

Besides, in the case that took place in a federal agency, governance was required by law. Back then it wasn't as obvious as it is today that some federal agencies find that to be a rather irrelevant point.

In both cases, things had changed almost before the ink on the agreement had dried.

Case Study 2: Violent Insurgency

Setting Up the Struggle

One organization hired me after numerous rounds of interviews because the top-most executives insisted they needed things to change quickly. Plus, they wanted to hold their managers accountable and shake things up. If that ruffled a few feathers, so be it. Unquote.

As we started the usual assessment of what was already in place, the lack of familiarity with any form of control became swiftly apparent. The executives who served on the existing governance board complained that program managers were presenting ludicrous business cases and downright false progress reports.

But it wasn't the culture to do anything more than make sharp comments. So everyone kept their jobs and their bonuses, which simply motivated more of the same.

In his blog post, *Cypher's Syndrome*, Ricardo Guido Lavalle laid out a broad description of deliberately selecting a parallel and imaginary universe over the reality of what's occurring.

We definitely had that going on. (You can find a link to the article in the References annex.) Before the PPFMO had time to gain momentum, the key executives moved on to other careers. The program managers (under the impression that the good old days of the Wild West would return) rejoiced.

And things did have to slack off, but not as much as they hoped. The executives on the governance board that had been formed still wanted to meet, still wanted their information cleaned up, and still wanted investments to start performing.

But they weren't going to waste time taking sides in what appeared to be a civil war within our business unit. As long as they didn't appear to be impacted, this wasn't even a secondary issue for them.

Without much peer-level support, the sponsoring executive also had to adjust his expectations. Suddenly bereft of allies, the PPFMO had to retrench and settle in for a long guerilla conflict.

Damage Control

You won't hear this phrase often: "Luckily we had to answer to regulators." But it was lucky for the PPFMO in that most people agreed that we needed to minimize the damage with external audit agencies whose earlier demands for punitive penalties had led to the PPFMO's creation in the first place.

At least we had that to fall back on, because with its highest level champions out of the picture, the PPFMO was being challenged to have an iron-clad basis for wanting information. "The governance board wants it" wasn't a sufficient reason. "The regulators will shut us down if we don't" worked much better, as long as we didn't abuse it.

Each step was challenged to show the actual value of taking that step (i.e., "If we give you that, what are you going to do with it?"), which was annoying. But in retrospect, it was also useful as it caused us to question the practical value of many industry-accepted best practices, and kept us focused on deciding which battle would yield the best results over the long run.

So how bad was it? At one point a program manager accused the PPFMO of doctoring the audio-visual record of a board meeting he hadn't attended by removing the section where the board supposedly had approved one of his projects. And removing all of the comments he would have made in the meeting to make it look as if he hadn't attended and the subject hadn't been discussed.

Set aside the fact that tools like Camtasia that might make such an action feasible today simply didn't exist anywhere but Hollywood and big-media studios. Even having a recording tool was a pretty big deal then!

The fact that nobody believed him wasn't the point. The point was that the environment was so bizarre that one could say such things without being sent for psychiatric evaluation. (I could share dozens of similar stories, but you get the idea.)

At about this time, the Army called me to let me know they needed someone with my skill set in the Middle East. It wouldn't be optional, but it wasn't decided on either. When I mentioned this to our sponsoring executive, his first reaction was, "You wouldn't want to go over there. You'd be going to work every day wondering which of the people you're trying to help will be ambushing or sniping at you."

We both pondered that for a minute, then in unison said, "Sounds familiar." Even though we laughed, it wasn't all that funny.

Plebe year at West Point had conditioned me to accept far more abuse than that. It was harder on the PPFMO staff members. The managers would regularly drop by their cubicles and threaten to "get them" if they didn't roll over and turn the red lights on the status board to green.

What a testament it is to those staff members that they believed deeply in their professional responsibilities, and never once gave a thought to doing so even though the threats greatly upset them. (I could give their names, but that would also reveal the miscreants, which would serve no purpose. You terrific people I got to work with know who you are, and God bless you for your strength and integrity!)

You have to accept that none of this abuse is about you personally. It's simply about a predictable reluctance to accept accountability and relinquish some level of autonomy.

We arrested the downward slide when we convinced the remaining executives that they needed to exercise some process oversight. That inflection point began by demonstrating that at the rate things were going, the entire organization was going to grind to a halt.

Either the overruns on the ill-conceived projects were going to eat up the operating budget needed to keep the lights on, or the escalating operational costs were going to put an end to the funds needed to undertake critical projects.

Unfortunately for the organization, we didn't win the battle at that proactive point. We gained credibility only once the forecasted crisis point actually occurred at about the time we predicted. Now the executives got really interested in making investment decisions in a more conscious fashion.

So we were eventually able to hold the line at gaining board approval for the budget and significant projects. Once the board had approved that work, the members became curious as to how the work was going (that dynamic is at the heart of *The Pasta Principle*).

The Path Upward

So yes, things were pretty bad for quite a while. But as time went on, small triumphs outweighed the resistive load.

Although it was frustrating at the time, I have to give credit to the PPFMO's sponsor who faced constant demands to put an end to the entire process. The PPFMO was always amazed that the sponsoring executive wouldn't hold the other directors accountable for their constant failures, which were amply documented even by the limited processes and metrics that were in place, and even though these failures were making the sponsor look bad.

The sponsor explained to me, "I only have so much political capital, so I'm not going to spend it on that."

I don't remember what the capital was spent on — if I ever did know (executives do many things behind closed doors). In spite of all those failures going on, the sponsor never got fired, so it must have been invested wisely.

We kept moving in the direction where we were headed, and most of our flare-ups were internal. Over time, our executive's greatest contribution was that the PPFMO had a long enough run to become institutionalized.

We worked with the more cooperative program managers to bring up the standard of play, while working to chip away at other people's resistance. We convinced them that they at least needed to know when they'd receive work from each other.

At first, the status reports were based on just an end date and the program manager's say-so. But later, we got into costs when we identified that contracts were getting out of control. As we regained control (which meant more deliveries for more people), most managers accepted the value of basic PM practices.

This is when I discovered *The Pasta Principle*, which served me and the PPFMO well, and would later form the cornerstone of *The Simmer System* (you'll read about it in the chapter on core principles).

We developed a program-based budgeting process to allow managers to forecast their own budgets instead of only being told what they were.

As noted above, those forecasts demonstrated that either the operational costs were going to consume the entire budget and push the project work off the table completely, or the other way around. And "eventually" was about to happen. At that point, people at all levels began taking an interest in portfolio management.

We also agreed that if our customers were willing to accept scheduling slips (which our managers always blamed on changes in requirements) and fund the overruns, then we wouldn't worry much about the original estimates and baselines, provided the changes were approved in writing by the customer at least three months prior to the planned delivery dates.

This sounds pretty permissive on paper. But it's not so easy to ask the customers to fork over another million dollars or more **and** admit that it's all their fault. So it became a self-controlling brake for which the PPFMO couldn't be blamed.

Notice how elegantly the zero-sum principle works: no fingers pointed, no excuses needed … and no magic money forthcoming.

All of these things took time, effort and patience under enormous pressure. But over the long run, we got the results we wanted.

True, it cost the organization several million wasted dollars compared to what could have happened by becoming more efficient more quickly. But even more money would have been wasted had they continued down the original path, which is what would have happened had the PPFMO been ejected as its predecessors had been.

Stability for the Long-Term

It took about a year from the time when we really started working to gain agreement on minimalist processes to get to a point where all projects but one were developing lean but well-supported business cases, delivering limited but useful status reports, working to a baseline, and either delivering to the baseline or providing adequate notice of issues.

Then the PPFMO took on responsibility for managing the support contracts, which gave us excellent visibility and the capability to do something about it.

This demonstrated another core principle: Purposeful Humility (taking on tasks nobody else wants if they lead to your objectives).

Once we demonstrated the vendors' costs could be kept under control and they could be required to deliver, the PPFMO procedures started looking pretty good (and then everybody wanted control of their contractors back).

Eventually we achieved a solid Level 3 on the maturity model scale that we preferred. We wouldn't go any higher, because that would have required "quantitative" portfolio management techniques that didn't work in our context. In reality it's as high as most organizations ever get, and it was certainly a lot higher than somewhere below level zero (you can learn about "anti-maturity" on the resources website).

If you like thrillers and mysteries, you may have picked up on the casual mention of that other project and are wondering what happened to it.

Well, the auditors got hold of it, as they promised to do, to such an extent that in an unusual move the organization tried do something about that manager. But something went wrong during the human resources process, and the effort at discipline ground to a halt. Nothing happened. That's how it goes when you're process-averse.

Perhaps the surest sign of success was during a return visit to the organization where I saw that almost all of the practices we'd put in place were still in existence and essentially unchanged.

In fact, my host related that about a year after my departure, some of the hard-line cowboys had attempted to reset the clock only to be told, "Why would we change that? We've always done it that way."

Case Study 3: Building from the Grassroots

In another case, a similar scenario played out with a little more finesse on both sides, and quite a different outcome.

Setting Up the Struggle

In this case too, the executive support vanished along with the promised resources even before my arrival. (If I ever write an autobiography, it'll probably be called *Things Have Changed Since We Last Talked*. Sorry, now it's copyrighted!)

The executive leading the organization sponsoring the PPFMO – despite having stripped it of its resources – still expected it would bring about the originally intended improvements. (I was to learn this was typical of the organization's habit of wishful thinking.)

He also wanted to stop, or at least slow down, the constant raids on his budget over and above the total reductions forced by the nationwide economic climate.

The root cause of many of the problems was that this executive went to great lengths to avoid saying "no" to anyone or anything. He'd commit to doing something whenever anyone higher or lower walked through his door, then reverse himself for the next person without informing anyone but the person he was talking to at the time.

Over and over, all this reversing and un-reversing conducted in secrecy had the place looking like a carousel: there's a lot of noise and movement, but the entire structure isn't going anywhere.

It also meant the CFO couldn't take seriously any of the group's budget estimates, or its statements of the impacts in the event of cutbacks. So the cuts kept coming and the lights stayed on, indicating there was room for more cuts.

Damage Control

In this mercurial leadership climate, the line managers operated with minimal oversight and paralyzing uncertainty. The constant shuffling of resources and priorities made it impossible to get anything done.

Of course, they became very frustrated. Trying to do anything other than handle the crisis of the day made them amenable to the PPFMO taking on a role that was little more than coordinating discussions between them.

Getting things resolved without having to take them up the management chain was far better than having to ask for approvals that meant nothing and had life-spans measured in hours.

One-on-one meetings with the line managers evolved into group meetings where the managers coordinated among themselves while I skimmed the information I needed to piece the elements of a PPFM solution together. We developed the lists and forged the collaborative agreements you'll be reading about, and reported on the status of each of the known projects as the information revealed itself. The foundation for PPFM (and *The Simmer System*) was being built.

The Path Upward

Working entirely by consensus on what information the managers needed to do their jobs, we took continuous steps forward each month.

First, we reported that the projects existed, then we agreed on when each group would be handing work off to the next and what that work product was. Then we settled on what the overall product of each effort was supposed to be and when it might be ready. We didn't get into detailed step-by-step planning; it emerged as time went on.

After we gained visibility over everything that was going on (and quite importantly, everything that was supposed to be going on but wasn't), it became clear that the issues with resources (in the form of bottlenecks and churn) formed a major part of the problem.

So we added the capability to see that picture and better forecast resource needs, which in turn had a strong impact on contract costs.

Once we identified what the work would be, we devised a supportable budget estimate that clarified which costs resulted from what activities, and the consequences of any change in the budget.

The higher-level executives were enthusiastic about what we had accomplished, remarking that it was the first time they'd ever seen the organization produce a budget that made sense. And the first time they'd received sensible answers to questions about possible reductions.

Since the overall financial environment remained weak, they went ahead and cut the budget anyway. But this time, because the organization was able to discuss the cuts in terms of the practical impacts, we were allowed to apply them to the priorities we had developed.

Stability for the Long-Term

Unfortunately, this case study doesn't have a happy ending. If anything, it shows how quickly things can disintegrate if you let your guard down.

The PPFMO sponsor was replaced during the upward path phase. The successor was very experienced, intelligent and extremely serious about the proper role of a managing executive. Sounds good, right?

This new executive came from an organization with very mature processes. The top executives hoped the newcomer would fix the still-struggling organization by dropping in those processes. Remember the point from Chapter One: you can't just force-fit best practices onto an organization that isn't ready. (At this point in the book, you can probably guess that approach never got off the ground.)

All the positions reporting directly to the new executive were still occupied by the former executive's inner circle. They didn't inspire the new executive's confidence enough for him to confirm them in their positions. But a much-rumored reorganization never came, at least not for many months.

That led the rest of the organization to wonder whether it would be wise to express any concerns with the way things had gone on before (and, in retrospect, that caution was well-advised). So the inner circle was able to ward off efforts to reach further down in the chart to get an accurate pulse of the organization, or perhaps to find replacement managers. As you've seen, the middle tier was where progress was actually being made.

One positive result of the new executive being unable to find anyone he could rely on was that once again the supporting master contract was turned over to me because nobody else wanted to do it (remember Purposeful Humility?).

Going forward, we made giant strides in project delivery and cost control. It wasn't rocket science. In fact, I didn't do much of it myself. Most large consultancies and contractors have perfectly adequate governance capabilities. But if they can make more money by not using them, then that's what they'll do.

In this case, once I made it clear we weren't going to allow uncontrolled contract growth or unsubstantiated current expenditures, the vendor brought its normal management capabilities back into play.

We ratcheted back a forecasted $5 million overrun, a quarter of the total budget, which the contractor achieved without having to lay off a single person. Holding the line on costs doesn't always require slash-and-burn tactics if you can get to the problem far enough out in front, which is what the governance process should do.

Meanwhile, I solidified the foothold we'd gained by rearranging the contract to give control of the work to those program managers who'd gotten used to working together. When it was time for me to move on to another assignment, I figured that by the end of the contract term, over 24 months of rational management would have been enough to sink in.

However, as so often happens, Murphy intervened. Frustrated at the inability to put an effective organizational chart in place, and/or to get managers to think in the structured way he was accustomed to, the new executive departed shortly after I did, leaving the organization back in the hands of the original inner circle.

Process-averse organizations can move with surprising speed when they want to, partly because they don't have to worry about following processes.

The contracts were quickly rewritten to place them back into the hands of the very person who'd originally let them get out of control. The organizational chart went back into the safe, with responsibilities being allocated and randomly reshuffled on a verbal basis.

A critical project that during my tenure had been confined to the testing phase because of its inability to prove itself was unleashed after my departure. Two years later – and after tens of millions more dollars had been spent on it – they remained no closer to their goal.

With oversight on hold once again, project performance returned to irrelevance, budgets turned back into a grab-bag, and the CFO went back to micromanaging (and raiding) the business unit's budget.

You should do what you can to lock decision processes into other more durable processes such as long-term budgets, contracts, personnel hires and the like.

But as you've seen, those things can be changed. And when things fall apart, they do so in a hurry. So don't worry about your legacy – just do the best you can with the time you have.

I'm not telling this story out of any resentment that the new-old regime shoved back under the rug all of the good things that had been put in place.

I'm including this story because it's important to understand that the collegial progress under *The Simmer System* was still trying to take root within a durable organizational culture.

It's only a seedling. Given half an opportunity, that culture will wash it away.

In this case, it did.

Finding and Using *The Simmer System*

*"Experience needs distance,
and what you write of at a distance tells not so much what you
were like as what you have discovered since."*
~David Wade, London Times, 1982

Early in this process of professional growth, I made things easier in successive experiences by borrowing lessons from previous ones. I didn't know at the time that I was refining *The Simmer System*, because I hadn't figured out that I *had* developed a system.

It's hard enough to make sense of things when you're in the middle of the action. Harder yet is seeing the reality behind events that don't conform to your worldview.

It's tempting to attribute "evil" or unprofessional behavior to people who do things contrary to your values. The problem with that approach is it makes it difficult to find points of constructive cooperation.

Most project and program managers bring a certain professional and ethical point of view to their work.

The Defense Acquisition University maintains statistics on the Meyers-Briggs profiles of program managers who come there for training. Meyers-Briggs defines four general attributes of personal behavior (extrovert-introvert; sensing-intuiting; thinking-feeling, and perceiving-judging). The permutation of those factors yields 16 possible different preference sets.

When I attended in 2010, the track record was an astounding 87% match on just one of these 16 possibilities! That particular set of tendencies (ISTJ) values facts over opinions, logic over feelings, and following the rules over exploring alternatives.

What that means is governance professionals have a remarkably common view of how things should be, and that viewpoint is quite different from the wide range of attitudes found in the other 93% of the world.

Because of the "judging" focus, they tend to view those others as slackers, rebels, troublemakers or incompetent twits. Combining this observation of widely divergent views of reality with David Snowden's Cynefin theory explains what happens next.

The model suggests four basic conditions that may exist in an organization. When the condition is known, the appropriate response is fairly clear.

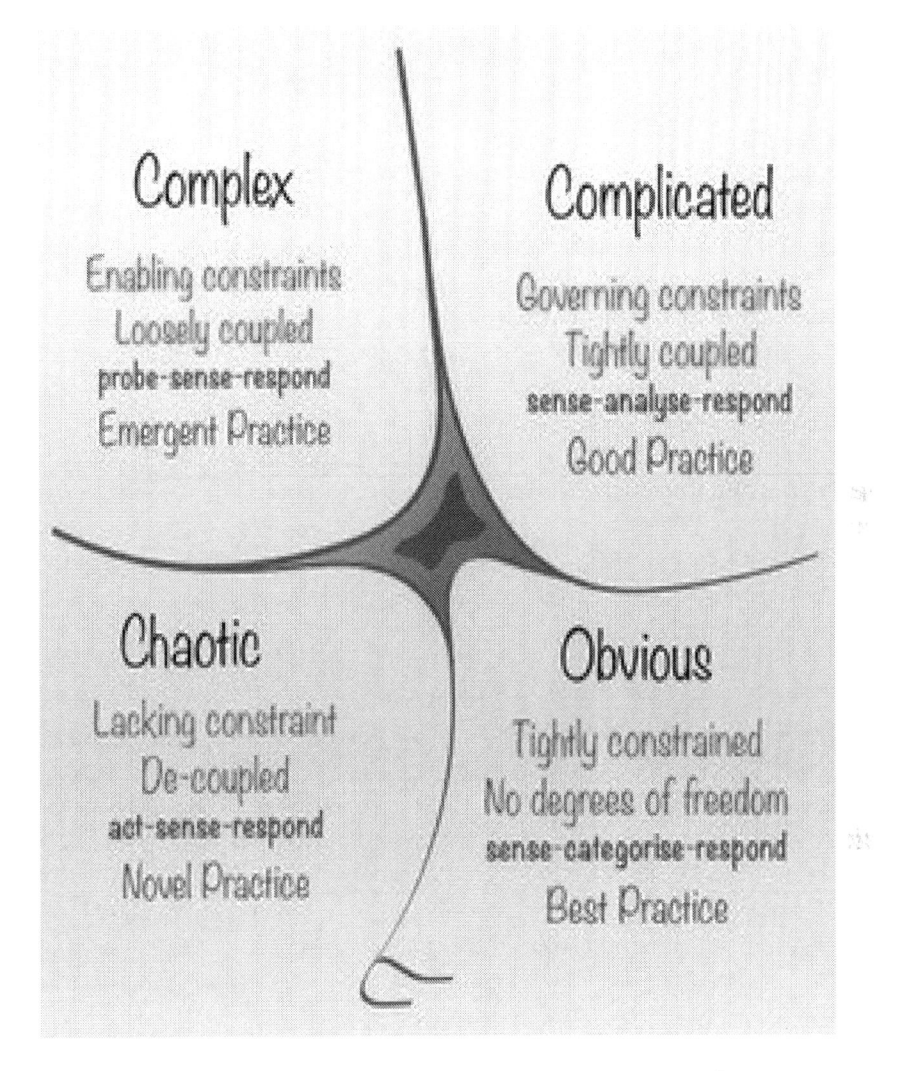

Complex
Enabling constraints
Loosely coupled
probe-sense-respond
Emergent Practice

Complicated
Governing constraints
Tightly coupled
sense-analyse-respond
Good Practice

Chaotic
Lacking constraint
De-coupled
act-sense-respond
Novel Practice

Obvious
Tightly constrained
No degrees of freedom
sense-categorise-respond
Best Practice

Image credit: https://en.wikipedia.org/wiki/Cynefin

There's also what I would call a non-condition ("disorder") in which it's not clear what the situation really is. Under that circumstance, people revert to their natural tendencies.

Here's where Snowden's work provides the critical insight: The boundary between obvious and chaotic is catastrophic. Applying an obvious solution to a situation that's actually chaotic will quickly drive that system to complete breakdown, and vice-versa.

You can find a more detailed analysis of the applicability of Cynefin to the process-averse organization at www.Simmer-System.com. The essentials of that analysis are:

- Organizations exist to turn their core business activities into "obvious" situations.

- Process-averse organizations have failed in efforts to routinize their activities. It devolves into "disorder" because nobody knows what they *should* do, so they do whatever comes naturally to them personally.

- Driven individuals (the ones we call "type A") are all about taking action. Any action will do as their world has no concept of cause and effect, and every day is a never-ending series of emergencies. Every event requires a new invention and discovery process. A "chaotic" response to non-chaotic situations eventually causes chaos to emerge.

- Less-driven individuals in these organizations see the disorder and lie low waiting for the storm to pass, hoping for someone to tell them what to do.

- Enter the project manager, armed with a set of professional practices that provide a perfect "obvious" canned response to any situation. Since the business processes fell apart, the organization is now acting in a chaotic manner. Remember, trying to apply obvious solutions (best practices) will fail miserably in a chaotic situation.

Building Theory with Experience

Unfortunately, we didn't have this handy model to call on, so we didn't know about the Complex quadrant or the appropriate responses.

The PPFMO had to learn on its own how to get the organization to swallow the medicine. The PPFMO started gaining traction when it pushed a little here and gave a little there, saw what was working, then moved to capitalize on successes.

After a few experiences of this nature, I worked out where best to "push a little," and where the hot buttons might be hiding that you want to stay away from. Now you have *The Simmer System* to help you cut down on those false starts and set off in a direction that's likely to work.

After seeing yet more organizations struggling through PPFM implementations for the second, third and fourth time – and hearing from PMs in other companies about similar problems they were encountering – I realized that while my experiences had been different on the surface, things that worked underneath were quite similar.

The first part of the system I grasped was *The Pasta Principle* (further explained in Chapter Four), which looks for opportunities to implement any aspect of PPFM that will stick at first.

The principle is that if you can get something started, everything else of importance will eventually be carried along with it. (The rest of *The Simmer System* is basically a set of "how-to" actions that harness *The Pasta Principle* to keep the action moving forward.)

At one organization I joined a program that was so large, the very thought of it had put the various component managers into a state of shock-induced paralysis. It was approaching its first anniversary milestone with lots of resources, but without progress and no plan.

Our team got it moving by convincing the program participants to define handoffs (a Collaborative Agreement you'll read about in a later chapter). From there we moved to other agreements that ended up producing a defensible schedule and budget. The program components began making observable coordinated progress.

In another case, we had allowed a business unit to continue using a proven process checklist rather than forcing it to switch to an elaborate lifecycle model.

In a matter of weeks we leveraged that information into a solid tool for cost estimation and tracking, which had been a bone of contention for a few years.

Here's the last war story (at least for now).

Case Study 4: Waking Rip Van Winkle

At another organization where managers had abdicated their responsibilities, and operations had gotten out of control, we asked people to define the program in terms of what they were going to do to support one or more general organizational goals in the current month.

Then the next month when we agreed on the next steps, the program manager was able to reprioritize some actions and suggest others.

Making a rough guess at the difficulty of the tasks, we estimated the total number of tasks that could be taken on, and tracked the rate at which the tasks were completed month-to-month. In short, we reverse-engineered an Agile process around an operational activity.

Within four months this organization was producing more in one month than any previous quarter (some might argue a year). It had a clear plan for the remainder of the year, and a demonstrable backlog for the upcoming year.

(If you're wondering about the title of this case study, it refers to the legend of the man who, like this PPFMO, went to sleep for a very long time. In his case, 20 years.

In the PPFMO's case, let's just say, not *that* many! You'll get a few additional details in the next chapter in the scenario called "Benign Neglect.")

Bottom line? This approach has worked in a wide range of situations.

The Simmer System provides key principles to adhere to, and critical agreements that will lead you to eventual success. What you have to do is work out how to adapt it to specific leverage points available to you.

Of course, it sounds simple when reading it on a page. But there's nothing simple about dealing with the personalities and politics of an organization.

What's in it for You?

Well, your sanity for one thing.

The Simmer System will...

- help you get project, portfolio and program management working in your organization.

- greatly reduce the pain and conflict typically involved in trying to induce a major behavioral change.

- get results quicker than you imagined possible.

- ensure that after you've worked through this process, the results will stick.

Will it be quick, easy and painless? Of course not. The processes described here will take months. They will require the most challenging but ultimately the most rewarding kind of work.

You'll be building symbiotic relationships with your peers that will help you to guide them to help themselves. For that same reason, it probably won't be totally pain-free. There are always challenges whenever you have to depend on getting other people to do things.

Incrementalism has a bad reputation because it often means "excessive timidity that ends up not accomplishing anything." In *Let It Simmer*, I'll be advising you not to take steps that are so small that they become irrelevant.

Yet you can't take such big steps that your entire effort becomes unacceptable, and you and your program are escorted out by security. Even the CEO can't mandate an organizational culture shift.

Grant Baldwin's four-minute video, where he describes his initiation into this reality when seeking to make a mark on his school before graduating, puts culture change into a context everyone can relate to. (There's a link in the References annex.)

He wanted to do something dramatic, but the best advice he got was: "keep it small and keep it local." Despite his own reservations, he was surprised to find that the most effective thing he did was to invite the new students to sit at the "in-crowd" lunch table.

Aside from the immediate benefit, others started treating each other more respectfully. Although it wasn't dramatic, it had a huge effect.

Since incrementalism has to occur over a period of time, you'll be annoyed at its leisurely pace. You might be able to create a Gantt chart showing how you could implement governance activities faster. You certainly can on paper, but not in reality.

In reality, this process is just as fast as any other way you've been offered, especially once you factor in the annoyance and delay of having to begin again when it doesn't stick the first time. Or the second, if you're still around to do it.

You'll still run into some interpersonal challenges even when using the collaborative approach, because some people are just that way. In any organization (particularly a "process-averse" one) there are a good number of them.

However, they will be far less painful than those that occur as a result of trying to force-fit these disciplines using whatever top-down mandates and backing you think you have.

Next Steps

Before you find out how to get that working for you, let's make sure you're properly prepared by being aware of some of the obstacles you're likely to encounter.

For instance, if you're going to take a road trip you'd first consult a map to learn the route. Along the way you'd watch for traffic alerts so you don't run into a construction zone.

That's not negativity – it's planning.

Negativity would be refusing to set out on the trip. *I have too many other priorities. There will be too many hassles. All my lunch buddies will stop talking to me. When we get done planning it, people will probably sabotage the whole thing anyway. Nothing much is going to change after all that, so why bother?*

However, there's a grain of truth in the negativity. If you aren't convinced your initiative is worth the trouble, you won't convince anyone else of it.

So the exercise for this chapter will be to remind yourself why you're doing this.

EXERCISE 2: SETTING THE FEEL-O-METER

Remember the happy working environment you envisioned earlier? Knowing where you are now, you're going to set a baseline so that when things get sticky (as they will from time to time) you can remind yourself why this is worthwhile.

I know this might not be your favorite exercise. So I've kept the questions short and simple, and your answers can be short and simple as well.

First, for your current situation at work, describe the first emotion-type word that pops into your head without over-thinking it:

When I think about my work, the emotion I'm feeling is _____.

When I think about my colleagues, the emotion I'm feeling is _____.

When I think about being in my current job five years from now, the emotion I'm feeling is: _____.

When I think about the possibility of finding a different job, the emotion I'm feeling is _____.

Now, take a breath and shake off the questions you just answered.

Ready for more?

Assuming that everything *The Simmer System* has promised you so far has happened, visualize how the workplace would be, then describe it in a few sentences:

_____
_____
_____
_____

Now you'll answer the first questions again with that new frame of reference (*The Simmer System* was successful in fulfilling its promises, and you're in the new workplace).

Your processes are working to the extent you foresaw in Exercise 1. Again, don't overthink it.

What emotion-type words pop into your head when describing...

When I think about my work, the emotion I'm feeling is
_____.

When I think about my colleagues, the emotion I'm feeling is
_____.

When I think about being in my current job five years from now, the emotion I'm feeling is _____.

When I think about the possibility of finding a different job, the emotion I'm feeling is _____.

In these first two exercises, you'll get an initial sense of where you and your organization's PPFM practices are and where they could go. Save the answers so you can review them later to see how things turned out.

If Exercise 2 worked the way it has for others, you've established that the current situation isn't quite right.

Because it represents a paycheck – and in the new modern economy that's always a consideration – you may have seen it as necessary in order to tolerate your situation. Given the fate of other PPFMOs that may have pushed too far or too fast, you're right to be a bit cautious.

The Simmer System will guide you to the necessary changes, while minimizing the resistance that would put the PPFM back on the shelf to detoxify.

(By the way, you should do this whenever considering any approach to improving your processes in any business domain, and not just PPFM.

If you don't feel the new world you've visualized would be a better place to be in, then when you finally go on the journey you won't have enough enthusiasm for the future to overcome challenges you'll surely face.)

Chapter Three

There Be Dragons Here
(How to Deal with Seven Common Monsters That Can Swallow Your Initiative)

Why would an organization resist doing something that's clearly in its best interest: establishing an effective governance process?

An organization is made up of people. People resist changes, often with good reason. No matter how bad things seem to be at the moment, they've seen salesmen with rose-colored glasses before. They fear that once the enthusiasm fades and the smokescreen clears, the alternative reality will prove to be little or no improvement. Meanwhile, they have to put up with disruption.

Does the following scenario sound familiar?

Organizations that need to improve the speed and costs of delivering their products and services often turn to PPFM for help.

There's a broad consensus that such practices offer real benefits in the form of cost reductions (eliminating redundancies, choosing the most cost-effective solutions, etc.), and in competitive advantages (speed to market and improved satisfaction of customer demands). So the organization gives it a try (remember Yoda?).

After many months of honest effort entwined with wrangling and dissension – and after hundreds of thousands (if not millions) of dollars have been spent with apparently no effect – the initiative slowly fades into obscurity.

People breathe a sigh of relief as they slide into old habits. If they're not laid off, the former staff of the PPFMO is scattered as fillers across the organization. Perhaps the external pressures have diminished such that the company has enough resources to limp along despite its inadequacies, or perhaps things continue their slow downward spiral.

But eventually the stakeholders make themselves heard once again, executives are pressured to produce results, and the organization decides "Hey, let's start a PPFMO!"

*This time it's different because they've turned to **you** to make it right.* This time they'll have selected someone who's going to defeat the monsters in their path not by charging straight at them (which hasn't worked too well in the past), but by recognizing them.

(I don't have a lot of personal experience with dragons. So I'll take the word of J. R. Tolkien and the imagery of Peter Jackson in *The Hobbit*.)

When dragons are aroused, they can burn you to a crisp, which is about the only course of action they consider. When they solve a problem, it stays solved!

But they'd rather be snoozing comfortably on whatever resources they've accumulated.

Dragons are fairly light sleepers, ever-alert to whatever or whoever is trying to grab their loot. To get past them you want to minimize the disturbance, especially if it's your intention to grab control of some of their loot, which is precisely what a PPFMO does.

You won't have Bilbo Baggins' invisibility ring. So if your disturbance is very slight, and doesn't appear to signal a raid on the resource pile, the dragons might just open an eye as you pass by. Or accept you as a helper.

A subordinate one perhaps, but at least they won't burn you to a crisp. Maybe as a plaything, they'll give you that very piece of loot you were hoping for.

In fact, they may like you so much they won't let you out of the cave and back to your real job. Since at present you're contemplating the possibility of becoming a crispy critter, that might sound like a good problem to have.

So onward to learn how to escape traps that might have been laid for you.

Change is Always Hard

Regardless of how much sense something makes, it can't be obvious to the rest of the organization, or they would have already done it by themselves.

Many books (including the project management classics) emphasize the need for top-level support in making a change happen.

But the root of success goes much deeper. Very few leaders are successful in transforming their organizations by ordering it to be so, or through the power of persuasive speeches. Or even through collective involvement. People just prefer things to remain stable in their personal lives and at work.

> *"He'll sit here, and he'll say, 'Do this! Do that!' And nothing will happen. Poor Ike – it won't be a bit like the Army.*
> *He'll find it very frustrating."*
> **~President Harry Truman, commenting on General Dwight Eisenhower's election to the U.S. Presidency**

Organizations reflect the preferences of the people working in them, and crave stability while wanting to be efficient in order to be effective. These desires result in processes that can be repeated rather than being reinvented. They are the very concept of *bureaucracy* (in the positive sense as first defined by Max Weber) as they institutionalize those practices that work.

While bureaucracy should permit change for processes that are provably more efficient, it intentionally impedes changing a successful trajectory at the whim of one or two zealots who believe they have a better idea.

When people use the word "bureaucracy" negatively, they mean an organization that has come to value stability and caution much more than it desires competitive efficiency. Competitiveness holds little value for very large market-dominating corporations, and none whatsoever for government agencies, which explains why so much "bad bureaucracy" is seen in those settings.

One way or another, organizations are designed to strongly resist any substantive change. Effective organizational change requires one simple driver: There must be a compelling reason obvious to everyone involved. Even if the change might bring improvement for some or all, the magnitude of the benefit must dramatically overshadow the effort required to achieve it.

After all that effort, if things aren't greatly different from what's currently happening (and the change might not succeed anyway), then why expend the effort? Why take the risk that the new approaches might end up making things worse?

Let's say you've been able to make the case that the benefits really are worth the effort. The dragons, however, aren't team players. It's all about them. They have little concern for the interests of the whole organization unless their own interests coincide. So they'll still lie on top of their hoards of money, not because they have any useful plans for it, but because it has become theirs. They are ever-vigilant to make sure you don't take it away. If you try, they will try to burn you to a crisp. It's not personal – it's just what they do. And here is where they lurk.

Seven Causes of Failure

Professional risk managers identify many kinds of risks that can cause an initiative to fail. In PPFM and governance, several reasons for failures keep popping up, both in published case studies and in the many organizations I've worked with. Almost all of those failures stem from the same root causes: The organization doesn't have a robust management posture, and won't embrace the need for change.

These organizational management risks fall into seven general areas:

1. Executives aren't promoting the seriousness of the issues

The PPFMO can't drive a conversation about the "big threat," as it's a minor staff appendage often seen as concerned only with its process mania and irrelevant to the rest of the organization.

If necessary, the leaders of the PPFMO initiative must expend every nickel of political capital to get the organization's leaders to articulate the major threat to the organization the PPFMO is intended to solve.

For the root problem to be a credible threat, it must be something that could have a heavy impact on something the organization values, whether that be jobs, funding, or elements of the mission.

That's something an executive can understand and articulate, and make sure people do something about.

2. Fear of Undermining Authority

It's wise to question who's going to benefit from the change, as it's seldom in the interest of key people. The simple fact is an organization rewards the behavior of successful managers.

People running the organization got to their positions because they were a good fit for the culture.

You can wave best practice documents at people all you want, and lecture until you're blue in the face.

But you can't change personalities, ethics or ambitions.

Instead, you must tailor any shift in the decision-making process to recognize the current leadership's interests, rather than being seen as a means to undermine them.

3. Fear of Transparency

In many organizations with weak processes, managers make decisions in secrecy even though there are no secrets to protect. They don't trust their own competence, so they don't want anyone knowing what they decided or why. Everything they do is "bad" politics (one-on-one, behind closed doors, behind backs). This is just as common in larger commercial organizations as it is in the public sector.

These types of concerns are difficult to overcome because they go to the heart of the organization's culture. For these managers, your effort needs to focus on recording their decisions rather than the decision-making process.

In the long run, it doesn't really matter **why** they decided something, but it does matter what they decided.

The rest of the organization can't carry out the leaders' wishes if nobody knows what they are.

4. Fear of Accountability

Managers may not want to be held accountable for their decisions and/or for the work they manage, which is by far the most common reason for fearing accountability. In truth, very few people desire such accountability if they can get by without it. (Before casting too many stones at "those people," let's admit that applies to you and me as well.)

The big question then for the PPFMO director is whether this reflects the overall corporate culture. The PPFMO doesn't have the clout to force accountability onto a managerial structure that rejects it.

However, people are likely to be a bit more cooperative with those on whom they actually depend to do their work. In any complex organization there are cross-group dependencies that need to be honored, whether it's customer deliveries or handoffs between functional areas.

That's the leverage point where it's possible to gain agreement on monitoring those events. Once this falls into place, the rest tends to follow.

5. Fear of Rigidity

Organizations often resist instituting governance processes they fear will be too rigid, diverting resources to achieve process compliance instead of working on timely delivery of quality solutions.

In addition to the burden on resources, managers fear a tedious change management process that prevents adaptation to changing circumstances. Those who have been through a by-the-book implementation have every reason to hold this concern!

Successful implementations must emphasize the amount of tailoring possible to reduce the process burden, the existence of a bypass option with a signed waiver, and the endorsement of agility.

It won't be enough just to say these things: people will draw their own conclusions from what happens with the first two or three initiatives required to undergo the process.

Learn from the earlier case studies. Only ask for what you need, know what you're going to do with it when you get it, and be willing to explain it to others.

6. Lack of Supporting Processes

Delivery of goods and services requires support from organizational elements outside the project team, such as finance, contracting and facilities.

All too often, those groups only know one way for doing things they've used in the past. They also have pocket veto power by failing to take action. Or worse, by incompetently performing their tasks.

The PPFMO must work with these groups from the outset to understand them, and take advantage of whatever processes *are* working. Over time, the PPFMO effort can be a catalyst for improvements in those support areas as well.

7. Maturity Model Dogma

Many professional associations have developed maturity models to portray ascension through progressive levels of competence. Of course, consultancies are happy to provide long-term support while helping you try to climb the maturity ladder.

There are a couple of problems with the maturity model concept. One is that reality doesn't operate in a convenient linear fashion, so a step-wise approach isn't always practical.

The more important problem is that there's no inherent value in achieving the pinnacle of maturity (and to be fair, the model builders made no such claim). No matter how elegant it is, a process that doesn't add value is nothing more than an overhead burden.

If blind adherence to practice standards and maturity models is a form of religion, it has a countervailing heresy: the small number of writers who have considered Anti-Maturity.

These writers suggest that it's a waste of time to try to climb the maturity model framework, as long as the organization itself hasn't adopted the necessary values. At its source, that culture shift is what *The Simmer System* is all about.

The good news is all of these processes are intertwined. Over time, the impracticality of following some processes and not others will become clear.

At that point, the organization will accept additional constraints in order to improve the processes that have proven their benefit.

The trick is to make sure the set of processes selected in the early rounds create benefits with the least possible amount of disruption, so that the overall effort gains credibility and the good will needed for acceptance of further refinements.

Taming the Dragons: More Case Studies

In an ideal situation, risks would be recognized and a plan of action would be developed to avoid them. But the situation seldom is ideal; otherwise, there probably wouldn't be a need for a new PPFMO initiative.

Most likely, vulnerabilities in the organizational culture have led to this point, and the culture encourages reactivity rather than conscious decisions.

The odds are the journey will already be underway before the captains of the ship trouble themselves about details like reading a map.

Whether you're going to try to avoid these monsters, or just want to be prepared when you encounter them, the approach is the same: Take small enough steps to avoid spooking the dragons, and large enough ones to get you past them. Sounds pretty mystical, right?

Now you're going to see examples of how to use this in practice.

Case Study 5: Killing Your Own Initiative With Kindness

Sometimes executives' desires to help a situation do more harm than good. A large commercial organization was very late on a major business initiative and heavily over budget. The company's top executives – who had large amounts of shares, and stood to make a great deal of money if it succeeded but lose a lot if it failed – had made public commitments to achieve the project by a certain date that had come and gone.

Though they'd been doing everything they knew how to make the initiative succeed, one PPFMO had already been disbanded and another put in its place.

Symptoms and Causes

The solution had become impossibly complex as the underlying platform was ill-suited to the task. Senior executives, who kept having good ideas, visited the vendor site to brow-beat the vendor to get their ideas directly implemented. Often the project team would have no idea of what those ideas were until they showed up as new features ... or more often, as calculation engine meltdowns and delays in deliveries.

Executives had also launched different project teams that were unknowingly working on conflicting approaches [***transparency***].

Staff members had good reason to believe that raising issues would be viewed as ***undermining authority***.

The PPFMO had insisted on change proposal documents in the past [***maturity model dogma***].

But that idea faded as staff members considered themselves too busy to do the analysis [***fear of rigidity***], managers were afraid of suggesting problems might exist, and executives refused to participate [***fear of accountability***]. So issues were neither raised nor addressed.

And there was no method of proposing and analyzing needed changes to the plan, unless you could get an executive to demand the vendor to make the change.

Meanwhile, time continued to tick onward.

Solution and Cause Overcome

Analysts warned of a significant impact on the company's share price if the initiative was delayed once again [***compelling reason to change***].

The PPFMO realized that something needed to be done and dropped its insistence on completing change proposal templates [*dogma*]. Instead, it developed a decision paper clearly explaining why the project was at a point of no return, showing what the options were and asking for a concrete decision.

This document, with its business language, was easier to grasp for managers and executives already focused by the potential loss of lucrative stock options.

The executives reached a very clear decision: launch something that will work well enough to make some sales on time. If what you're doing isn't needed for the launch, stop doing it!

Formal status reports became appendices to a more powerful demand for managers' clear commitments. Are you going to deliver by the date you're now saying [*transparency, accountability*]?

A formal contract management process with the primary vendors replaced the sponsor's ad-hoc directives. Related initiatives (such as the staff retraining effort) were included in regular coordination meetings [*supporting processes*].

Outcome

By tailoring governance to conversations that the company could accept, the initiative launched on the announced date with the product fully operational, although without some of the more exotic features executives had hoped for.

Investors leaving their capital in the company had become placated enough so that the offering could be refined in a more orderly manner over time. And it was.

Effective governance isn't an all-powerful magic bullet, and it can't rewrite history. By launch day, the company had spent nearly as much in recovering the project as it had intended to make in the first three years of operation.

Unfortunately, the experience wasn't healthy for everyone's career, which is what accountability can do for you. Fearing the consequences of being held accountable is also why many managers in a process-averse organization oppose transparency.

Unfortunately, this organization wasted millions of dollars before it started holding people accountable.

Case Study 4 Revisited: Benign Neglect

Let's look at an example from the other end of the complexity spectrum at a non-IT program. Governance failures aren't the result of being in certain industries; they're the result of organizational cultures.

In this case, an organization within a large enterprise operated a relatively small but important program responsible for maintenance of some significant assets. A decade earlier, this organization had done sterling work establishing the initial inventory of those assets and eliminating a great number of obsolete items (nearly 90% of the initial inventory!)

With the program in a stable maintenance mode, executive attention focused on problems elsewhere, which unfortunately led to the program staff resting on their laurels. In fact, resting so deeply that they had fallen asleep on the job. (Well, not literally, because most of the time they never showed up at work long enough to fall asleep.)

Symptoms and Causes

The program staff had completely abdicated its work. The supporting contractors budgeted, planned, and managed their own work. Records were stored on personal computers rather than in the enterprise's shared files, and the program maintained no meaningful metrics [***transparency***].

Questions from senior managers received multiple answers, all of them wrong and sometimes intentionally so [***accountability***]. Given a generally fixed budget, unit costs escalated while actual work done slowed to a crawl.

Customers didn't know how to get things done through the PPFMO staff, which had no plans or process guides, because the staff didn't want to commit to following them [*fear of rigidity*].

Their fear was well-placed. The few they had produced were lazily and blindly recycled from much larger programs, and entirely inappropriate for the situation [*maturity model dogma*].

Though managers further up the line became concerned, strong corrective action was inconsistent with the corporate culture. They had put up with this obviously deteriorating situation for over two years before taking any action.

Nobody in the organization ever got fired over anything. Even in the case of a near-100% outsourced activity (as this program was), contracts were renewed, no matter how poor the performance.

Those trends weren't likely to be reversed over this small program. If things got so bad that litigation ensued, the enterprise had enough money that it would delay, deny and eventually pay up [*lack of compelling reason to change*].

Solution and Cause Overcome

Due to bureaucratic inertia, the PPFMO contract lapsed. In the hastily cobbled-together bridge contract, a PPFMO contractor received an interim contract with re-competition to follow [introducing a *compelling reason*].

Seeking to relieve the higher-level managers' most immediate frustrations, the PPFMO contractor staff began documenting the answers it provided, then loaded the data into the client's SharePoint site [*restoring transparency*].

Soon, missing and bottlenecked actions became clear. The PPFMO deflected pressure to build a detailed Microsoft Project schedule and formal plans before taking further action [*fending off dogma*].

Instead, we used Agile month-to-month plans [*avoiding rigidity*] to get the gaps filled and bottlenecks opened [*instituting accountability*].

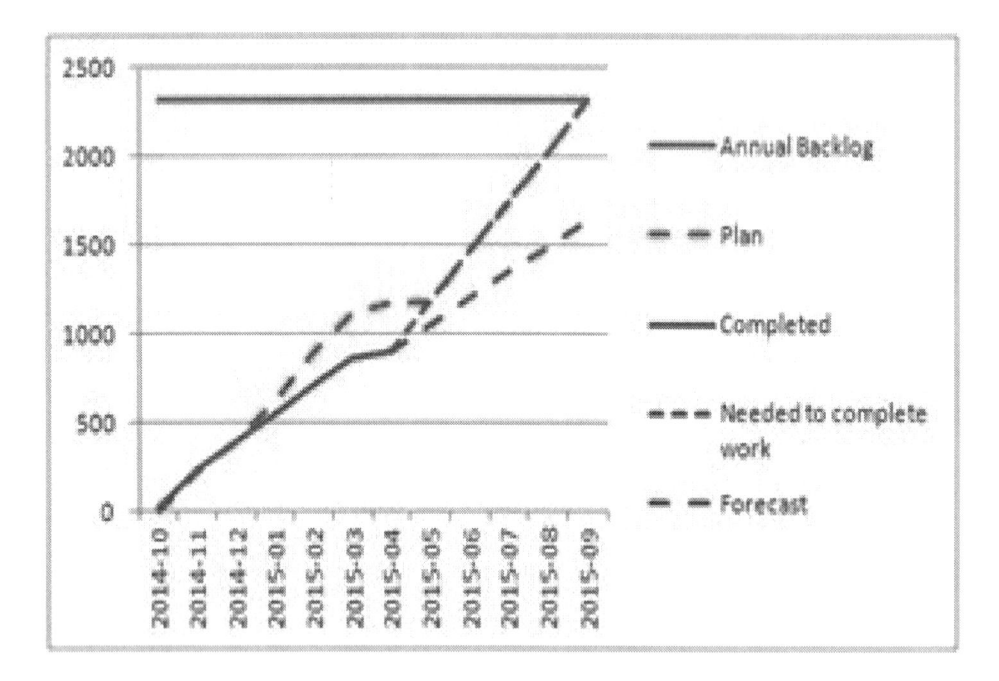

The PPFMO added critical provisions allowing for planning and oversight, as well as flexibility in supporting contracts [**better supporting processes**].

(Yo, Sherlock, I said you shouldn't try to deduce which case studies fit where in my bio. Data in this book are adjusted for illustration purposes, so any dates only mean the book was written in 2015.

Again, it doesn't matter who did what and in what year. This sort of thing can and does happen in every type of organization as time goes by and people move around.)

Outcome

Within four months, the PPFMO had gone from a 30% oversight rate to having solid documentation and repair plans for 75% of the assets.

Plus, senior managers had a simple status dashboard they could use to understand the true status of the program. For the first time in two years, they were gaining confidence in the information they were getting.

While many key issues and actions remained unresolved, they were at least recorded and tracked. In short, because the program had turned the corner, it was now positioned to sustain reasonable standards of effectiveness.

Taming the "Dragons" in Your World

A "hot button" is pressed to cause a full-scale, irreversible response to a situation that poses so great a threat that only an immediate and all-in response will do. There are no halfway measures, no abort features, and no apologies.

Remember what happens when you awaken the dragons. They launch their fire first and ask questions later! Even if you might have rendered it some useful service, it's too late. You're now a crispy critter, and so is everyone around you.

You and your governance ideas are aimed at making meaningful change in a strong, long-standing culture. All of the situations described above are the results of fears that arise when the culture realizes that something is happening in its environment.

Tripping over one or more of those fears in effect presses the "hot buttons" that awaken the associated dragons, and creates an instant and usually catastrophic defensive reaction. So try not to press them if it can be helped!

The Simmer System works by knowing where the fear-induced hot buttons are and deliberately working around them. You sneak past the dragons, rather than crunching blindly and noisily through the darkness.

You don't try to snatch control of their money; you help them manage it themselves. You gain collaboration and reduce fear by working with your fellow managers on problems they want solved, instead of trying to impose on them your solutions to problems whose existence they've not yet acknowledged.

The two cases I've discussed show that significant organizational culture issues can be overcome with some flexibility and a lot of patience. Once you recognize the root causes, you can take actions that recognize, avoid and bypass those buttons by taking advantage of opportunities the culture provides.

Here are some ways to get past the dragons that may be standing in your path. Any one of them can prevent your PPFMO from succeeding. Not all of them will be present in every situation. But you can't afford to assume that they aren't there.

Change Blockers	Workarounds
No compelling reason to change	Before suggesting to executives that they aren't providing enough support, develop evidence of ways in which the organization does not appear to be taking their initial pronouncements seriously. Work with them to get a strong, simple re-statement of the problem, and set up periodic review meetings to make sure the lower managers are carrying out their response actions.
Undermining Authority	When explaining any proposed governance process with the current decision-makers, take care to explain their role in the process, showing how they will continue to have decision authority.
Fear of Transparency	Emphasize that people can only carry out decisions if they know what has been decided on. Give in on the actual amount of information that is released; for instance, knowing how or when it was decided is a best practice but not necessary.
Fear of Accountability	Gain agreement on the points at which accountability - that is, delivering on commitments - is necessary. Focus at first on timeliness of handoffs; don't worry about detailed task tracking until the big things are taken care of.
Fear of Rigidity	Explain how processes can be tailored and even waived where needed. Lead off with simple efforts and simple compliance requirements.
Lack of Supporting Processes	Work with the proponents to tweak their processes, rather than fighting a losing battle to seek wholesale changes. Meanwhile, use approaches that make best use of whatever processes the organization does have in place.
Maturity Model Dogma	Avoid trying to achieve a target maturity level, or to build out a complete level. Pick the most feasible and effort-efficient elements of the model and implement those.

Next Steps

"The plan is nothing. The planning is everything."
~General (and future president) Dwight D. Eisenhower

This chapter discussed some of the risks that may affect your change initiative. Although all of them could occur, some will and others won't. You can't know which is which, so you have to consider them all.

Recognizing them, avoiding those you can, and preparing for those that you can't avoid are the elements of "risk management." It won't prevent the risks from happening, but it'll make sure your initiative doesn't get derailed by things that could have been foreseen.

The next chapter describes the four core bedrock principles of *The Simmer System*. Sometimes the next steps aren't clear because a situation can shift, which can make it hard to follow the sequences of specific steps.

So join me in my discussion about how following these principles will keep you focused on the goal and away from pointless detours and dead-ends.

But first, let's make sure you understand the risks that surround your PPFMO effort.

EXERCISE 3: ASSESSING THE VOYAGE

Now that you understand more about what's lurking in your territory, you're close to heading off on the quest to bring some order to the environment.

So how difficult a journey should you expect it to be?

Place each of the potential obstacles on a risk grid, such as the one in the workbook, where 1 is low and 5 is high. You can also adjust this grid to whatever configuration your organization may already be using for a Risk Matrix:

PPFMO RISK ASSESSMENT GRID

	1	2	3	4	5
5					
4					
3					
2					
1					

(You can find intermediate worksheets and the matrix in electronic form on the resource website: www.Simmer-System.com.)

Chapter Four

The Four Core Bedrock Principles

"In matters of style, swim with the current; in matters of principle, stand like a rock."
~Thomas Jefferson

During the violent insurgency case study in Chapter Two, one of the program managers, who also sat on an intermediate governance board, had several projects that were falling behind schedule.

I was stunned when out of the blue he said, "Why are we bothering to track these delivery dates anyway? It's not as if anyone really cares." At first I thought he was just pulling my chain (which, if you remember from the case study, wasn't that unusual). After all, he was a fully certified project manager.

I instinctively responded with, "If nobody cares, why don't we cancel the project and put the money to better use? Then we'll start working on it again in five years, if anybody cares by then, and finish it sometime after that."

I like Spockian logic. Even when I don't like the answer, the consistency of it appeals to me. That's because I am left-brained.

Right-brained people ("feelers") hate logic and despise processes. When someone says something that seems illogical – which makes the person sound unprofessional and untrustworthy to you – a response based on your logical view of the world can sound snide, unfeeling or dismissive. That's how it feels to them anyway. Even when such a response is richly deserved, if the idea is to have a conversation then I wouldn't recommend this as a tack to take.

Besides exposing a fundamental difference in philosophies, you will now recognize that in being flabbergasted at this heretical statement I had fallen into the trap of "best practice dogma." However, in this case it provoked the correct response: "Five years is ridiculous! We need this done in two years at the latest because…"

Through the ensuing conversation we learned that the incessant delays were not news to his actual customers. At least in his version of reality, they had actually caused the slippage by changing their minds, or being unable to make up their minds, about what they wanted.

In some cases it was due to alterations in the underlying regulations they had to include in their business processes.

By entertaining his thought, rather than dismissing it as obstructive (even if that had been the intent), we could begin a serious discussion. We moved quickly from "who cares when we deliver?" to "we have to deliver in the next two years." And we had exposed a significant issue that needed to be addressed with the customers.

A few board members pointed out the meter was still running on the contractors who were producing these solutions. Sooner or later the program would be demanding funds to top off its contract accounts. That concern, and the discussions of how to deal with it, led to good outcomes:

- We decided if the customers came to the table with their own money (thereby conceding their responsibility for delays and costs), we would re-baseline.

  Otherwise, the customers would be notified the project would have to be halted until they could stabilize their requirements enough to justify resuming the work. Either way, the decision would be transparent.

- We had a cordial discussion about the fundamental principles of all three of the PPFM disciplines. A recalcitrant program manager agreed to provide (somewhat) realistic forecasts, and the PPFMO came to a deeper understanding of the limits of pre-defining the situation.

Given that particular organization, the second outcome may have been of greater value than the first.

****

A fledgling PPFMO will be tested early and often. Remember, it's not about you or the practices you aspire to deliver. It's purely about control. People will do what they can to subvert control so they can go back to doing what they were doing, which might work fine for them but not for the rest of the organization.

Mark Suster's excellent blog post, "What You Can Learn From a Scorpion" (the URL link is in the Reference annex) is based on Aesop's fable about the scorpion that stabs the frog that is ferrying it across the river. He explores the notion that people do what they do partly because they can, and they like exercising that power regardless of the cost.

Some people take counterproductive action because it's their assigned role and they're unable to see the larger picture. Whereas others act badly because that's just who they are. Even people favorably disposed towards you can find the transition from leisurely chaos to rowing in time to the calendar's drumbeat to be exhausting.

When a bug bites you, your first response is to scratch your skin, which makes the bite fester before you get around to applying ointment to take out the sting. It's human nature to seek relief by getting rid of the symptom rather than solving the real problem.

Red Pill, Blue Pill? Just Give Us the Magic Pill!

In one engagement, after the typical early struggles we achieved notable success in spreading enthusiasm for project management across the rank-and-file. That happened when we got the issues register (which included the age of the issues) added to the agenda for the executive project review meeting.

At the meeting, astonished executives took immediate action. Long-pending decisions were made, and resources were refocused to their assigned tasks. Responding to not-so-veiled allusions by the executives about one obvious solution to apparently having to do the managers' jobs for them, mid-level managers became interested in clearing action items and issues before the monthly status report got to the executives.

The project started humming along, and we recovered almost half of a six-month delay in a few weeks. People worked like beavers on what was undoubtedly the company's most important initiative. This was a really big company, so that's how important the project was.

After a few months, some of the people who'd earlier set themselves up as human roadblocks conceded the process was working. We took it as a sign of success when one of the managers said, "You know, this project management stuff is working pretty well. But it's really wearing on my staff, and a lot of other stuff isn't getting done." (Remember, this is the company's top priority with billions of dollars at stake.)

"Couldn't we go back to the way we were before, with you guys laying the project management stuff on top of it, so we can go about our business?"

This shows the difference between compliance and understanding. They had completely missed the point! We were finally seeing progress because the company **was** now going about its business, rather than the sub-group leaders going about theirs.

People want a magic pill (like "Lose 30 pounds in 30 days without dieting") that makes everything better with little to no effort or change on their part. Sorry – that's not going to happen with *The Simmer System*. There *will* be work, and there *will* be change.

The way to get your colleagues to accept the burden of work required, and to limit the amount of resistance that typically comes with change, is to have them work on things that solve *their* problems and let them decide to change themselves.

Guiding Compromise

Warning: The Simmer System can present challenges, because for a while it will ask you to make compromises or take half-steps in the interest of moving towards an ultimate goal.

When you do that, you'll be acting in a way that's less than the established standard of practice. Is that allowed? Maybe a better question would be, when does it not happen?

Most professional best practices come with a set of principles. Many have a formal code of ethics that you may be asked to sign as part of your certification. Such a code has the advantage of having to exist only on paper.

Many things look good on paper, but reality offers more challenging situations.

In order to make **some** progress in an environment that doesn't always embrace **any** known code of ethics, *The Simmer System* openly advocates making many compromises while adhering to a subset of core principles that must not be compromised.

No way. Values are values. Without values, you have nothing. I'm going to stand on my principles. I like that; it sounds nice and clear. But it doesn't work that way.

Any value system consists of a set of guiding, non-negotiable principles. But it gets more complicated. Any complex system – including societies and religions, and most organizations – has an equally complex value system, such that some of the principles conflict with one another.

Latching on to one stated value usually brings you into gross violation of a different principle contained within the same complex system.

That might have been as hard to follow as it was difficult writing it. So maybe an example would be better. Most systems include values such as:

- Be tolerant of a wide range of opinion. You get better solutions that way.

- Our way is the best way to do things. It has proven to be so. Any attempt to do otherwise (perhaps even "to think otherwise") is an unacceptable deviation from the norms of the group.

Be honest. Doesn't your company, your church, your professional code say exactly this? In everyday situations, we understand this and get along with the contradictions.

The downside? People looking to discredit the PPFMO process to make it go away will choose not to understand. They will latch on to these inconsistencies to prove you're incompetent.

Compromise tempts you to abandon some aspect of your principles, perhaps exposing what your true principle really is (the one you won't relinquish). But once you've compromised an "unshakeable" principle, especially in a public setting, there're no way to stand on it in the future with any credibility, and it threatens your ability to stand on any other principle. Your "red line" drawn in the sand has been washed out in the tide.

You and the PPFMO can get past such criticisms by refusing to compromise the important things. *The Simmer System* relies on identifying fundamental principles that will help you decide when to give ground without affecting them, and when enough is enough.

In the case of PPFM, those principles are:

1. **Integration:** From a process governance perspective, everything relates to everything else. As you improve in one area, the others will eventually be drawn along for the ride (aka: *The Pasta Principle*).

2. **Zero-Sum:** Governance can't work if undisclosed alternative channels are tolerated, with the key word being "undisclosed."

   Your processes keep things honest and transparent by building a Zero-Sum environment. When everything is on the table, nothing happens under it. When every shift in direction requires adjusting something elsewhere, decision-makers have no choice but to consider at least one other set of consequences of their decisions.

3. **Integrity:** (This is preaching to the choir for those of you reading this book.) The PPFMO must deal in facts, only facts, and just the facts. In these early days, any re-interpretation by the PPFMO will be attacked as a deliberate distortion. Just let the facts to speak for themselves; that will give the board plenty to do.

   The worst possible scenario would be a situation in which the PPFMO feels its position to be so weak that it connives to alter data or records to reflect the way management wishes things were rather than how they are. If that's the case, please shut the PPFMO down now and save overhead expenses.

4. **Purposeful Humility:** The PPFMO can make a lot of mileage by taking on tasks nobody else wants. Or doing some aspect of their job for them as long as that can be used as a leverage point to advance the PPFMO's objectives. If it doesn't, then don't fritter away your limited resources.

Notice that "adherence to published best practices" isn't one of the core principles. That doesn't mean they're rejected – it's just not their time. Sticking to these principles is your means of getting to the place where best practices become a viable option. But they aren't until you get to that point.

Much of this book emphasizes "hacks" to establish various aspects of PPFM. It's not a matter of cheap tricks, or diluting the professional standards of practice. You'll get to that standard in the end, but you have to get to the end first. You're going to get your colleagues to devise and infuse the professional values and practices of their own accord. These hacks present ways to get them to undertake activities of value to them, which also happen to lead towards your desired destination.

The Simmer System is about moving the effort forward without creating so much ill will that ordinary reluctance becomes active opposition. You can't have a happy ending if you get thrown out of the movie theater halfway through the show.

The Peril of a Restart

Newly-emerging organizations turn to seasoned managers and executives to help them transition from the idea stage to ramping up to efficient, competitive manufacturing or service delivery. Unfortunately, it's not always successful.

An experienced manager from a well-run, sophisticated organization may have difficulty adjusting to the chaos that comes with early maturity cycles in management and governance.

It may be even harder to make an impact in an organization stuck part way up the curve, because they'll have many shelfware processes (manuals that people seldom read and/or follow).

In an organization that doesn't bother to follow any published processes, why should yours be treated differently?

Managers in process-averse organizations that have been through earlier failed change initiatives have learned some lessons from that experience.

Proposed changes...

- May reduce their autonomy.
- May promise wonderful things in the long-term, but are certain to entail a great deal of work in the short term.
- Seldom deliver all (if any) of the benefits their champions claim.
- May be dictated from on high. But they have to be executed at the lowest level to take effect, so they can be fought off.

One way or another, the change agent and/or the executive sponsor can be defused:

- Once the change agent is removed, the initiative ends.
- Some managers may learn that "dirty tricks" (bad politics) can undermine the change agent.
- If dirty politics doesn't work, inertia is also powerful.
- If lower levels ignore the change initiative, it will be a while before the change agents complain to a high enough level to make any difference.
- Once the highest level does find out, not much will happen.
- If lower levels claim the initiative is getting in the way of doing the customers' work, the sponsors will tell the change managers to back off.

- Once the initiative has been delayed to a glacial pace, eventually the change agent will grow discouraged and leave, or the high-level champions will move on or lose interest.
- Once the change agent leaves or the sponsor loses interest, the initiative goes back on the shelf, and any policies and procedures that were launched can be ignored.

In a restart, any new approach will have to be adopted by consensus. There are too many people who know how to get around any process they don't want to follow.

It's not very likely that you'll start out with a true consensus in any organization, least of all one dedicated to the principle of each manager doing their own thing.

So you'll have to grow this consensus from the bottom up and spreading sideways, working with colleagues to accomplish agreed-upon tasks that move you in that direction of best practices.

You should be warned that agreeing to not implement (or deferring implementing) best practices in favor of doing what works could earn criticism from purists within the organization.

You'll be amazed at how many people who only recently refused to have anything to do with any processes or practices now denounce you for heresy from the best standards of the profession.

These accusations have nothing to do with you or the proposal you're making. If these "sudden converts" knew all this before you arrived, they certainly didn't put that knowledge to use. They just don't want to see PPFM succeed, so they'll use any pretext to filibuster or undermine your efforts.

Now that you've seen why you need principles to guide you through a wilderness of unpredictable situations, let's take a closer look at the principles themselves.

THE FOUR CORE PPFM PRINCIPLES

1. INTEGRATION: THE PASTA PRINCIPLE

The basic premise of *The Pasta Principle* is that regardless of which individual strand is pulled on, all of the strands stick to it and become badly entangled.

Bypass the Swamps – Take the Trails

Throughout this book you'll learn about steps to prevent the organization from trampling the PPFMO along the way. You'll learn about them in the order they're likely to occur, and an order that minimizes the resistance. But the order doesn't really matter as long as you're finding ways to keep moving forward cooperatively.

Each of those steps generates positive momentum toward a reasonably effective governance capability. Regardless of the actual order of the steps, the process will result in the creation and continued viability of that capability.

Many people will tell you that incrementalism can slow the process of achieving anything useful. You and the organization know what's right, so "ripping the bandage off" will make it quicker and hurt less in the end.

Logically, that's probably true. But in your case, that won't work. For organizations with a history of PPFMO initiatives on their third or fourth cycle, moving faster in a more aggressive (but therefore more controversial) approach is likely to be interrupted by a year or two of exile.

Experienced PPFM implementers – especially those who've had the luxury of operating within process-mature organizations – tend to worry about this approach because it doesn't include the full spectrum of PPFM solutions.

The more complex the solution, and the bigger and broader the change, the stronger the resistance will be to yet another layer of overhead. That is true in relatively mature organizations as well as those that are less mature. In fact, the more mature the organization, the better its processes are in fighting off unproven changes.

Long-term success with more sweeping visions must build from early success in solving the problem the initiative first set out to solve. The best way to achieve early successes is to pick targets that can be reached with the resources on hand.

Don't get bogged down plunging off into a straight-line approach. Take the trails that are already in place and make some progress. If you keep heading in roughly the right direction, as guided by the other principles, you'll eventually come out of the swamp.

The "Pasta" in the Principle

Briefly allow your mind to wander from the "exciting" topic of program management and governance, to eating a plate of al dente linguini heaped with a delectable, messy tomato sauce.

Eating pasta doesn't require a great of finesse, but there are certain approaches that won't work well:

- You can't swallow the entire mound of noodles and sauce all at the same time.

- You'll be at the table for hours if you pull each noodle out one at a time.

- You wouldn't enjoy the mixture of flavors if the cook gave each ingredient to you to eat one at a time.

A good way to eat pasta is to stick your fork into the noodles, then swirl them around to catch the sauce. Some people twirl them on the fork; some people use a spoon to get an even stronger spooling effect. If some of the bits you hoped for fall off, you just get them in a different bite.

Having the noodles and sauce together tastes wonderful, and can be accomplished without too much mess. On top of all that, the mechanics of the twirling just makes the whole thing seem even more "foreign" and sophisticated, which is twice the fun!

It's not just the eating that has a technique to it. The best results when cooking the noodles involve attachment of one component to another. In business you don't implement a practice then forget about it, just as you don't take freshly-cooked pasta and dump it into a colander so all the water goes down the drain. Cooks save the starchy water to add to the next batch of sauce or pot of pasta, as it helps the sauce stick to the pasta.

Always keep this *Pasta Principle* in mind while implementing your PPFMO: Like tangled noodles on a plate, almost all aspects of governance activity are connected to most other facets of governance. You can't eat all of it in one bite, and you can't implement just one facet at a time (the "change control" sub-process seems to be a favorite nominee for this) without invoking other aspects of the solution.

Nor can you select in advance which pieces of the solution to emphasize and de-emphasize. You have to go with what you can get and build from there.

You may be able to leave out some essential ingredients in your organization. But once you're into the implementation phase, some ingredients are already mixed in, and some ingredients take too long to cook to add them in at the last minute.

You won't be able to pre-plan which ingredients to add and when, so just go with what you can get going. As long as you've got the basics, it will work out.

Chefs adjust basic recipes according to the qualities of the ingredients and cookware to ensure a perfectly cooked meal. Likewise, you'll be adjusting your governance approach, specific tools and solutions according to the receptivity of the community your PPFMO is to serve.

Variation is not a bad thing. You'll discover the perfect sauce when it differs in some way from the good enough one you made last time using the same recipe (maybe even this one). You just need to remember what you added that made it perfect!

Any Noodle Will Do

Why do I keep insisting these things will work themselves out?

Let's focus on one noodle in the PPFM "bowl." Saying "I want to know what's going on with the top priority projects" implies many PPFM activities.

(Please don't tackle this as the first item on your to-do list just to avoid thinking about what to do. While it's a bona fide example, it may not apply to your situation or be the best place to start.)

To resolve this particular request you'll need to:

- Define "priorities." That will open some good discussions, such as "whose priorities?" and "how do we know?"

- Define "what's going on." Since this presumably means "progress against what we thought was going to happen," you'll need to clarify:

    o What you thought was going to happen (the baseline);
    o What is really happening (current status);
    o A means of portraying all this (status reporting and dashboards); and eventually,
    o Issues management to deal with things that aren't proceeding as expected.

Wow! That covered a pretty good chunk of the Project Management Body of Knowledge (PMBoK), and it was just a simple problem that needed to be solved.

Before too long, as the new issues management process begins to work, resolutions will demand action in other areas of the PPFM spectrum:

- Why are contracts consistently delayed?
- How could we not have understood this effort was dependent on that other effort?
- Why are these three top priority projects dependent on an initiative that's not on the list?

And so on.

It may take several months before you've covered the spectrum the PPFM purist might have desired. But the difference is you'll actually have it in practice, and the organization will be on its way to PPFM effectiveness.

By contrast, taking the purist approach would, after a year or more, find the organization still lingering over the review, comments and resolution process for a full-featured PPFM policy and procedural guide that took several months to create but has yet to be published.

Achieving success by taking many small steps is more likely to get you where you were going. But it's not without risk.

The Slippery Slope

Earlier, I suggested that *The Simmer System* exposes you to the risk that comes with all compromises. You have to give up something you want in order to get the thing you want more.

If the elements of the governance solution truly work together, then in the long run you can't afford to bargain those elements away.

The Pasta Principle suggests you can afford to make many short-term concessions, because eventually the things everyone has agreed upon will force most of the other governance practices to come along for the ride.

But what if they don't?

You have to move forward on the basis that you're going to find a way to get the organization culture to shift enough to accept the basic premises on which governance rests. This doesn't require a large stretch of the imagination, because PPFM practices are mostly codifications of common sense.

Sooner or later, with your help it will become obvious the organization is facing pretty massive inconsistencies. Managers are going to want to resolve those issues, as long as it can appear to be their idea.

That is the core of *The Simmer System*. The practice that you deferred as part of an earlier compromise will be an obvious solution to the problem. In fact, you'll probably be blamed for having given up on it.

Now, that's the kind of problem you want to have! When this occurs, you'll be in a strong enough position to take the hit and accept "yes" for an answer.

2. ZERO-SUM

> *"If you have all the time and money you need, and no particular goal to meet, you don't have anything to manage. This situation isn't a management problem, it's a leadership problem."*
> ~**Paul Dienemann, Program Director, Logistics Management Institute**

Decisions are only relevant when there's something to decide. In a business or government organization, most decisions boil down to money. The organization's values and priorities are clearly spelled out by who gets it and who doesn't.

Project managers and regular line managers often consider funding as the product of a mysterious external force. Of course that's not the case, as money doesn't appear out of thin air. Even the government has a process for printing more when it runs out.

Managers obtain funds in similar ways in both the public and private sectors:

- They plan for it in a long-range forecast against which the organization can make allocation decisions.

- They must raid their own accounts.

- They must get a higher-level manager to squeeze it out of a collective forecast or budget. That manager in turn raids another funded activity that will experience its own difficulties.

  There's nothing inherently wrong with this approach; in fact, it's sometimes the only way to add money to an activity. But it does lead to a series of knock-on actions, all of which are unexpected and some of which turn out to be unfortunate. And of course, some other program loses funding thanks to you. There will be payback one day.

- There is another way. In a non-Zero-Sum world you can find a sponsor who has wads of cash squirreled away in off-the-books accounts, and get them to give you more money when you run out of what you were originally given. In a process-averse organization, this is precisely what happens in most programs most of the time.

Within this last scenario, management tolerates imaginary practices (such as elaborate rituals leading to the preparation of budget submittals that are almost completely unrelated to the actual expenditures) for the simple reason that they create confusion, which in turn eliminates transparency.

The Simmer System provides a way to start off showing executives that governance doesn't force them to give up their decision rights. If anything, it ensures that their decisions are more likely to be carried out.

Exactly What is Zero-Sum?

Zero-Sum (and the transparency required to ensure you have that situation) is a core principle that can't be compromised.

A Zero-Sum situation is one in which all the resources are defined and included, and there's no slush fund that you can go to for extra money. This doesn't mean the finances of the entire enterprise have to become clear: it will work for you if you can get clarity about just those that apply to the business unit the PPFMO supports.

The project management community pays tremendous respect to the "iron triangle" of cost, schedule and scope. That too is a Zero-Sum game. You can't make a change in one without affecting the other two.

The fundamental problem managers are supposed to address is finding the balance between those three constraints. The entire governance process becomes meaningless if program managers or executives have unaccountable funds to throw into or withdraw from programs and projects at will.

Creating a Zero-Sum situation forces a conscious choice of "more for A" and "less for B." Action proposals must consider all sources of resources and funding, so that any action's equal and opposite reaction and the related trade-offs are considered and revealed.

The fact that an increase has to be offset by a decrease establishes the creative tension between the manager demanding increased funds, and the other managers who will have to relinquish some of their funds.

The PPFMO doesn't attempt to resolve this balancing act, as that's up to the various proponents or the governance board.

The PPFMO did take the action needed to make a decision possible and necessary, because Zero-Sum created the boundaries that caused that opposing reaction.

The best place to take money from is the one that causes the least damage from being short-changed. That's often not the case. Money generally gets taken from the activity that presents the least procedural hurdles.

In an earlier chapter you saw how the PPFMO itself can be subjected to excessive and unproductive conflict. Here I'm discussing good conflict, the kind that sets up creative tension (the equal and opposite reaction) forced by the fact that you can't afford everything you want.

An open discussion about how to allocate resources across conflicting priorities is the best way to ensure the strengths and weaknesses of the alternatives are fully explored.

Of course, such conflicts shouldn't disintegrate into arguments in the boardroom. But creative tension forces a careful assessment of costs, benefits and risks to the extent that managers will shape their programs to make them more viable and valuable to the entire organization.

Many organizations view any form of direct conversation with horror, let alone actual conflict. If the alternative is conflict, many would prefer to do nothing and allow more time for the parties to reach common ground.

It's quite surprising how many things don't have any time urgency about them. When things need to be speeded up a bit, a compromise between solutions can yield a quick and amicable resolution.

Getting on with business is a good approach whenever the outcomes don't really matter. *The Simmer System* itself suggests that early in your PPFMO's history, you should see any compromise as a win. It's one less battle you'll have to fight.

However, in organizations where outcomes do matter, compromise runs the risk of sacrificing essential outcomes, or sweeping major risks under a rug in the interest of harmony (does the Challenger O-ring sound familiar?).

Either way, it's important to recognize that the tradeoffs and compromises were reached only because you defined the Zero-Sum boundary. In the 'old days,' managers would privately go to the controlling executive to get non-disclosed funds from a "secret pot."

Today, with Zero-Sum in place, each decision has an offsetting consequence that needs to be considered. That doesn't mean the PPFMO controls every aspect of the funding. It's not about telling people what they must do; it's about knowing what they're doing.

An Alternative to Zero-Sum

The term "Zero-Sum" can be a bit controversial. In the 1990s, management theorists got it largely drummed out of polite society because it was too confrontational. But it is in fact the essence of the project managers' beloved "iron triangle."

Most organizations that have struggled to deliver on their commitments, and have turned to PPFM as a solution, have also had difficulty grasping the rigidity of the iron triangle. They spend their time fighting short-term fires they themselves set when they:

- Shift funds from the most important effort to the most immediate problem, thereby robbing Peter to pay Paul.
- Allow delivery dates to drop further behind, usually to the customer's annoyance.
- Skip effective procedures and ship defective products, hoping the flaws won't surface until the stock options vest, or until after the next election.

In process-averse organizations, executives and managers have a lot of money tucked away. In one of the case studies in Chapter Two, the executive retained complete control of the funds. That's not an uncommon situation, and not always undesirable. The problems occurred because he handed the funds out, then took them back in near-random fashion without telling anyone what he had done.

If any significant work can be launched without anyone else knowing about it, then it doesn't matter whether the board approves or disapproves the work it gets to see. In that situation, the managers have worked out how to bypass any kind of executive governance. It's an alternative.

Many organizations use it, but that doesn't make it a good one.

Don't Worry About Being a Big Zero

The need to set up the Zero-Sum situation doesn't mean that PPFMOs (or governance boards) can only exist at the top-most level of an organization with purview over *all* funds. That would be a "big zero." Most readers aren't going to start that way. Start out as a small zero.

A lower-level organization can have a successful PPFMO to reduce some of the fluidity within its own sphere of operations even while dealing with the reality that higher levels of the organization are in relative chaos.

Realizing their sponsors are victims of higher level dysfunctions, some PPFMO teams run aground on the shoal of organizational politics by trying to unnecessarily fix issues at higher levels, which can awaken the dragons guarding that turf.

That higher-level staff office may not have the intention or even the capability of doing its job properly. But pointing that fact out can generate a lower-to-higher turf war that will end badly for the subordinate staff office. *That would be the PPFMO*. You've got enough dragons to deal with as it is, so don't go around inviting others to the party.

Federal agencies deal with this all the time. They have to make multi-year plans, even though the Administration and Congress are unable to provide an environment that goes much beyond the next three months.

Some agencies have allowed this situation to send them into managerial paralysis, as if it was a new and unsolvable problem suddenly dropped into their laps. Most agencies know this problem has been going on for at least 35 years, and they have devised ways of dealing with it.

There's a popular misconception that planning is more difficult for the public sector because of annual budget cycles, which is complete nonsense. Corporate revenue is highly uncertain. It comes from selling the next bottle of Coke or the next Tesla automobile. Who can be sure when that will be?

They'd love to have the certainty of knowing what their revenues would be for the next 9 or 12 months. So this concept of creating a small-Zero-Sum bubble is even more critical for companies.

Without it, you can't make any decisions.

Zero-Sum Doesn't Eliminate Managerial Flexibility

The Zero-Sum approach doesn't eliminate decision-makers' prerogatives, as they can still hold funds in reserve and reallocate them as the need arises.

When money runs short in one initiative, decision-makers should be free to reallocate funds from elsewhere. If the process shows where the funds are coming from, and the consequence of any change, the decision-makers can determine priorities and choose how to allocate/reallocate funding to achieve the best outcome.

Making transparent decisions doesn't eliminate back room meetings or promises, if that's what the manager wants to do. It does, however, allow everyone in the organization to understand what the executives decided, what funding is available for what initiatives, and most importantly, what each person is accountable to do.

It also means that seeking additional funding might come at the expense of a peer manager, which will require considerably greater fortitude and more compelling reasons than sneaking into a budgetary grab-bag in the dark of night.

Don't confuse hidden funds kept off-budget with "fat" buried within the declared budget. Fat is not such a big problem for you, because at least it's tagged to a particular effort.

It's an efficiency issue, and can be trimmed off with the help of a little benchmarking.

Hidden funds are sources of money that not everyone knows about, and have managed to elude the prioritization process. As long as those funds exist, bad politics will trump governance. Why ask for permission when you can get money from your buddy?

If you're successful in establishing the Zero-Sum reality of a limited budget, and are transparent about it, the competition across program areas will begin to sort it out. Sure, the program manager can siphon funds to undertake pet projects. But pressure from the other program managers will enforce reasonable boundaries around the obvious fat.

Many management texts focus on efficiency as the measure you should be following. Please don't fall into that trap as you're not there yet. Remember that in the previous year this same organization had difficulty delivering anything at any price.

Discussing efficiency tends to point a finger back at the individual managers you're trying to win over. That discussion will just generate further resistance rather than winning additional allies. Besides, it's a matter of definition that if you don't deliver your efficiency is zero. You can imagine the reaction that will get, so don't bring that up either!

What the organization needs to do is to build the habit of delivery, which is easy to evaluate, is non-judgmental, and has a concrete impact on your customers.

Over time you'll be able to trim that fat and decrease program overhead. You'll find benchmarks the PPFMO can use to compare those program costs back into submission. This approach may be intolerable in a more mature organization, but that's not the situation at this point. Usually, it's more of a problem trying to get total visibility in the first place.

Once you've defined your world, the time will come when forcing tradeoffs within your available funding simply won't meet some urgent and unexpected need.

Every level of every organization has some sort of mechanism to obtain funds that higher-levels of management reserved for themselves. Before releasing funds, higher level managers want to know what the funds are for, what caused the need for them, and what will prevent the problem from occurring in the future. In other words, that mechanism is part of a functioning governance process.

Zero-Sum doesn't have to possess a completely leak-proof wall. You just have to know the money is coming in, and the quantity and purpose.

Then you can add it into the budget wherever it fits. Ideally, the process makes it difficult to obtain additional funding from outside the governance board's boundaries, and makes the actions to do so fully transparent.

Zero-Sum in Practice

The Zero-Sum universe can be defined as those funds the decision-makers and anyone below them can conveniently get their hands on. Once that universe becomes evident, the governance board considers all activities for which it is responsible, and determines how best to allocate the funding for those activities.

Packaging those activities into initiatives defined at the highest possible level will provide the executing managers with as much latitude as possible to produce optimal results, while leaving room to deal with issues and capitalize on opportunities.

High level initiatives, that would include both operational and project-like activities, are the programs the governance process guides.

In actual practice, because most of the organization's programs have been in place for a considerable amount of time, it will likely have no more than one or two new initiatives. The definition process will be more a matter of refinement and rationalization than a complete visionary effort.

The flip side of this coin is to avoid the temptation to further elaborate the funded initiatives at the next level down. Organizations often believe that specifying the allocation of funds at deeper levels – and managing completion of the sub-efforts – will yield more fidelity to the original intent.

This isn't true for any particular initiative, unless the managers have reserves to address unexpected deviations from the plan. And it's certainly ineffective while managing multiple initiatives across multiple sub-organizations.

In the natural order of things, certain activities will cost less and come in faster than expected, while others won't. Micromanaging from above removes any incentive to produce the under-runs that could resolve funding issues for equally probable overrun situations.

A later chapter will go into more detail about planning and managing programs. But for now, an effective decision-making process for allocating and overseeing an organization's activities depends on understanding there's no "magic pot" of money to dip into.

Managers are held accountable to execute initiatives within the allocated funds. If they can't do that, they need to reallocate within their available funding.

Managers who need more funding might be able to get it if the program is of high enough priority and the situation is sufficiently problematic. But they'll have to explain their needs to the governance board.

If approved, other managers will have to cut back on their own programs to support those requests.

3. INTEGRITY (AND COMPROMISE)

*"I have never lied to you.
I have always told you some version of the truth."*
~Jack Nicholson as Harry Sanborn in the movie,
Something's Gotta Give (2003)

Integrity. It's easy to live it, but hard to get it back once you let it go.

The Simmer System suggests compromising now to achieve goals in the future. By definition, a compromise means giving up some portion of what's important to you. If you draw lines in the sand – but then move them rather than engage in conflict – your pronouncements over what's right and wrong, and acceptable and unacceptable, lose their effectiveness.

Once you've shown you'll fold in response to progress, every simple statement of what procedure has to be followed is open to challenge. People will assume you're grandstanding, and that you'll back down as soon as the going gets tough.

Of course, if you take the opposite approach and try to hold the line on everything, the organization will refuse to deal with you. First, you'll be frozen out of discussions, and your processes will be bypassed either openly or covertly. Then they'll get rid of your PPFM program, the PPFMO and you. Nothing will have been accomplished through this martyrdom.

One solution might be to resist taking any positions at all, doing the best you can with the openings the situation provides. This may sound very collegial. But there's always at least one opponent who will happily portray your failure to endorse any standards of practice as evidence that you're incompetent and need to be replaced.

That's why *The Simmer System* calls for compromise on anything except these four principles.

Basic Integrity Issues

For people with integrity (which I assume would include any executives, managers and professionals who would be interested in reading this book), the hardest part of any ethical discussion is accepting that there are people in this world – especially among the ambitious – who don't share the same code of ethics. Not only do they exist, but they are all around you, even in your very reputable organization.

I'm not suggesting that organizations are filled with frauds and criminals. However, what a process-averse organization does have is people who are used to getting what they want without being questioned.

Through general chaos, senior managers and executives have been able run their operations as they see fit. Because they've never been held accountable for their actions, they say one thing and do another, and it goes unchallenged.

They will say, and may well believe, that their methods are dealing with reality as it is, not as it could be. And that all of their decisions are aimed at the best interest of the organization. Since the organization is badly flawed, there may be some truth to this.

Managers in immature organizations value their autonomy and self-image far more than the consequences to the organization itself. As a result, the PPFMO receives daily opportunities to alter, shade or obscure the truth. Or at least to become an accomplice in doing so.

Depending on the relative strength the governance process has achieved, managers will (in order of preference) demand, threaten, wheedle or plead for the PPFMO to:

- look the other way when a project team submits misleading or false information to the governance board;

- ignore situations where managers are clearly acting contrary to the board's decisions; or

- change reports so as not to cast a manager in a bad light.

All I can offer is just say no!

If someone insists on turning in information the PPFMO knows to be inaccurate, there should be an obligation to say so.

It may be better for all concerned if the PPFMO has a process of validating what is turned in, and that process results in an indication (such as a status flag) to show that the material hasn't undergone the required review and validation.

That's a little less sensitive than coming right out and saying the program manager is being deceptive, and the board will get the message, especially if you trained them on what to look for.

At that point, it's up to the governance board to decide what to do with it. If board members consistently show little interest in the fact they're being handed bogus information (yes, that happens), it will be time to make a value judgment as to whether you're a good fit for this organization. It certainly doesn't need a PPFMO.

We've Got Pictures

The PPFMO doesn't buy itself any peace even if it surrenders to the threats. Right behind the bullies you'll find the blackmailers.

Most professional certifications (such as the ones you may have) and many professional societies require avowal of ethical codes, and many of those refer to upholding the standards of practice.

The Simmer System exposes you to some risk in that it might suggest a degree of suspension, if not outright toleration, for the compromise of professional standards if they are highly prescriptive.

The PPFMO must assess and often question a program manager's business cases, technical plans, status reports and so on. That questioning must be framed as – and must in fact be – an objective search for the best possible representation of the truth.

Even so, managers who have been used to doing whatever they want will often see the questioning as an attack on their competence or integrity and will counterattack.

"How dare you suggest I don't know what I'm doing? You're the one who hasn't got a clue. These processes you're putting in place don't even conform to [pick your standard]. What kind of incompetent are you, anyway?"

In addition to those who have been subjected to the PPFMO review, opponents of the entire governance effort will join in simply because the opportunity presented itself.

Any compromise you make inevitably places you and the PPFMO on the side of not doing what best practices call for. Opponents who originally demanded those concessions will argue that everybody wants to do the right thing, but are being prevented from doing so because the PPFMO is so incompetent it's not following the best practices.

And because it's incompetent, the PPFMO must be constrained, if not shut down, until the organization can find more competent staff to operate it.

Dishonest attacks are very convincing to the uneducated observer. So you need to be prepared, as this **is** the approach your detractors are most likely to follow.

Handling the Heat

You and your PPFMO are going to get attacked as a means of delaying or killing off the effort to institute governance, which comes with the territory. You're not making any progress if it isn't happening, because your efforts still aren't seen as a threat to the status quo.

You can't prevent them, but you can place yourself in a better position to deal with them:

- Accept that this is the way it works when you try to bring change into an organization that isn't sure it wants to change.

- Compromise proactively, not defensively.

- Cooperate with enthusiasm when people want your help. Listen to your colleagues' points of view, as sometimes their heretical ideas make a lot of sense. Then stand your ground on these few principles.

If you are the PPFMO director, I'll add another action you must take: try to protect your people. Hardcore opponents will try to pressure your staff members in hopes of dissuading them from doing their jobs properly.

Confront the bullies in private if you can, openly conceding that you don't agree and the two of you will continue to battle. But warn them not to take out their frustrations on the PPFMO staff.

If that doesn't work, then call them out as needed and escalate to the sponsoring executive, the inspector general, labor relations office, or whatever tools are available. This is one area where there can't be even one inch of give.

Make Sure It's Not About You

When your competence and integrity are attacked to cover people's dishonesty, it's difficult not to feel angry and abused. So it's good to remember that it's not about you. Well, let me restate that. You need to make sure it *isn't* about you.

Find people who will give honest feedback, and will let you know if you're over-reaching or standing too high on your best-practice pedestal. Perhaps the way you approach things annoys people.

Whatever kind of constructive criticism they provide, pull your big-boy or big-girl pants up and make amends as best you can and as quickly as possible.

People you can trust while being respectful in their comments can be hard to find in the workplace. Plus it can be embarrassing to ask for assistance. So make friends early before people start taking sides. (And use the community at www.simmer-system.com.)

Provide a Safety Valve

The existence of a decision process doesn't mean it can't be changed, or solutions can't be tailored to meet demands. The point is to have a set of standards that includes documenting when, why and how to accept a departure from the standard, which could occur through a waiver of process or one-off approvals to deviate from it.

But in either case, it needs to be documented, and needs to follow a consistent path from one instance to the next. (This concept is so important that it has its own chapter later in the book.)

Even the CEO needs to sign off on the waivers for their own projects; in fact, they should be the first to do so to show no one is exempt.

As soon as the PPFMO gives in to temptations for just one stakeholder, even if it is the CEO, every other stakeholder will find out about it and demand the same amnesties. So provide an emergency exit door, but don't keep it propped open.

Know Your Material

Don't get caught out of position.

You'll lose credibility if you're demanding something that's neither desired nor required. If you're asking people to provide you with something, you must be crystal clear as to the external force that demands it or the internal imperatives that need it.

"It's required by regulation" means you're able to cite the specific sections of the laws or regulations that require it, and the words in that citation need to say what is required. If that's not the case, then your request is only one of several ways the requirement can be satisfied. Then it should be clear that what you're proposing is the least burdensome response.

If your request supports something the organization wants to do, then you must be very specific as to what you're going to do with it. "We need it to do an analysis" rightly draws the question as to what analysis, requested by whom, and how the information requested contributes to that effort.

"The CFO needs it to submit the annual xxx return to the IRS" is a much more powerful argument. Managers are put into a difficult position if they refuse to provide specific information that supports a specific organizational process.

If you don't know the answers to those questions, find them before you ask people to do work for you for purposes you can't explain. Doing so will build your credibility.

Getting caught not having done your homework will put all of your data-gathering efforts at risk, even those that have already been accepted.

Know What the Best Practices Are

If your organization is aligned with a particular standard of practice or maturity model, you need to know it backward and forward. Know when a compromise is going to go against the standard, and make sure this is noted at the time of the decision.

Most of the standards don't actually call for specific implementing techniques; usually they call for processes and capabilities. So you can defer the implementation of a particular activity until a later date, which is an acceptable practice. Nobody implements all aspects of a complex change all at once. Just add the item to your PPFMO development plan as a deferred action.

Provide alternatives and solutions "until we find the best way." Eventually either the PPFMO will have disappeared (not your preferred outcome), or *The Pasta Principle* will have taken over and the issue will have been resolved.

Running through the PPFMO's current and expected practices with the governance board on a regular basis will create legitimacy and support for your decisions (use the worksheet in the Exercise at the end of the chapter to help you frame the discussion).

The more often the board reviews and endorses the PPFMO's approach, the less likely managers two or three levels lower will attack the board's endorsed approaches. Many executives who couldn't care two hoots about governance processes will inflate like a bullfrog at the idea that someone is criticizing "their" actions or decisions. They've just been invited to a game most managers will not want to play.

Agree With Enthusiasm

Finally, you might get the chance to be a bit devious yourself. For instance, if challenged on less than complete implementation, you can use *The Pasta Principle* to your benefit.

"Oh, we're ready to take that on now? That's great! Let's use your project as the pilot to show everyone else how to do it right. Shall we have a kickoff meeting with your staff tomorrow?"

You never know. They might be so surprised they're getting what they're asking for (which is exactly what you want to happen), that they'll forget it was the last thing they actually wanted.

Which segues quite nicely to the fourth principle of Purposeful Humility.

4. PURPOSEFUL HUMILITY

Is it an oxymoron to be both purposeful and humble at the same time? If so, be an oxymoron!

Doing Jobs Nobody Wants to Do

As you saw in the case studies in Chapter Two, you can win friends and gain ground if you relieve someone of a task they don't want to do.

Many PPFMO directors who are having a hard time gaining cooperation have their staff do the PPFM tasks line managers refuse to do.

Although I discuss doing exactly that in the next section, that's not a good idea as a general rule of thumb. A PPFMO's role is to support people who are actually doing the work, so those people must "own" their work.

Business cases, cost estimates, design documents and even change proposals (or at least the supporting analyses) are fundamental to the line managers' decision and production processes.

The PPFMO can't possibly know those processes better than the managers do. So why would they want to rely on analyses conducted by the PPFMO? Try to resist this urge. It's a better solution to relieve the program managers of functions that aren't part of their core work but reinforce yours.

The PPFMOs in the case studies were fortunate to get hold of the contract management functions for key support contracts. While contracts are necessary for the line managers to get their work done, contract administration is not a core skill for that group, certainly not on a level with the "PM" activities mentioned in the previous paragraph.

Since the contracts are often the means by which most of the organization's work is completed, what could be a better source of information than the person doing the work? Even better, it's usually the case that they aren't paid unless they do provide it in their periodic reports.

That precise approach won't work in every organization, especially if program managers work out that your control of their contracts means they can't conceal progress data from you.

As with everything in *The Simmer System*, if one door is closed, *The Pasta Principle* will ensure that another door will open somewhere. So look for those opportunities.

All of the things a PPFMO does are basically overhead or back office functions. In a happy coincidence, the things program managers would rather not do are also back office functions.

Unless line managers work out that having the PPFMO execute a back office function will provide more information than they might have been willing to share, there's usually little resistance to an offer of relief from an overhead burden.

Assuming Tasks Program Managers Won't Do

The PPFMO will often spend more time getting a program manager to do the minimum amount of work than it would have taken to do the job themselves. Don't count on winning a friend by doing their work, as it's more likely they'll expect you to do everything else.

As noted above, as soon as you take it over, they view it as a sideshow that is not really relevant to their jobs, which is a dangerous attitude towards governance.

Even so, there can be benefits from getting the job done right. In the earlier case study with the rogue project, taking over the drafting of the project plan paid off in several ways. The external auditors were satisfied with the process (although not with the answers). More importantly, the PPFMO locked in the project's baselines.

Though it continued to wage many political battles behind closed doors to recover its autonomy, the dynamic had changed. All of that project's subsequent battles were uphill, and had to be framed in terms of undoing what had already been submitted to regulators.

The other advantage was that once a good number of teams were participating effectively, then by picking up the slack for a couple of project teams, the entire organization was included in a regular system of reporting and documentation.

Once that occurs, the governance board becomes familiar with the reports and documents, and is able to reach conclusions and decisions more quickly. It also makes it easier to see when a program delivers an inadequate product. Ideally, the governance board has been primed to treat "no data received" as a crime far worse than "somewhat over budget."

Quite often, program managers won't like the way their work is being depicted to the executive board, so they'll want to change that perception.

Your PPFMO, far from being spiteful about it (and oh, how tempting that is!) will work with the program manager to show how their activities can get out of the "black" hole. Black is a good color to use for "no data received" as it tends to stand out on a chart even more than red. Once you get some data to work with, you can show them how to move out of a red or yellow condition into the green.

Remember, your goal isn't humiliation of the former opponents; it's to get their work functioning effectively. If everybody is a true green, your work here is done. Once the program manager starts playing your game – even while stretching the rules as far as they can go, and perhaps a little beyond – you've won. Accept the win, and repress the urge to hold a victory parade. A little humility goes a long way.

Limitations of Humility

You can overdo the generosity tactic. Sooner or later you'll run out of resources. Some of the PPFMO's opponents would be pleased to see it become so bogged down with irrelevant tasks that it can't effectively carry out its oversight role.

Weigh the value to be gained in giving up your own resources to doing other people's jobs for them against the impact of losing time to manage the functions you're supposed to perform.

As a somewhat extreme example, you may gain leverage by taking on Human Resources' function of helping line managers write position descriptions. Not only can you make sure the processes for staffing key initiatives keep moving forward, but you can also use the opportunity to add in requirements for basic understanding of PPFMO concepts.

Perhaps you can even slide in a mandatory element about project outcomes on annual performance reviews. That can certainly generate positive returns, as many managers are more concerned about their performance reviews than about the performance of the total organization.

However, position descriptions can take many rewrites, or expand to include running the staff's annual review or other time-consuming activities. This does little to advance your agenda, and may threaten your ability to carry out your core tasks.

So choose where your time is best spent.

When Does Compromise Become Surrender?

When you're considering whether to accept less than a best practice approach to a situation, at each point ask yourself:

- *If I concede a point now, will The Pasta Principle eventually bring it back into play as the inevitable consequence of the other practices we **have** agreed to do?*

    If yes, then let it go for now. You'll get it back later.

- *Will the compromise [usually about funding or reporting] create hidden pots of money? Or is it just that we can only see the larger pots?*

    As long as there are clear performance outcomes that are tied to all the money pots and visible at reasonable intervals, then it doesn't matter how many pots there are or how frequently they render status reports to you.

- *Will the result of the decisions we make still be out in the open after this compromise?*

    If so, don't worry about how that sausage got made; just worry about how much it weighs.

- *Will the information be truthful? Or will it be shady and misleading?*

    While you can compromise on the volume and sophistication of information offered to the decision-making board or anyone else, *do not* compromise on the truth. And not just the literal truth, but the truth in context.

The proper question to ask isn't "Is this in accordance with the XYZ standard?" The proper questions are "Will this work?" and "Will it move us towards the goal?" If it will do both of those things, then go for it.

Things that could have been fixed early on become very expensive to retrofit later. So for the future, remember that every deferred standard of practice carries an additional burden of magnifying its impact as time progresses.

But for now, every deferred standard allows you to move forward with a set of processes that *have* been accepted. That's a good start.

At this very early stage in the PPFMO's life, you're going to have to accept many compromises, which is fine. After all, you're starting with little to no information on any of the initiatives.

Just make sure that you and the decision-making board are aware of and understand possible future consequences. If nothing else, they may give you the leverage to ratchet back those concessions.

Next Steps

In this chapter, you've been thinking about what positions are going to be important to you. The exercise will ask you to be more specific about how that will apply in your particular organization. You intend to fight until the end to retain these.

Inertia and culture have some powerful forces lined up against you. They've fought people in your position before, and they obviously won. To hold your red lines, the PPFMO may need some powerful allies of its own.

Getting help from those higher up in the organization, with a better view of the organization and its needs as a whole, could go a long way to help.

The next chapter discusses what such top-down support can do for you, and how to get it and make the most of it. Spoiler alert: sometimes, you don't get it. (What? You didn't read Chapter Two?)

Let that possibility tumble around in the back of your mind when you're deciding in this chapter's exercise what exactly you're going to fall on your sword over. That's a decision you only get to make once.

EXERCISE 4: DEFINE YOUR RED LINES

Prepare yourself for the challenges that lie ahead. For each of the standard skill areas in the PMBOK (again, *Project Management Body of Knowledge*), consider the following for your PPFMO practice:

- What's the next step forward?

- What elements of best practices have already been consciously deferred?

- What should the "red lines" be in terms of elements that must or must not be given up?

- Which of the core principles applies to the situation?

(You'll find a template for assessing these situations at www.Simmer-System.com.)

Extra Credit

For each process category, write down the potential consequences of the deferral decisions you've made. Then, how are you going to deal with those residual risks?

_____
_____
_____
_____
_____
_____

Chapter Five

Top Cover: The Executive Support You Need (But May Not Get)

This chapter talks about the one thing that will be most helpful in making your PPFMO succeed: *executive support*.

It may also be the one thing that in a skeptical organization you won't get, at least not until some form of governance has proven its viability, at which point that support won't be needed to keep things going.

The Simmer System[SM] came about, at least in part, in response to this very problem.

What is "Top Cover"?

If you're a veteran, or if you read military and/or history books, "top cover" means aircraft flying in support of ground operations or lower slower aircraft to protect them from being attacked from above, and to blast away resistance occurring below.

When you get into something that's too heavy to handle, you can call in the 'top cover.'

Many people would prefer not to use military metaphors for any reason. So you might not like the use of one for this very critical aspect of the PPFMO effort.

But you can't avoid the fact that the entire reason you need something like *The Simmer System* is the issues surrounding efforts to substantive changes in organizational behavior are all about conflict.

If you're a people person, you might prefer to think in terms of win-win. *Kumbaya!* Wouldn't everyone?

The Simmer System sets out from the beginning to minimize, delay or bypass (oops, another military metaphor) areas of potential conflict while producing win-wins wherever possible. Sometimes it just doesn't work that way, and conflict is forced on you. In the case of a PPFMO, "sometimes" will be "almost every time."

Denying it doesn't change that fact, but it may impede your ability to deal with it.

Why Top Cover is Needed

> *Butch Cassidy: Ah, you're wasting your time. They can't track us over rocks.*
>
> *Sundance Kid: Tell them that.*
>
> *Butch Cassidy: [after looking for himself] They're beginning to get on my nerves. Who are those guys?*

A PPFMO and the governance practices it supports provide an organization-wide method of prioritizing and viewing the entire spectrum of activities, which will necessarily impose limits on the freedom of action at lower levels.

By this point in the book, you know that the equal and opposite reaction will set in to try to subvert the process. So like it or not, you can expect some level of conflict. Resistance will be fierce at the beginning of a PPFMO's life, partly in hopes of making the constraining change go away, and partly out of fear of what it might become.

If the PPFMO survives those initial contests, some people will continue to resist control long after the PPFMO initiative is running smoothly on all cylinders.

Of course that's annoying, but it's just the way some people are. However irrational their response may be, it can be devastating (refer once again to Mark Suster's blog post about the scorpion and the frog; the URL is in the References annex). At that point, most opponents are pushing the envelope to get a bit of relief; only a few are really trying to be annoying.

Though resistance may continue, at least the perspective will be clear. If the conflict is about the legitimate order defending itself against a gang of crazy radicals, the question will be which side is which. Without top cover, the change agents (the PPFMO) become the "crazies."

You can try to avoid (or at least minimize) conflict through *The Simmer System*, but there are always opponents who can't be co-opted or placated. They will seek you out. Maybe they foresee the degree to which governance is a threat to their autonomy. Maybe they've previously experienced overly rigid PPFMO implementations. Or maybe they just love to fight.

It doesn't really matter why. If the cooperative approach is being rejected, and if the PPFMO is to move forward at all, then one of two things has to happen:

1. This resistance has to be overcome by coercion, since it doesn't respond to logic.

2. The PPFMO will have to concede the field in the short term. Instead of fighting a pitched battle it can't win, it undertakes its own subversive campaign. It must operate within a zone where its activities aren't perceived as a threat, at least until it is too late for opponents to do anything about it.

Every organization change management book and process I've read goes with Option 1 (coercion), although of course without actually saying so. But they insist that introducing a change begins with, and depends on, a firm commitment to the change from the top level of management. That's a polite way of saying "people who can coerce compliance from those at lower levels." At least in theory.

However, you're not in an organization that is well-described by theory. I use the word *skeptical* in the book's subtitle to be kind, and to avoid turning off potential readers. In reality, it's dysfunctional. It can't produce, at least not at an expected level. It's irrational, or at least highly erratic, which is why it's being pressured to consider introducing PPFM in some form.

People don't like to be called dysfunctional. If your boss found you reading a book called *How to Introduce a PPFMO in a Dysfunctional Organization*, he or she would probably become quite offended, especially if you're charging the book purchase back to the organization.

Now, a title like *PPFMO in a Skeptical Organization* might just pique the boss' curiosity (so order a few more!)

In this book, I call these organizations "process-averse" because it goes directly to the root cause. So let's start with the worse-case possibility, then go on to discuss what you might do if in fact executive support might be available.

Socked In: No Top Cover Today

It can happen that you don't get the top cover you want. Now you have to make a choice:

1. Wait until you have the cover you think you need to get the job done. Step back and focus your marketing efforts on the sponsor and other executives to ensure they understand the need for change and the benefits of your proposed approach. If you never get the cover, then the job never gets done.

2. Going without top cover will make things harder. But the questions to consider are:

- How important is this change initiative to you?
- Are you really on a deadline?
- How critical is the top cover?
- How controversial do you expect your initiative to be?

Of course there's the possibility, just as in one of the earlier case studies, that the people who **should** be the top cover **are** the problem. In that case, you'll need a cooperative grassroots effort to make the change without having to ask for permission.

Just because you think you have your top cover lined up doesn't mean it's going to show up after you get into the battle.

Recall from the case studies that in several instances I was brought into situations where that support either wasn't there or disappeared. That's the way it goes in skeptical organizations.

Why Top Cover Could Be Missing

It's already been determined the organization is dysfunctional. Aren't the managers and executives there to prevent that, or to fix it? All too often, they might like things just the way they are, even if that means running the organization into the ground.

The corporate executives and the union bosses in the giant automakers in Detroit did just this for decades until they ran out of money. In the process, they made progressively worse products and deceived their shareholders with elaborate financial shell games. But they took home very nice bonuses, and destroyed their companies and the city in which they were based.

This also happens on a small scale. I once worked for a company whose future depended on renewing and growing a strategic contract. We had the right contacts to expand the work we were doing. Alas, the company president believed (perhaps with justification) that our customers didn't understand what they were doing.

So he made it his mission to harass them in increasingly shrill tones until he was banned from the customers' premises. It should come as no surprise that the option on our golden egg wasn't renewed.

You've seen the case study in Chapter Two where we built the bones of what eventually became *The Simmer System*. Managers were frustrated at not being able to get anything done due to the executive constantly changing his mind without telling anyone.

That executive wasn't a bad person. Quite the contrary. The problem was a desire to please everyone. *"Can't we all just get along?"*

No, not when giving some people what they want means others won't get what they want. Something has to give. Making those choices is what managers and executives are for, but not all of them are up to the task.

The lack of cover doesn't necessarily mean your sponsors are weak or are part of the problem. It could just mean you didn't consider that they also have challenges to deal with. Sometimes it's just a matter of opportunity cost.

"Dad, she's touching me! Make her stop touching me!"

Photo Credit http://www.kmart.com

To me, a Baby on Board sign on a car window means "Stay clear! Driver might make irrational movements at any moment!" as they can be distracted by what's going on in the back seat.

In business, it can mean your attention is diverted from something important to deal with someone else's problem or potential problem that's of no great consequence, except that it prevents you from dealing with more important things.

The PPFMO's sponsoring executive has more things to think about than the PPFMO. Much as the sponsor may want the initiative to succeed – and much as the executives may want the benefits of going better, faster and more efficiently – face it, *everybody hates a whiner.*

Ideally, the PPFMO would run practically hands-free with minimal calls for executive action. The more of their time you demand, the more they'll wonder if it's worth it.

If that time is further consumed in battles with other executives upon whom, on other fields on other days, the sponsor is going to depend for support in other unrelated matters, the sponsoring executive may decide that it's better to let this governance business slide for a while.

The whiner effect doesn't apply to just the executive level – it works on the peer level as well. Nobody likes a sneak.

Whatever the real work of your organization is, your peer managers are the ones who actually get it done, and over the long haul you depend on them for information and cooperation. The more you turn to higher level support, the more you'll alienate your peers. So you need a process that works without constant monitoring and micromanaging; otherwise, it will quit working the moment you turn your back.

What if You Don't Get the Cover?

Sooner or later you must get some top cover. The PPFMO has no intrinsic value. Its job is to support a decision process of some kind, however immature. If there is no such process in place, and there isn't going to be one, then either shut the PPFMO down, or revise its charter to turn it into nothing more than a forum for cooperating and coordinating among the program managers.

By demonstrating value early on, you may provide yourself with the case studies needed to win over sponsors and decision board members. Until those materialize, you can operate in stealth mode, but your effectiveness will be correspondingly limited. So keep working the problem.

What can you do if you don't have any top cover? You can apply the jujitsu nature of *The Simmer System*: collaborate, cooperate, adapt.

- Encourage people to use appropriate project management practices to guide their group-level work.

    o **What to watch for:** Independent project teams will become frustrated at the inability to resolve issues that go beyond the project.

    If it appears that nobody who counts (which doesn't include the PPFMO) cares about the progress or lack of progress of their projects, and nobody is going to help deal with problems, teams will start abandoning their project methods.

    o **Opportunities:** The PPFMO, which isn't as heavily consumed in day-to-day activities, might be able to provide a brokering role between project teams and the wider organization.

- Encourage and provide logistical support for a grassroots effort among program managers who have some role in the overall funding process to plan, organize and coordinate the work among themselves, and get things done despite the lack of approval or oversight processes.

    o **What to watch for:** Without organizational priorities to provide the longer-term stability that processes need to take a firm hold, sooner or later an ambitious manager who doesn't play along will force others into defending their own programs, and the whole cooperative process will fall apart.

- o **Opportunity:** Publishing the cooperative work product early and often will lock in the decisions, and make it obvious if someone tries to upset the process.

- Involve stakeholders in portfolio management (i.e., in the prioritization process). It's much harder for an internal manager to start undoing commitments made at the stakeholder level.

  - o **What to watch for:** If high-priority project work isn't moving forward, but lower-priority work is moving, it means somebody is reprioritizing the work behind the scenes.

  - o **Opportunity:** Again, publish, publish, publish! The more publicly the organization commits to deliveries, especially to the customer community, the more it will feel obligated to make those deliveries happen.

- Get tacit support from the executives. Even if they aren't willing to provide active support, they may agree that things would be better if there were organized. See if you can shape their thinking about how things should be brought forward for their approval, at least as an individual decision-maker if not as a collective board.

  If each individual executive functioned as a de facto governance board, the program managers would end up doing even more planning and coordination than might have been required in a board review, because now the program manager has to satisfy all of the questions that these mini-reviews might generate.

  - o **What to watch for:** Back-sliding. Every time an executive permits (or worse, encourages) an alternative process, or an off-the-cuff decision in order to meet some expediency, another nail goes into the coffin of a structured decision process.

  - o **Opportunity:** If the executive positions change, there is always an opportunity for support to build. Remember, the executives may be withholding open support for various reasons, but they may also provide behind-the-scenes support.

All of these actions can help. But they're stop-gap measures until you can get some traction. Eventually, your PPFMO must provide something useful at the organization level, meaning that the executives recognize it as the source of valuable information and demand the PPFMO's services.

Let's face it, if you can't get the cooperation of a critical mass of the program managers, and the initiative can't get any traction with the executive group despite doing all these things, then the organization is beyond "not really ready" for the change to accountable practices, no matter how rudimentary they may be. It actively doesn't want to do it.

Which should make you question why you're trying to make it happen:

- If you're doing it because you were ostensibly hired to do it, then set that thought aside for a while. Validate it with the executives who hired you, if they're still around.

  Now that you've got a better feel for the organization and the challenges, re-interview them and yourself just as if the job search for a new PPFMO director was still happening. Only now you're better informed and perhaps they are as well.

  You may find that the objectives are radically restated now that people have a better sense of what this means for them. Whatever the restatement is, validate it with the program managers and then fix that problem.

- If you're doing it because you were an insider before the PPFM initiative began, and you welcomed the opportunity to set right issues that were making life difficult for you and presumably for your peers, then reexamine how you're going to do that.

  Reengage with your peers on the specific issues you confronted at that time, and remind them of the hassles you were all going through. Revalidate that they still have those issues, and get consensus as to what to do about it, then do it.

- If you're pushing best practice solutions because that's what you learned to do – and you think it's the right thing to do but nobody is buying into it – then it's time for some creativity.

  Plan A isn't working. Try something else. You need to do something different (say, Simmering!), or stop to reassess your strategies.

- It's even possible that you've been following *The Simmer System*.

  Even though I'm flattered, there will be times when the recipe doesn't seem to be working for you. If that's the case, contact me and/or the community at www.Simmer-System.com to get situation-specific advice.

This whole governance thing isn't about doing something because that's what this or other books say. Nor is it about doing what the contract says. It's about getting results.

If your top cover works, it will be because you've successfully managed a balance between making sure appropriate support is available, working things out on the ground, and knowing when the situation is critical enough to ask for help.

When compromise and accepting partial successes is still inadequate, you find yourself pushed to the wall of the Core Four principles.

The Sky's Clear

So much for what to do if your top cover is weak or missing. Let's hope you have a bit more than that to start with. If not, perhaps the foregoing suggestions have enabled you to build that support.

If you get that top-down support, then you have several things working for you:

- It removes the "not my job" response. The organization has made it clear that making this change work is everybody's job.

- Failing to cooperate in the change effort is going directly against the express wishes of the manager's manager, and the executives in the chain above that.

- You now have a legitimate reason for measuring and reporting on the success of the initiatives the change is about, as well as on the progress of the change effort itself.

- As your top cover, higher-level executives have the necessary firepower to blast away any corporate obstacles, and/or deal with individuals who don't want to go along with the program.

Confirm Your Support

To make the PPFM initiative successful this time around, you need to make sure at least one of the organization's "heavy hitters" really does support it.

The individual being referred to here is in the position to make the PPFM initiative work, and to make sure that those whose support is needed are also on the bandwagon.

This person may be a CXO, or in a smaller initiative (or a larger organization) a department head, who may have the necessary position power.

In practice, they must have the responsibility for all activities the program or portfolio will include. That way, there aren't any mysterious external forces that can be blamed if things don't go as desired.

The Battle Rages On

The fact that you now have executive support of some kind for your PPFMO doesn't mean the battles are over. It just means you'll be in a position to participate more effectively.

In his article "7 Responses to Reasoned Resistance," leadership expert Dan Rockwell explores ways in which a disingenuous response may appear and how to deal with it (URL in the References annex). The pushback will generally appear on the surface to be reasonable inquiries. At least until the stakes are high and imminent, organizational communications always appear to be very reasonable on the surface, even if the implication is a middle finger salute.

For instance, we've all seen one of the tactics he cites: "[One source says] 'When I don't want to do something, I ask lots of questions.' She uses distraction and foot dragging to escape change, so her questions seem like concern."

Respond positively and logically without a kneejerk reaction to those aspects of the pushback that merit any response. Though Dan provided several useful responses, the three most pertinent to this situation are:

- Tell me again why this idea won't work (reasoned resistors won't open their hearts until they feel heard).

- What makes staying the same better than trying something new?

- I hear you on what we can't do. What can we do?

You can rectify some of this through your charisma and interpersonal relationships. If you're on the left-brain side of the house (I spoke earlier of the extraordinary congruence in Meyers-Briggs tendencies among program and project managers), you may not be able to count on those assets to take you all that far. So you'll need some help. Good top cover can make up for a lot of charisma.

The Real Reasons for Resistance: Autonomy and Disbelief

A stakeholder who doesn't see an upside to "what's in it for me?" isn't going to be a supporter of a change initiative or any other initiative.

If you accept the premise that governance and the PPFMO will help the organization to operate more efficiently and effectively, why is top-level support so critical? Better efficiency makes the organization more profitable or competitive. Or in a public or nonprofit entity, it frees up more resources for more projects.

How can anyone be against that?

At any level of an organization other than the actual delivery teams, just how tightly coupled is someone's job security to the actual performance of the organization? When you look around, you'll see the answer is: "not very."

The fact is, organizations consist of people, and they exist to serve the interests of those who run them. With few exceptions, people at the top got there through methods that worked well for that particular culture and vice versa. So why would they want to change that?

This isn't just limited to those at the top. In fact, it gets worse as you step down the ladder. Those at the very top are already fairly secure, so they can tolerate a degree of innovation.

Your most violent opponents will come from those in the next layers down: those who have neared the top.

If a change initiative can alter the equation of power, it can also undermine the aspirations and values of anyone who's climbed a significant way up the ladder. The last thing they're going to embrace now is a rules change.

The odds are a new PPFM initiative is being pushed by a few visionaries who have gained the trust and support of one or more of the CXOs. Nobody else has bought into it yet.

Even though those CXOs have great top-down power, they're going to have to use it aggressively to allow this small band of warriors to overcome the inertia created by the rest of the management layers.

Adult learning theory has shown that commitment to change typically occurs only after a serious emotional event. Knowing objectively that an action can cause the organization to lose ground against its competitors, or that the action is required by law, isn't enough.

In an organization, about the only serious emotional event you can have is that you believe you could be fired or your job could disappear in the immediate future. In the commercial sector, these are often very real possibilities, and they are at the root of many change initiatives.

The number of people who do indeed eventually get fired, and the number of companies that do go bankrupt even after all those explicit warnings, just proves that people will go a very long way before accepting the existence of an obvious threat.

Apparently it hasn't been presented in a way that fires off their emotional responses. (This also explains why change is extremely difficult in government agencies, where the one thing people are pretty sure of is they're not going to be fired.)

Even where organizational dysfunction has a specific impact on the ability of project teams to get their work done, don't expect automatic grassroots support.

Most governance initiatives are launched to produce a top-down benefit, such as eliminating redundant efforts or shaving costs. At lower levels that's seen as a cut-back, not a benefit. You'll need to sell hard to overcome that history, and convey a message that something is in it for the performers as well as for the executives.

Once launched and funded, the only way for a program or project to benefit from governance board intervention is to raise an issue that needs to be resolved to stave off potential failure. In most organizations (skeptical or otherwise), capable project managers are very reluctant to hint at the possibility of failure. Driving the process solely by means of red lights on the dashboard won't be popular.

If people are fairly competent and motivated, then project teams and project managers will (within the limits of their knowledge and abilities) work out how to get the job done, with or without top-down guidance.

Your help is only going to be accepted if it actually provides solutions to their issues. They won't want to stop what they're doing to provide you with information which by definition they already know.

So you'll do yourself a big favor by integrating what already works, even if it means more effort on the PPFMO's part, rather than by demanding they do something in a way that might be slightly better.

If you use their own data to hold them out as "deficient" on a dashboard based on criteria that are only pertinent to the PPFMO, you'll have lost them forever.

Remember, the organization's work and delivery of products is done in the line divisions, and not by the executives or the PPFMO. So you have to find ways to make the governance program acceptable to those being governed.

Get a Charter

One of the best practices consistently shared across most methodologies is to make sure an initiative has a formal signed charter before spending too much time and energy. However, the only time the charter might be referred to is when stakeholders point out that whatever you're trying to do isn't in it. Or when project teams object that they weren't given the promised resources.

In many years of doing this kind of work, I don't recall too many instances where expectations or resources were corrected to match what the charter said. What I do remember is hearing "That was then – this is now."

With or without a formal charter, an initiative achieves success because it has active, observable leadership support. Leaders constantly inquire after its health, and come down like a ton of bricks on responsible parties if the resources they need aren't available. Not the resources called for in the charter, but the resources they need right now.

In these instances, a charter serves no purpose. All the project manager has to do is amicably suggest the other manager may well have a good point. "Maybe we should pick up the phone and bring Mr. Big in on this very enlightening opinion so we can get a resolution and move on." You then both agree to move on instead of bothering Mr. Big. But you can't resort to that strategy too often.

Plus, you can't have more than one or two initiatives with that sort of status, or you're back to the chaos of not having any priorities at all. For the rest, a bit of evidence of interest from Mahogany Row would come in handy.

The point isn't about getting the charter signed. The point is if you can't get closure on getting it signed, your initiative doesn't have a great deal of status with the intended sponsors.

If they won't do something as simple as signing the charter, do you think they'll go to war with other senior players who renege on their resource commitments?

In Japan, executives sometimes sign a charter upside down to indicate they don't really support or oppose it. That's pretty transparent! Wouldn't it be helpful if everybody could be that honest about their intentions?

Having a charter doesn't prove you have real support. Being unable to get a charter definitely means you don't have support. So by all means get a charter. Just remember, it won't prove they care, nor does it mean you'll get all the support you've been promised. At least it'll show they don't really hate the idea.

Sample Charter

Headings like "Sample Charter" are tempting to template hounds who are just skimming the table of contents. *Hey, skip the context. Just give me a form to fill in and we're off to the races!* So it's better to understand the templates before inflicting them on anyone.

Just before writing this section, I saw an elaborate charter establishing the operating role for a governance board. It had sections for key deliverables and baseline costs. But nothing whatsoever about the board's responsibilities, or how they would accomplish them. The author had re-used a project charter template without giving any thought to the content. It's not enough to have a template; you have to have the right one, and you have to understand what the content means.

Very few templates can be used as-is, and they certainly shouldn't be used without thinking about what the organization's trying to accomplish. Even the lack of detail in a simple template speaks loudly to the organizational governance philosophy. Tools don't work well if they're not suited to the job you decide to use them for.

A template document is intended to speed the process along, so an effective charter needs to reflect the environment in which you'll use it. Since a charter is usually a fairly concise document, it can be difficult for a template to contain more than just the headings.

So whenever you choose a source for your template, provide an example of a properly completed document so you can show people what it should look like.

(You can find an example of a completed governance charter at www.Simmer-System.com. Though it may give you an idea of things to include, please don't copy and adopt it as-is, as it won't match the organization's way of doing things. You'll lose credibility and it will be ignored.

However, you can use it to get an idea of the scope and tone of the language that might be in your document. Then custom-tailor it by using the suggestions in the next section.)

Making the Charter Mean Something

Your charter is a communication from the sponsoring executive to the stakeholders.

Successful politicians and executives may say a lot of words. But when you listen more closely, you'll find they get ahead by suggesting too much and committing to too little. Don't for one minute think that private corporation executives are any less political than their public sector counterparts. In fact, they may be better at it because they have to pretend they're not. So don't fall for politically correct mumbo-jumbo.

If the executives' hearts aren't in the game before the hard parts have surfaced, they'll cave when the going gets tough. Clarify things from the beginning by keeping things simple and specific.

Keep the charter in basic English (or whatever your business language happens to be) – not in multisyllabic "bureaucratese."

For instance, all anybody really needs to know about a governance board is:

- What's the point of the group or effort?
- Who's responsible for it? And which of the executives is the sponsor?
- Who's allowed to participate in it?
- What decisions can the group make?
- How do decisions get brought to the group?
- Are there any constraints on the types of decisions it makes, or how it must make those decisions?
- How are its decisions to be enforced?

These questions don't have to be answered with long-winded explanations. State them clearly and succinctly in no more than two pages.

Keep in mind that the mere existence of the charter isn't enough to keep the initiative in business. Because change is hard, sponsors need to remain engaged with the initiative for as long as possible to witness the initiative's benefits; otherwise, the organization can backslide into whatever is easier to do.

Many Charters Are Better Than One

A PPFM initiative will require multiple types of charters. In logical order – though not the order in which they will appear – they are:

- Charter of the governance board by the executive leadership
- Charter of the PPFMO by the governance board
- Charters of programs by the governance board
- Charters of projects by the program offices

Since you're not starting from a green-field organization, the charters won't appear on the ground in that order. So let's take them in the order in which they'll likely appear, and put *The Pasta Principle* to work!

Project-Type Charter

Project management is probably the best-established of the governance disciplines, so people will be most familiar with a project-type charter. Its intent is to obtain approval (let's defer the question from whom for a moment) for the necessary resources to implement the initiative and the outcomes it will achieve.

A project itself has no viability without the endorsement of a program since there would be no funding and no staffing. Some organizations will charter just the exploratory phase of an initiative, which is an interesting idea. Just don't overdo it, or the budget will be consumed with early analyses for work that can't possibly be accommodated.

Naturally, the PPFMO should be the first to undertake the processes it proposes to create for everyone else. It should set the bar somewhat above the minimum standard as an example for the rest, but not so high as to terrify them.

PPFM Initiative Charter

A charter for the organization's PPFM initiative will be quite different from the one used in a project. Much of the typical project charter focuses on setting baselines for the solution, cost and schedule, as well as specifying where the resources will come from. All of that may be included in a PPFM charter, as it's useful to set those expectations. But it's even more important to look at the non-quantitative expectations.

The most important thing is to clarify the desired outcomes, which the PPFM initiative manager *and* the organization need to respect. If the main problem is that the CXO is tired of not having key initiatives completed because people are working on other things, then after being turned from an issue into a positive statement of the outcome the charter should establish three to five objectives that clearly address that problem.

All of the initiative's efforts should be aimed at a rapid, pragmatic approach to dealing with that problem. Once it's been solved, the charter can be revised to address the next most pressing challenges.

Charter of the Governance Board

The PPFM initiative will also have to develop another type of charter in which someone empowers governance boards to make their decisions. There may be several such charters in a sizeable organization that needs to use multiple layers of boards or parallel boards.

You need to remember you're likely dealing with an organization that's not by nature process-driven, so getting the "deciders" to commit can be a major triumph.

In a clear and concise communication via an email or memo, announce the new group and its role. (Having the signer speak in first person *I, me, my* sends the message that 'the boss wants this to happen'.)

Program Charter

Logically, and in conformance with the PMI practice standard for program management, the organization should charter the programs before issuing project charters. In reality, that doesn't happen much because most of the programs are already in existence.

With all of the other decisions that need to be reached, documenting why you're doing something you've been doing for a while seems like a fairly low priority.

Actually, getting program charters in place would eliminate the need for many of the project-level decisions the governance board has to make.

Program charters would also expose the service level agreements that should underlie the operational aspects of the programs. Those activities consume some 60 to 80% of the total budget, so there's a lot of benefit to having those commitments defined.

As a practical matter, the organization is going to need a lot of training to grasp these concepts. So don't let this issue stand in the way of progress in other areas!

In all of these efforts, don't overcomplicate the situation with elaborate lengthy documents.

Sweeping Away Obstacles

In a more mature organization that already has a formal process for publishing policies (even if they're ignored), enlist people who manage the process to help you get your charter through it in a relatively timely manner.

As much fuss as people make about the difficulty of getting a proper charter in place, it's actually the easiest part of getting executive support. It doesn't take much effort for an executive to put a signature on the charter.

Much more important is getting public commitments to the charter. You'll need a bit of lead time, but you must get executives to attend a meeting where they'll make an appeal about how important the initiative is for the organization's future. They typically like to do that sort of thing and the organization wants to know if they really mean it.

A key rule executives should put forward is that things will run into difficulties from time to time. They will want to know when those situations occur so that they can remove any obstacles in the initiative's path. The only unacceptable behavior is to insist that things are going great, then at the last minute declare a major budget shortfall or slippage. Green-green-green-green-**red** isn't an acceptable pattern.

Any challenge that prevents progress needs to be immediately brought into the open, and escalated as needed until the problem is solved. In a maturing organization, there may not be an obvious path to raise, then escalate, an issue.

Therefore, the PPFMO must provide that path and make it highly transparent. Even if no other aspect of governance is working, this one item can make or break the PPFMO.

On the positive side, the high point in a PPFMO manager's career might be the moment when a project manager sees the light as a result of reporting a "red" project issue, and gets the attention from leadership to resolve problems people have known about for months or years.

This, of course, can be a truly uplifting moment for all concerned. It will also generate more converts than any amount of preaching by the PPFMO or by the executives themselves.

On the other end of the spectrum, if managers dilute issues for fear of offending anyone – or if issues make it all the way to the governance board and nothing happens to make them go away – the PPFMO is on its way out.

No amount of Gantt charts and Risk Spider charts can override evidence that the organization doesn't care very much about getting things done.

People already know what you're going to say. What they want to know is what you're actually going to do.

One of my most enduring lessons from my successes with establishing a PPFMO was when delays had become so bad, the project team finally screwed up the courage to include the issues register in the progress report to the executive level.

Whammo! Instant resolution appeared for many issues that had lingered for months – sometimes closer to years.

After that, the project team members wanted to bring up all the issues that they had given up adding to the issues list after many months of inaction. This is a good problem to have, in that the PPFMO gains instant credibility. But it immediately faces another test from the opposite direction. So one of two things is about to happen:

1. If the issues are largely external, continuing the pressure will convey the message that the other executives' organizations are falling down on the job.

    Even if that's true, you can only present this message a few times before it annoys them. Then instead of cooperation you get defensiveness.

2. If the sponsor is brave enough to assume the risk, confessing to and then fixing a mistake is an act of noble honesty. Repeatedly making the same mistake suggests incompetence. If most of the issues are internal, continuing to raise them can make sponsors look bad to their peers. They will search the organization to find the buffoon causing the problems, which would be you, the messenger.

You'll get detailed micromanagement to ensure the issues are rectified before reports go forward, which is probably what should have been happening all along. That's fine, as long as it doesn't devolve into taking all the issues off the list to avoid oversight, which puts you right back where you were in the first place. In fact, it may have been the reason the last PPFMO before yours became a "casualty," and the reason why yours might be next.

At the executive level, one of the highest priorities is to tend to the politics, because almost everything at that level is subjective, regardless of what the numbers may say. An executive can't afford to be on the wrong political side of too many issues (even when they're right about the facts).

Finally, coach your sponsoring executives to go beyond paper involvement with their initiatives. All too often, it's assumed that participation is limited to signing the charter, giving a motivational speech, and responding to status reports.

That loses sight of the point that the sponsoring executive is supposed to be the person who, more than anyone else, really wants to get this initiative done successfully.

In addition to procedural actions, there's a lot to be said for the practice of "managing by walking around." Executives bothering to come down from the top floor to drop in on a project team is an unmistakable sign that the initiative is important to them.

They should make some impromptu visits from time to time, and get past the polished quarterly briefing by the program managers to obtain the unvarnished views of people actually working on the project.

Keeping Managers Accountable

Once the executive governance board has allocated resources and approved key initiatives for the programs, the members need to make it clear that they intend to get their money's worth.

There's no way to establish accountability without some degree of formality. A written record of what the board approves, and a periodic review of whether the activities will be delivered as approved.

The PPFMO *must* document the initial approval, although it may consist of nothing more than a date, budget amount, and a few lines of text on a spreadsheet as to what exactly is being approved. A verbal commitment can be a source of later debate, so it must be in written form.

When allocating funds, the board is in essence establishing a baseline. Therefore, it's up to the managers at the initiative level to deliver what was agreed upon. Or at the very least to declare the impact any circumstance can have on making such a delivery.

Project or initiative status reports from senior staff members also need to be recorded. They can be very informal, and can ask simple questions like "Will you be ready on xxx date?" as the list is reviewed.

You don't necessarily have to have elaborate analytical processes to confirm the performance of the work. As long as the top leadership has established the understanding that reports of good health followed by sudden major slippages could be career-threatening, you can be fairly certain the organization will provide reasonably honest assessments of how things stand.

Are you starting to feel the pull? If it gets this far, your PPFMO is definitely getting off the ground.

Keeping the Troops Motivated

The importance of senior leaders periodically visiting the teams doing the work can't be over-emphasized. If key initiatives are critical to the organization's strategy, how is it possible the executives have time to look at a cafeteria menu, but don't have time to look in on their crown jewel?

The PPFMO should encourage surprise visits by the executives to the staff. The director must emphatically state to all parties that they won't be dog-and-pony shows requiring advanced preparation, cleanup and PowerPoint presentations.

Therefore, the schedule should remain undisclosed, as the executives need an unfiltered picture of what's actually going on.

What about initiatives that aren't high on the priority list? Almost by definition, they're required to give up resources whenever one of the more glamorous initiatives runs into trouble. But in order to get resources in the first place, they must have served some useful purpose.

Therefore, it will be important to keep track of any deferrals that result from such reprogramming and the expected cumulative consequences. Today's discretionary expenses have a way of becoming tomorrow's "how could you allow this to happen?"

Most of the lower-priority activities are routine operations the rest of the organization depends on for daily services, even after being raided to prop up the innovation projects.

The PPFMO should consider ways to give those efforts the appropriate recognition, and make sure they're not cut so deeply as to result in failed capabilities that everyone needs to do their "more important" work.

Next Steps

In this chapter you've taken the necessary steps to get the support from your sponsoring executive, which makes the PPFMO official. You also prepared the appropriate charters so that people who aren't intimately involved with the project(s) can understand what they are all about.

Far more important than the PPFMO's charter is that of the governance board that gives it the authority to operate. In the next chapter, we'll take a look at what "operate" means from an implementation point of view. What should the board do, and how should it do so?

EXERCISE 5: SETTING THE STAGE

Now that you've seen how to get your basic principles established, your top cover lined up, and a charter for the governance board, it's time to get the board up and running by following these next steps:

1. **Develop a charter for your governance board**, which you can create with the information provided in this chapter. But you can also find an editable MS Word version at www.Simmer-System.com.

2. After defining the governance board's responsibilities, **put together key responsibilities for the PPFMO supporting the board**. (Don't over-think this. I'll come back to it in a later chapter.)

3. **Identify the stakeholders who can influence the PPFMO's success in the organization**. Include:

    - Sponsoring executive
    - Peer executives the sponsor must deal with regularly
    - Members of the PPFMO's governance board
    - Program managers running the projects and programs the governance board oversees

Now, identify and define the relationships between all these people (i.e., are they supportive or confrontational?) Maybe you should do this first in your head, and guard it closely if you write it down.

If you think you have any adverse relationships, you don't want to make that fact public! (You can find an example of this analysis at www.Simmer-System.com.)

Chapter Six

Ready, Set, Govern!

Setting Up the Board

You just completed the challenge of creating a charter for the governance board by identifying the scope of its role and who the affected stakeholders will be.

This chapter explains how to prepare the board for that role, how the PPFMO supports it, and the decisions that should be made (subsequent chapters will go into what the board actually does).

Board Principles and Roles

At the simplest level, a governance board...

- ensures that investments are properly balanced to achieve enterprise goals; and that funding isn't siphoned to a local effort nobody agreed to;
- ensures the programs' estimates of funding requirements are realistic and appropriate, and that the expected outcomes are delivered effectively;
- ensures that operational activities remain cost-effective;
- provides and enforces standards and processes for proposals, progress reviews and other board interactions to ensure a consistent framing that allows the board to notice the nuances of differences between investments; and
- devises some manner of ensuring that its decisions are carried out.

A Key Sponsor Role: Assure Attendance

This tiny topic gets its own section – it's that important!

The governance board members are senior managers and executives who were busy before the PPFMO initiative started. Making sure the organization runs well and spends its money effectively are among the numerous roles they have.

Almost all PPFMOs are put in place to facilitate the members' implementation of this one aspect of their responsibilities.

One of the biggest challenges the PPFMO will face is getting adequate time from the board members. PPFMO sponsoring executives must earn their money at this point.

The board will need several face-to-face meetings to form a good sense of its role and its own internal dynamics. Partial attendance won't do. The sponsoring executive is the only person closely involved with the PPFMO initiative who can cajole other executives to join the meetings.

"Well begun is half done."

The best chance of engaging and retaining board members' attention is to convince them through consistent action that their decision processes are important, will be respected and will not be bypassed. People tend to be interested in having the opportunity to make a difference.

It's well-known that you have food at a meeting if you want people to attend. That's not just for people in lower income brackets, as executives don't mind being fed either! (Unfortunately, if you're in a federal organization, you have serious constraints in this regard, so you'll have to get more creative.) This is probably overdoing it if the meetings become weekly events, in which case you'll need to make sure they are somewhat interesting. Consider guest visitors, videos or some other means of breaking up the monotony.

A much more serious aspect is that attendance will begin to decline the first time the executive level decides it would be more expeditious for a pet project to bypass the governance board. Members will realize their presence is irrelevant if key decisions are being made without them. Nobody wants to think of themselves as mere window-dressing.

The organization may get away with this one time, if you make sure the appropriate *mea culpas* are offered (and not by you. You don't count at this level, so the offending executive has to step forward.) If it recurs, the governance board will collapse like a pricked balloon with about the same noise.

If the PPFMO's sponsor achieves nothing else, maintaining an engaged board may be sufficient to keep the governance and PPFMO efforts successful. The potential for appearing in front of an executive-level board does wonders for a project or program manager's motivation to think their initiatives through with the appropriate due diligence.

Without an engaged board to incentivize effective preparation and to legitimize decisions, the entire governance initiative will fade quickly into oblivion. At least until the organization decides to try again in a few years.

Make it Live and in Person

Technically speaking, the discussions and voting processes could shift to an electronic process via a collaboration site or email. *Don't fall into this temptation!* Hold the line as much as possible on an in-person rather than virtual meeting.

In the rare instances where executives tend to their own workflow or inbox, the volume of material they have to read doesn't allow time for adequate attention to big read-ahead decision packages.

So those packages are often not read until the time of the meeting itself. If there's no live meeting, then on deadline day the executive's assistant clicks "approved" and shoves the still-unread package forward to the next step. That doesn't help anyone.

Most successful executives have the ability to quickly skim a fairly thick document while noting critical points and inconsistencies. In a live in-person meeting, they often do this with physical copies of documents which, old-school though they may be, lend themselves to skimming and note-taking.

In a virtual meeting, the executive reads an electronic document which is harder to absorb. Without the pressure from their peers during an in-person meeting, members in a virtual meeting can check their email, read non-related documents, and find other ways to distract themselves from the business at hand.

Even if the member never gets to the read-ahead, the in-person meeting serves an even more important function: the opportunity to sit down for 15 to 20 minutes to really pay attention to an investment, observe the program manager's and your colleagues' body language, and to decide whether the rose-colored presentation is really poison ivy hiding behind a pink smokescreen.

This is something that most executives are really good at, so don't take the tool out of their hands.

Live meetings, whether electronic or in-person, also prevent program managers from winning approval for the work by promising contradictory things to different sponsors during one-on-one sessions.

This isn't saying program managers are trying to be dishonest; they just might be focusing their talks on the considerations that each board member wants to hear about. And then they might forget what they told each person. It happens a lot.

Having many different versions of the same thing prevents the pieces from fitting together correctly if you haven't thought the process through. Quite often the program manager has become too focused on getting the resources to begin or continue their initiatives. Planning, budgeting and risk management can place second or even tenth in their attention.

Never underestimate the fear most people (including experienced program managers) have of making presentations at all, let alone to a board composed of their supervisor's manager's boss and unknown executives.

There's value in causing the program and project managers to make an effort to prepare their facts and figures to minimize the risk of embarrassing, unexpected questions in a public meeting that could expose a hole in their knowledge. Or worse, a flaw in their approach could cost funding and delay the program.

The PPFMO staff can gain points by making it clear they're available to the program managers to assist them in preparing for the board, and making sure that presentations make sense and meet expectations.

Eliminating public decision meetings in favor of an offline format removes the incentive to do the right thing. Without having given appropriate attention to the decision packages – and without a meeting where the program manager can be in attendance with the proper information (or subtly shamed by not having it) – everything can slide downhill.

Board members will have a harder time noticing the holes in the arguments, and won't be able to sense their colleagues' levels of comfort or discomfort with the proposed investments. They won't able to call a program manager to task for a shoddy or deceptive decision package and presentation. Busy program managers will spend less effort on making sure their packages are bulletproof, and the quality of the supporting analyses will decline.

Of course, the decision package itself doesn't cause a program to succeed or fail; the quality and amount of planning that goes into them is what's important. Without those, many initiatives fail before they ever begin.

That's not to say you should never have a board meeting unless you can do it in person, as technology has removed some of the impediments of geographic separation. It's often not practical or cost-effective to assemble the members together at one location. But you can convene an in-person meeting using Skype, web-conferencing and other tools so that live interfacing can capture people's body language. If you can't, then you can't. Just be aware of the limitations, and do your best to minimize them.

How Many Meetings?

When the board first starts having meetings, you may think there's no point in meeting often since there's a minimal workload. Try not to do that. The best approach is to schedule the same amount of meetings you'll have once the process is in full swing. That puts a recurring meeting on their calendars, and they'll get used to keeping that space open.

Besides, it's not as if there's nothing else to do. A lot of training and planning needs to occur before the initiatives start rolling in, which will create larger demands on the board. Having a relatively fixed amount of time for board activities will reinforce the idea of breaking the work into more aggregated packages (i.e., the programs).

In theory, the frequency of meetings should depend on the volume of work. But there's an upper limit to that. This governance stuff may be important now, whereas previously it wasn't. The executives still have plenty of other activities to undertake. Consider yourself lucky if you can get them together once a month (again, this is where the PPFMO's executive sponsors earn their keep).

There's some practicality to starting with a plan to hold at least one meeting per month. As an example, let's look at a typical board in a midsize company or agency. If the organization has 24 projects and/or sustainment initiatives, this requires at least 48 board presentations per year: one to get approval to do the work, and one to see how it is going (24 x 2 = 48). This means reviewing four initiatives per monthly meeting (48 ÷ 12 = 4).

Depending on the nature of the organization's work, more reviews may be appropriate. Or some initiatives may be complex and require extended discussions.

But wait ... that's not all!

Time will need to be set aside for general budgetary overviews, and for discussions of corporate policies, technical directions and other strategic topics. In addition, there will be instances where events require an out-of-cycle review of an initiative, or the board must consider and resolve an escalated issue. Now the agenda is getting longer!

Tossed into this mix, you'll need to consider how often you can re-review the same presentation if at first it doesn't meet the board's standards. However, if the board allows shoddy presentations to slide, over time they'll dwindle to the lowest common denominator.

It's critical to have a solid understanding of the kinds of decisions the board will make, the documentation they'll see in support of that role, and what acceptable solutions look like. The total number of decisions the board must make, and the time needed to make them, might need to be limited. You can do that by establishing rules, or by delegating certain decisions to someone closer to the actual event. The board may also want to include delegations or rules to account for emergencies where convening a meeting is impractical.

This reality is also a key reason why a program structure is needed in any but the simplest organization. Instead of adding more initiatives, push to establish programs so the board can limit its oversight to a manageable number of programs. Then they can do a better job of holding the program managers accountable for defining and managing the projects and operations needed to deliver their program's intended benefit within the overall resources and constraints the board provided.

Another important reason to have some time between meetings is to make sure the board's directions can be taken seriously. If the board can't hold the line on simple, specific action items, it's a natural reaction to backslide on compliance with more nuanced activities.

If the board meets every two weeks, many issues brought up in one meeting might legitimately not be resolved by the next meeting. Being deferred for a meeting or two inevitably turns into three or five or never. Providing a full month usually allows enough time to resolve almost any matter assigned by the organization's senior leadership, and therefore makes it reasonable for the board to crack down on a program manager who didn't get the matter resolved (or at least make significant progress) before the next meeting.

Over time there will be demands for more board involvement or at least for more meetings. As the governance process matures, issues might arise that could have been avoided if due diligence was initially done. More resolutions in turn require more paperwork and reviews.

The PPFMO director needs to remain vigilant to control the growth of paperwork and process time. The staff tends to develop tunnel vision about the importance and impact of review documentation. The real burden of oversight falls on program managers who have to prepare the information, and the board members who are supposed to review it. Both of those players have many other responsibilities besides reading and writing project documentation.

If you think you're providing the board with adequate information – and about as much as they can stomach – adding more won't produce added value. Fine-tune the decision packages to focus on material that gets initiatives back on the right track.

How the Sausage Got Made (Hint: It's Not in the Boardroom)

In order to provide effective support for the decision-making process, the PPFMO needs to understand how board members really operate.

Bottom line? Decisions aren't made in the boardroom.

An irony of the governance situation is that we seek to prove the existence of transparency and process consistency by demanding that evidence-gathering and decision-making be conducted in public with the proceedings in the record.

Yet, any observer can tell you this isn't where the critical points of those processes really occur. In fact, if it is all forced out into the open, it probably won't happen at all.

The best you can do is to get visibility of the final decision and the actual outcomes. You'll never know (and you probably don't want to know) how the actual "sausage" gets made.

Don't fall into the trap of thinking major decisions are going to be made at the meeting. Some horse trading and fine-tuning on minor items may occur, but the real politicking will have occurred prior to the meeting.

Unless a general consensus – or at least a strong majority – formed beforehand, the matter will seldom be allowed to come to a decision in public.

If that consensus hasn't occurred, the board members will table as much business as possible until they have the opportunity to speak with their stakeholders.

Meetings and reviews consume board members' time, and time and resources at the program and project levels. So why even have them? Didn't this whole effort begin with a commitment to bring decisions out into the open? Well, yes and no. The decisions – yes. The negotiations toward the decision – no, unless they create another decision.

Wouldn't it be interesting, and probably build even more legitimacy, to have full information as to everything that went into a decision? Shouldn't you get to see what tradeoffs were made to achieve a consensus?

Interesting, certainly. Productive? Probably not. But since that's not going to happen, don't worry about it. It's enough that the actual decisions are known.

The ritual of assembling a board meeting to issue decisions not only reinforces the decision process, but demonstrates official unity on the decisions themselves. Regardless of how an idea or proposal arrives on the table, the only way to get approval for the resources is to go through the board.

Again, please be warned against using an asynchronous process. If the decision meeting shifts to being held offline, it can appear the process has reverted to the secretive, back-door way of doing things that led to the need for the PPFMO and governance initiative in the first place.

(Notice I didn't say above that the decisions were being reached there anyway; I said consensus was being achieved that way. The decisions need to be "taken" in the open. Legitimacy is all about how things appear.)

The fact that members reach conclusions in private shouldn't be all that troubling. The purpose of the governance process isn't to think for the board; the point of a broad-based board is to avoid falling into a group mentality.

Members sit on the board to represent a broad set of perspectives and responsibilities. Each member needs to conduct their own due diligence to feel confident that if what they're about to approve won't benefit their part of organization, at least it won't harm it. As long as the board reaches reasonable, consistent decisions, how the data was collected shouldn't be a matter of great concern.

Senior managers try hard not to get into situations where the outcome is unclear. Nor do they take public stances without a great deal of groundwork done ahead of time to figure out where the board stands.

Whenever possible, members will have settled on a consensus solution before bringing a matter up in public. If a consensus is impossible, then a solution needs to attract a strong majority. If it doesn't, the meeting is likely to run out of time before the matter can be addressed, and will have to wait until the next meeting or the one thereafter.

For this reason, it's better that the charter doesn't try to force a majority vote system onto the board. Many are written to require unanimity or nearly so, with an escalation process to some higher authority to preclude a filibuster by one or two members who refuse to agree.

To justify using the time of high-priced board members, the matters brought before them need to address critical issues and substantial levels of resources. An approved initiative that fails will cost the organization a great deal of money. In the worst case scenario, it could cost a strategic advantage.

Yet all of the decisions must be made with imperfect information. When you have a fair chance of the decision going wrong, it's essential to have everyone on board from the beginning. On the heels of making a major decision where the outcome is uncertain, the perfect sentiment would be: *"We must all hang together, or assuredly we shall all hang separately."* ~Benjamin Franklin, 1776

Although the decisions seem important to the program and project managers trying to move things forward on behalf of the organization, it's surprising how often things can be left to cool for an extended period of time without the world falling apart.

These behind-the-scenes processes aren't purely self-interested politics. It's unrealistic to assume that board members will understand all of the intricacies of the initiatives based solely on a heavily-skewed information package and perhaps 20 minutes of presentation and discussion.

In reality, before they get to the meeting, most of the executives will perform a 360-degree assessment to make sure they're not being sold a bill of goods (which to some degree they usually are); determine the true level of significance of the proposed investments; and make sure other executives will support whatever action is being taken.

That's one reason you need to give them a week or more for the read-aheads. They have a lot to do after they've gotten the gist of the meeting material, and very little has to do with the specifics of the content.

Setting Up a Program Structure

Because of the corporation's size and the complexity of its activities, it's usually impossible for a board to spend an appropriate amount of time on each of the initiatives. So they must be collapsed via some form of aggregation.

There's value in understanding individual investments when they run into millions of dollars. Micromanaging the project teams to make sure they're doing their job defeats the purpose of the board, and assumes the members know better than the highly-qualified functional managers. It shouldn't be about knowing better; the decisions are really about whether the managers' intentions make sense on the surface and are well-supported in the details.

The key tasks in establishing program structure are:

- Determine the language
- Consider the capacity

Determine the Language

The first task in setting up the structure is to **define terms**. In order to ensure discussions are being held on a consistent basis, with the help of the PPFMO the board will need to establish a common vocabulary and set of standards to be used enterprise-wide. To begin, you'll need to define what the organization means by the words "project", "program" and "portfolio."

Don't waste time on exhaustive tweaking and combining of common project and program management best practices. Modify or add only the smallest subset of terms that must be understood in the organization's unique way ("must" and "unique" are important words in this context).

In addition, a term is worth defining if it's vague or used loosely in common speech. However, since people seldom read glossaries, you're going to have to find the best way to get the message out.

For example, consider putting a "PPFM Word of the Week" section in newsletters, interoffice email updates, or other program-wide communications to create retention.

Terms that are commonly used incorrectly and might benefit from such publicity include:

- **Planned** means planned. It's only as good as the information used to generate it. The eventual reality **_will_** be different.

- **Spent** is an example where the various shades of its different meanings can be extremely important. In the commercial sector, the handling of capital and operating expenses has major impacts on a company's profitability. In the government sector, an entire range of terms may sound similar to an outsider but can carry various meanings and practical implications.

  A project manager on a government project usually only has to deal with turning allocated funding into obligated contracts, at which point the work can begin and eventually will turn into invoices. The program level, with its multi-year, multi-investment perspective, enmeshes a program manager in terms such as budgeted, programmed, appropriated, allocated, committed, obligated, invoiced and expended.

- **Accrued.** With all of the government's elaborate money-tracking activities, the one term that really hasn't caught on (despite being perhaps the most important) is "accrued," which is well-understood in the private sector. Many people in government consider either obligations or invoices to constitute "actual" costs. Accruals are a much better reflection of what the project management discipline would consider an "actual cost."

  Invoices often lag too far behind to be useful for metrics, and obligations can be clawed back, as long as the costs have not in fact been accrued. Hardly any government organization bothers to do it that way (in fact, very few have any means of tracking accruals), because getting that money back too late to obligate it again would result in its being "lost," as well as generating a reduced budget for the project in the following year as a lesson to spend harder next time. The fact that federal projects never under-run isn't due to a huge coincidence.

- **Finished.** This should be an easy one, don't you think? Would you believe that as of July 2015, there were 255 million hits on Google for the term "definition of done"? "Finished" is a major component of Agile frameworks. Entire sections of Earned Value texts are devoted to explaining how to count whether something is done, and if not, how much of it is completed.

The earned value aspect is a bit off the end of the timeline for the purposes of this book, although not as far as people might think. Even so, you'll find yourself in robust conversations between project managers, testers and trainers, operations managers and solution developers to determine when work is ready to be handed to them. Even at the foundational level of *The Simmer System*, discussions of "done" are one of the key agreements described in a later chapter.

- **Approved.** Again, the PPFMO will need to fight to make sure this term is understood to include the phrase "by the appropriate entity." Everyone else will be arguing that a go-ahead from their boss' boss is good enough for them, especially if they want to stay employed in that job. Let the governance board members carry this water, as all too often the PPFMO gets caught in the crossfire.

- **Estimated.** Fairly mature organizations have difficulty with this term, while governmental agencies can't abide it. "Estimated" means the number is merely one point within a probabilistic range of values.

In my experience, the main reason many projects fail to meet their baselines is that neither the executives nor the project managers (or for that matter, the organization's financial system) understand or know how to handle the concept of a range of outcomes.

They convert an estimate to a single point of illusory certainty, and that becomes the baseline. Predictably, half of the approved work overruns such a baseline, or else estimates are so heavily padded that the single point now represents a 95% certainty number that may double or triple the amount really needed.

If you compound this error by trying to redeploy any saved program funds into an enterprise-wide investment pool, you've just removed the program manager's incentive to find those savings. So all you ever see are overruns. Check your local newspaper for daily evidence of this. Any savings will disappear to handle unforeseen or unapproved needs, and you've just abetted the exact lack of transparency you're trying to eliminate.

Happily, this situation is alleviated by focusing on programs rather than projects. At that level, if it's done correctly the allocation of funds owes more to the board's willingness to invest in a capability than it does to lower-level budget forecasts for specific solutions. Program managers are asked to deliver capabilities within the allocated funding, and they can adjust specific deliveries within the program as long as the core requirements are being met.

Consider Capacity: Don't Bite Off What You Can't Chew

A critical decision the board must reach is how to control the flow of reviews and decisions so it has enough time to consider the proposals put before it. But it must have enough meetings that "waiting for board approval" doesn't become the obstacle to organizational progress.

At the other end of the spectrum, a decision board that conducts perfunctory reviews before agreeing to whatever comes in front of it is a rubber stamp.

It's a waste of time for program and project managers to prepare and present briefings they know are meaningless. Even worse, such a process generates a disparaging view of the executives' competence, and it creates a dangerous liability for the organization which is assuming that board approval implies some level of due diligence.

So what is the workload that must be accommodated within the time available? In addition to setting policy, the board has essentially two responsibilities:

1. Determine at an enterprise level (however the enterprise was defined for this particular board) what investments are needed.

2. Periodically revisit each of the funded investments to see how they're doing, and/or approve further progress.

Clearly, the frequency of seeing any investment will depend on the number of review meetings and investments. At the most basic level, the board shouldn't be hearing about an investment's progress for the first time at the same moment it's deciding on whether to continue its funding.

This is certainly true for investments experiencing challenges, because the board is being asked to overlook these issues (about which it's been unaware until now) and provide the manager with more funding before it knows what efforts have been taken to resolve ongoing issues.

Given that there is finite time available, the only way to adjust the board's agenda is to adjust the number of investments it reviews, and the depth in which it reviews them. Once you do that, the review cycle in the vast majority of organizations (regardless of their size) settles into the same pattern.

Getting executive attention on an annual basis is about as much as one can expect. It's also the least one can expect. Even a massive organization like the Department of Defense manages to hold annual reviews of its investments.

Of course, they accomplish this by allowing the military departments to conduct their own oversight of a good proportion of their investments.

If there are so many programs that even an annual review seems impractical, it's time to establish lower-level decision-making authorities, and define some means of spreading the decision load.

Such a simple prescriptive metric can't apply across all situations. Still, it seems to work so well in practice that, if you find yourself at the other end of the spectrum, it's worth giving some thought to the situation.

If the number of programs is such that the board can plan and review them on multiple occasions throughout the year, then one has to wonder whether the "programs" aren't complex enough. Or whether the board isn't getting an appropriate level of information to be able to understand the key issues involved in a complex program.

Perhaps the board isn't taking enough time on its enterprise level planning and guidance effort. Maybe its review process has become so consumed by the detailed activities that it lost sight of the forest.

The bottom line is that it's better to have a thorough review of a few high-level, complex programs than it is to have many cursory reviews of the separated pieces of those programs. The latter way doesn't show how the pieces fit together (or worse, how they don't), and allows substantial issues that are worthy of the board's time to be hidden in a mass of process activity.

Respect the Existing Structure

In reality, every organization has already figured out some aspect of that problem, and organized itself into some sort of logical or at least pragmatic groupings.

Ideally, initiatives would be grouped into programs based on the common outcome they're trying to achieve, and the organization would already have named someone to be held accountable for that outcome (i.e., the program manager). This can be a very useful situation because it allows discussing the program with all of its initiatives in terms of how it plans to achieve its objectives.

Once activities are grouped into programs that deliver outcomes, the board can make decisions based on its concern for the outcomes without having to deal with a raft of issues that snake their way to other organizational groupings and impacts.

Remember that the earlier material on Zero-Sum warned about treading on other people's toes? Here's one of the places you might fall into that trap. If you set up the program structure without consulting the business architecture group, the PPFMO will be subject to the accusation that it's ignoring existing organizational artifacts and efforts, even if nobody else was paying attention to them, and even if those artifacts do not actually exist yet.

So what is a business architecture? It sounds like a product, and sometimes it is one, but mostly it's a process. The enterprise architecture group (which may go by many names, such as Strategic Planning Office) analyzes the organization's value streams and activities to identify how the organization delivers its products and services. If you use that as a program structure, then it's easy to place the initiatives into appropriate functionally-related groups.

A process-averse organization seldom empowers the groups that handle enterprise architecture, business strategy, or plans and evaluation to produce much that is useful. If they have, you should try to use it. If they haven't, they may appreciate your initiative being able to produce something for them.

Don't make the mistake of bypassing those groups if they seem ineffective, as they'll awaken if it appears you're trying to invade their turf and/or make them look bad. They may well be ineffective and even downright incompetent. But often their top-level connections will make them formidable opponents if they ally with those in the organization seeking evidence your PPFMO is weaving out of its lane and threatening to spiral out of control.

In a new governance initiative, it's more likely the board will make decisions along organizational lines. The representatives on your governance board will come from organizational groups, regardless of any other structure the PPFMO may have suggested. That's how decisions have been made, money has been allocated, and work has gotten done.

(Oops, what happened to the architecture? Well, your board is also made up of power players. If the organization is ignoring the architects, no problem. At least you tried.

The important thing to note is if there is an architecture, however unloved, or if the board has a preference for some other viewpoint, use one of those. If necessary, let them battle it out with each other. Just don't try to force some elegant structure you invented onto the process as yet a third option that nobody supports or understands.)

You should follow the board's preferred structure, because that's what *they* are going to do no matter what *you* say.

If the silos are strong – as they usually are in a process-averse organization – most of the work will be allocated to the divisions in a manner that is, if anything, too clean. Even work that should be an organization-wide initiative will be confined to one of the divisions.

Likewise, some initiatives will appear to be assigned to the "wrong" division for some long-forgotten historical reason. The object of the exercise is not logical purity. The preferred outcomes are that everybody understands how things are to be broken out, and that the division heads acknowledge their responsibility for these efforts. So let it go, even if it messes up your neat and tidy logic diagram.

The program structure allows the board to focus its efforts at the right level on the right issues, what the program benefits are, and whether they'll be delivered. This also allows the program manager flexibility to adjust resources to meet the demands of reality as it emerges.

There are always project-level investments that by their centrality to the objectives, by the amount of risk they carry, or by their sheer size are more critical than the rest.

The board should designate a few as being of corporate interest, and should conduct direct supervision, as these kinds of projects merit this level of attention.

In those cases, the board will accept even more involvement than it does for the programs, often reserving the right of phase-gate approval for itself as described in the following section.

Adopt a Business Lifecycle

The governance board will need to hold reviews on both a strict calendar basis (such as an annual budget proposal) and on an event-driven basis (i.e., when the time is most appropriate, given what is going on with the investment).

Ongoing operations that have no particular lifecycles can be reviewed by the board on a calendar basis (e.g. semi-annual), which requires little explanation other than to note that each investment probably has timeframes when it would be best not to conduct a large-scale review. For instance, it's best not to divert accounting managers' attention during the end of the fiscal year.

In midsized and larger organizations, the PPFMO may try to create a fairly complex review calendar while honoring multiple review blackout periods across many different functional disciplines. By contrast, evolutionary (project-like) investments should be reviewed when they reach certain milestones to consider whether they're achieving the desired goals or need to be redirected.

General Frameworks for Project-Type Lifecycles

After working with many organizations in many functional areas and industries, it's difficult to imagine an industry that hasn't developed commonly-used approaches to the business.

An IT project is different from building an apartment complex, which in turn is different from developing a training course. You may not be able to apply the same solution to all of them. But there's no shortage of examples in any of these fields as to how to get that kind of work done.

A structured model of the lifecycle of your organization's products provides everyone with a general understanding of how work gets done, and identifies consistent points at which it might be productive or prudent to inquire as to how the work is going.

The reviews conducted on an IT project may be different from those used by educators. But one would expect that all across the IT industry, most project managers would be able to give a pretty consistent definition of a Production Readiness Review.

Another insight gained from experience in a wide range of fields is that after the professional jargon is stripped away, the system lifecycle is pretty much the same in all industries. This may be the result of fairly similar professional education backgrounds across the project management spectrum.

Perhaps real-life situations are being force-fit into more or less appropriate concepts. Nevertheless, that is the case. The general phases of a project are somewhat the same regardless of what kind of project it is.

For instance, an organization delivering small IT applications was able to adapt the Defense Department's lifecycle model used for multi-billion dollar programs:

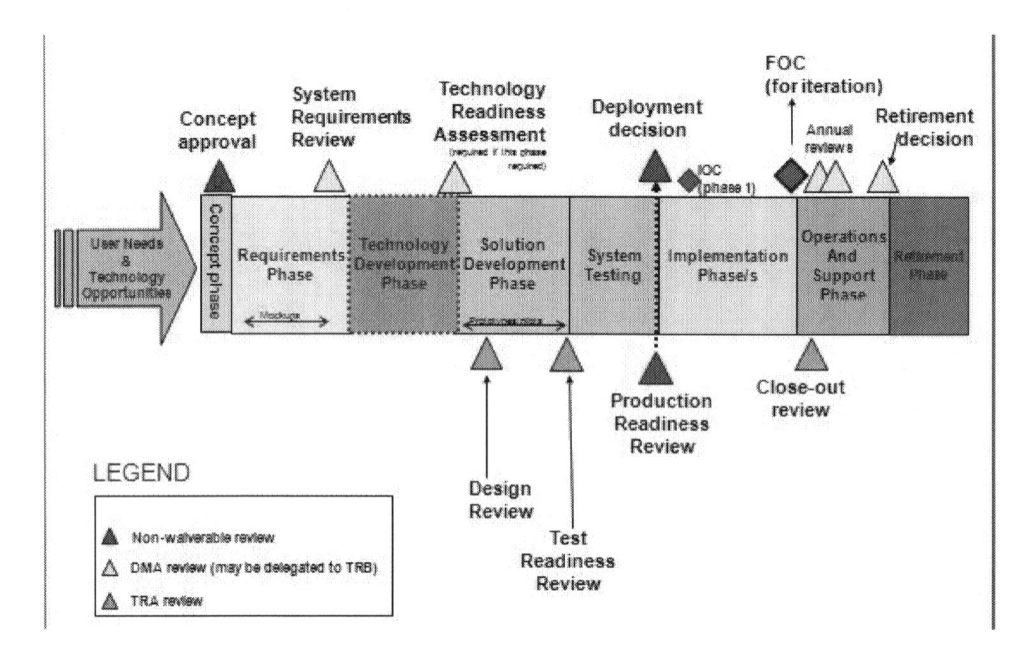

Of course, if you're following a different methodology, such as one of the Agile variants, then you have a different structure to fall back on,.

The greatly different styles of the two philosophies obscures a powerful fact. The proponents of these approaches consider themselves as radically different from one other, and they generally see the proponents of the alternative approach as hopelessly misguided.

But at the most fundamental level, the DOD model has 5 phases leading to launch, and the Agile model also has 5 (the conical node is really two phases). When you decode the phase names, they are the same.

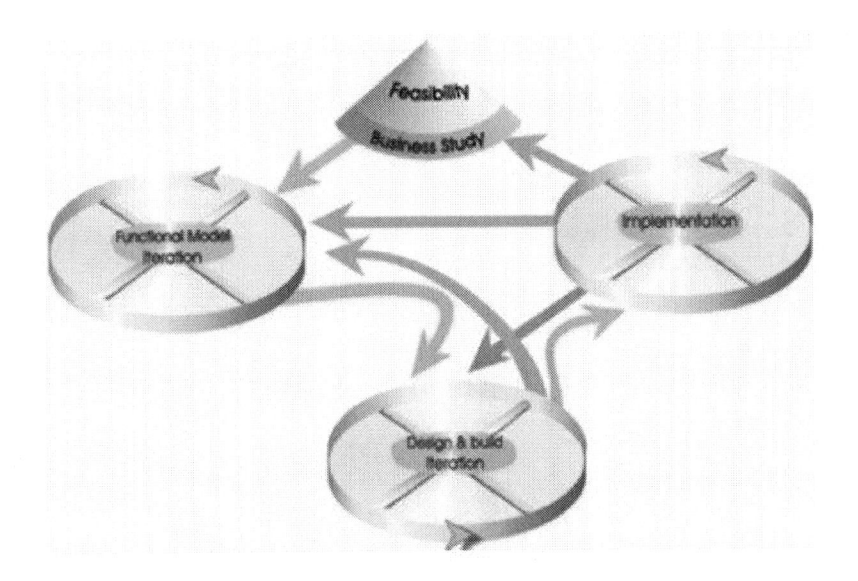

[Diagram: DSDM-style cycle showing Feasibility/Business Study, Functional Model Iteration, Design & Build Iteration, and Implementation phases connected by arrows.]

Now isn't the time for an extended discussion of the merits of one framework or another (the skeptical organization probably isn't really following one anyway, even if it has "adopted" one).

The point is to find or develop one or two models that reflect what the organization already thinks, then have the governance board require the use of one or the other or both, but not any other models. That way, everyone can use the same language when talking about where they are in their work.

Then over time, as people become more familiar with the concept of phases and reviews, the models can be customized for your organization, or replaced with others much better suited for its needs.

All of the major SDLC models (even Agile processes) include some form of phase-gate or review point (this is when a significant phase in the project or program development ends, and a decision is made as to whether they're ready to proceed to a different phase). The organization must also establish who has the authority to make such decisions.

The U.S. Defense Department's approach has an interesting feature (the chart is currently under revision, but hasn't changed much over the years).

It includes both Decision-Making Authority (DMA) reviews, which would be those conducted by a business-driven board, and Technical Review Authority (TRA) reviews that are (as the name suggests) more technical and have been delegated to the TRA to conduct.

While this might seem to be a rather advanced concept for less mature organizations, it actually has a lot of merit in limiting the amount of reviews the business leaders on your governance board have to conduct. Most organizations that achieve maturity typically end up operating in a very similar manner.

You may be able to find some wonderful integrated SDLC charts on the Internet, or your organization may have some developed already. These show the contribution of all sorts of functional units to the development of a product or project, and list a whole range of possible documents and other artifacts that may provide useful.

A word to the wise: Whatever you do, don't show these highly complex SDLC charts to people in your organization. You can caution all you want that it's just a schematic, and everything will be tailored down as necessary. But all they'll think is, *Are they crazy? Do they know we're not building battleships?* Stick with a simpler model at this point in the organization's maturity, then do whatever you can to make it look even simpler.

Once you have a solution, map the review requirements for all initiatives into a calendar to get a sense of the demands the proposed SDLC will place on the governance board (and on the initiatives).

The calendar should show the different types of meetings. At the program and enterprise level, the time scale might well be in months rather than weeks.

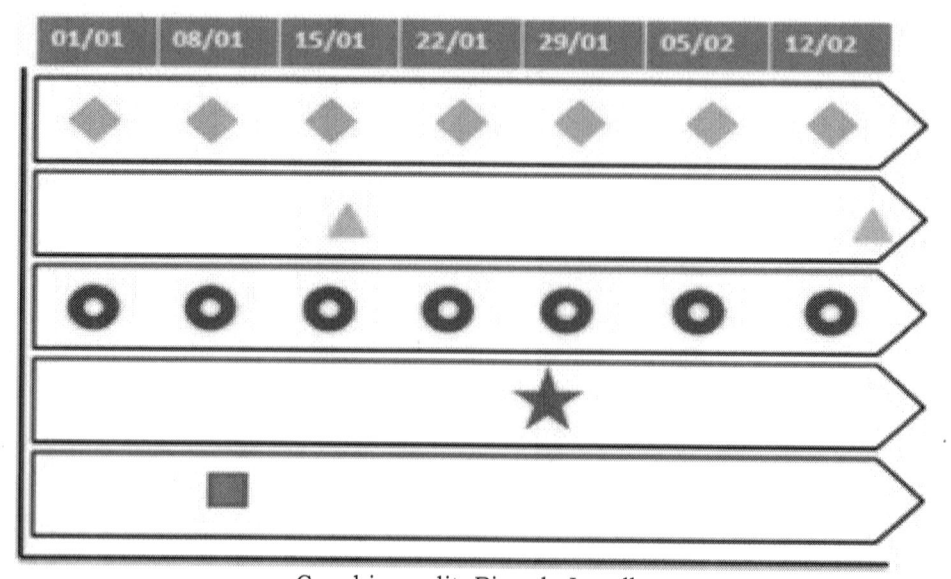

Graphic credit: Ricardo Lavalle

As mentioned earlier, if the number of meetings or amount of material reviewed in the meetings is absurd, the governance process will to have to incorporate some delegation and automation, or it will quickly bog down.

Tailoring for Risk and Complexity

"Tailoring" means reducing the amount or scope of reviews and associated documentation so they remain proportionate to the scale, scope and riskiness of the project. So those tailoring decisions should be based on the complexities and risks of the project.

In trying to keep things simple, a massive error many organizations make is to base the tailoring on the expected cost or duration of the work (i.e., exempting anything under a certain amount, often $50,000; or requiring less than two or three months to complete).

It should be obvious that the larger, more complex or riskier a project is, the more often it should be checked on to make sure it's on track, that it has everything it needs to be successful, and that it's still worth doing. One would expect a much wider range of issues to be considered on such projects.

That being said, the interplay of scope and risk offers an infinite number of possibilities.

Projects spending millions of dollars have been plagued with less issues and caused less organizational disruption than projects that cost nothing and do nothing more than turning on a feature of a nationally-used product that's already paid for.

One such project (a regular update of a simple $100 barcode scanning device) ended up presenting the most challenges of all the projects in a $40 million portfolio. It required no money, and was supposed to be accomplished in a matter of hours if not minutes.

In the end it crashed the network several times, required the purchase of tens of thousands of dollars of equipment that could operate with the new software, and consumed over six months of time (including dozens of high-level meetings) before finally being dumped altogether.

Besides, the PPFMO shouldn't lightly discard a learning opportunity that can help transition managers' thinking from "just do it" to entertaining the idea of planning and risk assessment.

Regardless of how you come to the conclusion that tailoring is in order, you still have to figure out how to do it.

Your organization may urge you to develop a "PM-light" methodology for the projects that pose a lesser risk. It might urge you to do that first, since that's where most of the projects are, while conceding that "maybe" the heavier methodology is needed for an occasional mammoth project.

If those larger projects already exist, you can be assured those PMs are using this cooperative suggestion as a form of filibuster (talking something to death) to delay the onset of oversight.

In a half-dozen different organizations in different industries, in my role as in-house or contracted PPFMO Director I asked my staff to investigate how to implement a "lightweight project management" approach that would allow us to decide in advance what documentation and processes would be needed for larger and smaller projects.

Every time they came back with the same answer: There's no special subset of issues that are only considered on "large" projects. Or conversely, there's no reduced set of practices that consistently covers everything that is appropriate for "light" projects.

All of the topics and practices remain relevant regardless of the project's scale and risk. Simpler projects merely require simpler answers to the same questions.

You don't cut a sleeve off a suit to make the suit fit a smaller person – you shrink everything in proportion. So when the process does emerge, either it will look like the heavy methodology (which will generate complaints and probably another rework cycle), or you'll have been snookered into culling some very important considerations which will probably come back to bite you soon enough.

At one organization we set up programs that contained initiatives. The governance board had delegated permission for division-level managers to act as decision authorities on those initiatives as long as the program didn't violate the baselines established by the board (an approach I highly recommend).

However, the divisional board decided that investments that required only the purchase of packaged items (no engineering or operational services) would speed through the decision-making process, which would require much simpler planning documents and waiving further reviews until the annual budget discussions.

In order to get this status, the project managers had to present how they'd complete the work. They'd have to commit to an achievable schedule for anything that would require purchase orders, and a more defined schedule if any design, development or testing would be required.

They had to submit a project plan reduced from the standard 35-plus pages to around 10 pages. But if any element of that plan received a "no", it would have to be considered a regular project.

Becoming even more streamlined, every year the organization required a reasonably robust program-level briefing to obtain budget approval. The program briefing included budgets, risk assessments and any other considerations relevant at the program level, as well as a description of the project-type initiatives included within the program and their estimated costs and delivery dates.

(Estimated, estimated, estimated! This information was provided so the board could understand the concept, not to have them set baselines for those subordinate projects.)

If programs containing those initiatives had already been voted on, why reinvent the wheel by having the piece-parts come back in to get reapproved?

Initiatives would be allowed to proceed to acquisition with only a rapid review by the PPFMO to confirm that what was being purchased would conform to what had been approved.

It would be up to the program manager to recognize when the conditions assumed in developing the program level plan no longer pertained.

There are many ways to tailor the process burden. The one you shouldn't adopt is to remove artifacts (and the thinking that would go with them) from the process altogether. Let them be smaller and incorporated into larger efforts.

You can always allow the PM to enter "N/A" (not applicable) whenever that's the correct answer, or respond with a paragraph instead of a separate volume. But don't let them remove the section heading. Some of the most spirited, beneficial debates during governance board meetings have begun with questioning how a particular item could possibly be "not applicable." Leaving the section out wouldn't have cued the same discussion.

Preparing and Supporting the Board

If you're lucky enough to be one of the few governance managers setting up an enterprise-level board, the members will be the true decision-makers within the organization. That's a pretty interesting role, but it isn't always a guarantee the decision will be accepted.

I was once on a project where I saw how the wishes of the CEO of one of the largest companies in the country were disobeyed by the bureaucratic action (or inaction) of a single staff member three or four levels down the hierarchy who had been given the administrative responsibility of managing our contract, but chose instead to leverage it for their own agenda.

That individual (and the VP above him) didn't agree with the CEO's approach (which interestingly had much in common with *The Simmer System*). They directed us not to carry out the monthly CEO-level progress meetings, which would have revealed that we had been diverted to an approach that the CEO had specifically stated he did **not** want.

We could have gotten around this by going over their heads. But the executives at our consulting company saw an opportunity to milk this cow with a huge team for many months, and went along with the staffer's scheme.

As you can imagine, it didn't end well. When the company didn't get the results it wanted, the CEO eventually wanted to know what was going on. The staff member and the VP suddenly developed amnesia as to how this had happened, and the contract ended bitterly.

That's how the principle of integrity works. Sometimes you can get away with cutting corners in the short run. Given enough time, it catches up with you. At least, I like to think so.

A Bolster for the Chair

For most of you, the governance role will be played by managers and executives a little lower down the hierarchy than the actual CEO. Depending on the size of the hierarchy, the members may not have had much experience in a group decision setting.

In the kind of process-averse organization I'm focusing on, the managers may not ever have had the opportunity to make substantive decisions in a structured way (remember, many things are done in back rooms).

One of the most important things you can do to support the board is to make sure it has effective leadership. Unless you're one of the senior executives who'll be setting this entire process in motion, you won't be able to do much about the board's composition.

Mostly it will be comprised of *ex officio* senior managers or executives from each of the main organizations included in your PPFMO's enterprise. Preferably it will also include at least one of the big three executives in your organization, or perhaps from your part of the organization, who will be the board chair.

If you're an internal PPFMO director, don't fall prey to the temptation to be the board chair if nobody else wants to do it.

Remember the principle of *Purposeful Humility*? Sure, you can use the board as a platform to drive your governance agenda. But its real purpose is to show that resources allocation and oversight decisions are being made through the consensus of the power players in the line organizations.

If you're the chair, the governance process becomes a compliance ritual that has nothing to do with actual business processes. So don't take the ball from the hands of the business unit representatives.

I've already discussed the role of the PPFMO sponsor in getting the board members to participate. You can assume the sponsoring executive took this effort on in the belief that governance is necessary and works. That executive could be an excellent chair for this group. But sometimes they aren't properly placed in the organization.

In that case, the sponsoring executive can support the board chair while staying in the background to prevent overshadowing it. It's better for the executive, rather than junior staff, to remind the chair that the board's purpose is to generate consensus and not have the chair drive all the decisions.

A more difficult coaching role – especially in an immature organization that prefers back room dealings to open discussion – is guiding the chair to encourage members to consider different points of view, and to be comfortable in having their decisions recorded.

In this game of chess, an investment of a few hours with an external coach might be worthwhile.

PPFMO Support for the Governance Board

I've spent quite a bit of time talking about how board members are often too busy to invest too much time in the minutia of the decision-making process, and still less in the supporting analyses.

One of the PPFMO's key roles is to act as the board's secretariat by cuing the actions, and making sure the supporting materials are complete, accurate and useful. Its chief responsibilities include:

- Planning and scheduling the agenda.

- Providing processes to streamline the read-ahead and decision-making processes to a necessary minimum.

- Guiding contributing program managers through the board process, with an eye on facilitating success rather than finding failures.

- Helping board members understand what decisions are being sought. (It's amazing how often a program or project manager comes away from a review without being clear on what they've been approved to do, if anything.)

- Highlighting the issues to make sure members know about them. Then it's up to the members to decide if they want to force a discussion or let it go. But at least they're aware of it.

- Providing processes that enable the board to assess the health of the organization's programs and initiatives in little more than the blink of an eye.

A key part of the PMO's role will be to shape the materials given to the decision-makers. No matter how lean and primitive your governance processes are in the beginning, over time they'll become more complex as new issues are discovered, and as fail-safe processes are introduced to deal with situations as they arise.

Beware of scope creep!

Bad bureaucracy begins when you try to write rules that preclude every possible situation from recurring. Quarterly meetings will turn to monthly meetings, and before long there will be pressure to make them weekly. It's not possible or even desirable for a high-level board to spend so much time on a small portion of their responsibilities, or to micromanage the organization's work.

The board must elevate the levels of its decisions to address only those initiatives that can be reviewed effectively, which in turn forces the work to be divided into manageable portions (in this context, the programs). The board holds the program managers accountable to plan effectively and to deliver results. In turn, the program managers hold the project and operational managers responsible for their work.

The more the governance board members have to delegate in order to preserve its available time, the more they need to be able to quickly assess governance matters and identify the critical issues for discussion.

This can't happen if they're expected to sift through mountains of "materials for advance reading," or squint at a dashboard that has evolved into a highly-complex maze of astrological symbols.

The materials offered to the board members must enable them to grasp the overall situation immediately, and see patterns that warrant further clarification and deeper discussions. So a substantial part of the PPFMO's role is to assemble highly-aggregated oversight metrics and useful decision-supporting information packages.

If there is no PPFMO, or even if there is, the organization may have a program analysis and evaluation group, or an enterprise architect, each coexisting in their areas of specialization.

(Don't start getting territorial on me now that you're starting to get some traction. There's plenty of work for everyone, so keep in mind *The Pasta Principle*. Everyone will get what they want as long as they work together to capitalize on any leverage the situation offers.)

The other half of the PPFMO's responsibilities is to be a friendly face for program managers, showing them how to navigate the board review and approval processes to maximize success without skewing the facts.

This approach gives decision-makers a presenter who is well-prepared to deal with important questions, and will keep things moving while exposing the proper considerations.

For a fledgling PPFMO, much of this will occur later in its development. In the early stages of establishing control, the first step is to start presenting useful metrics, beginning with your findings from the initial lists of basic information discussed in Chapter Seven. If those lists don't seem like much of a deliverable to a high-level executive group, remember that prior to this time they had no information to go on at all.

Keep your eye on the pasta bowl. You're about to pull out that first fork full of noodles!

Board Training

Use the early months wisely to shape the board's understanding and cohesiveness so they can move promptly and with confidence when the burden begins to accumulate.

The success of the organization's governance efforts, and the PPFMO itself, depends on top-level support. To get that support and have it applied in the right directions, the PPFMO should sponsor events for the board members.

Sometimes executives think they're too senior to need "training." Fine. Hold a seminar instead.

In the early days of the PPFMO, you'll be collecting data lists and engaging program managers in the collaborative ventures described in other chapters. While that's still going on, this is the time to bring the board up-to-speed so it can be prepared when the programs are ready to come to the table.

A trainer who focuses too much on the mature processes other organizations have developed will leave the board concerned that their burdensome new role will consume all their time and be extremely boring. They'll start drifting away before the first meeting.

Keeping that in mind, provide that knowledge in sessions where they can adapt a generic solution to something that will work for them.

These sessions can't be accomplished by purchasing just any offered off-the-shelf training for portfolio management or similar topics. Even training that's properly aligned with your general business model may go far beyond anything the organization will attempt in the next several months. That can risk making the whole governance initiative seem far too complex for the board members to support.

Training that's offered for generic board membership may prove useful, but look at the agenda before selecting such a provider. This kind of training often spends a great deal of time on how to read organizational financial statements, which may or may not be relevant to your PPFM governance. You don't have the luxury of wasting your board members' time.

When you do bring in outside speakers, they need to be clearly at least on a level equal to the level where the board members see themselves, if not higher.

Status is very important at the executive level. For at least a few of the early sessions, you should include a business executive who would be a peer the members can relate to, rather than a mere consultant no matter how distinguished.

Advice from them based on experiences similar to those of the board members will be greatly appreciated. Even better, if you can find one who's also funny, your initiative will be off to a roaring start (over time, we'll identify such resources at www.Simmer-System.com).

Beyond formal training, use the early months for collective learning where board members reach a consensus as to how they want to manage the business through the board process. The PPFMO should provide mockups of processes and template documents, while making clear they're only samples to begin the discussions.

Be sure to conduct a walkthrough to clarify how the organization and the information will grow and deepen as it works though the governance process.

You can refer to individual aspects of the Eight Agreements as examples of things that may pave the way. But don't refer to them collectively as 'The Eight Agreements" as if they came from scripture. You may decide not to do them all, or not to do them in that order. That's your own process for getting your peers to do things that are good for them and for you.

Remember, the exact agreements you reach may be different from the framework provided here. Executives – and life in general – resist being preprogrammed.

The discovery process should also incorporate typical scenarios beyond a "successful" case to understand the cumulative impact of rejecting initiative proposals, or making them return with more details. This will allow the board members to understand the need for grouping initiatives into programs.

What About Automation?

This is an easy question to answer while the governance board is still being created. No, no ... and no!

Don't set up an automated tool as yet – at least not a portfolio or project management one – because as soon as you set it up, it will demand to be fed. With limited resources and even more limited information, now is not the time to fritter them away on something you won't be able to use.

I've used Excel effectively to manage organizations with budgets up to $100 million spread across 40 to 70 initiatives. If you're encumbered by detail at the PPFMO level, then you're micromanaging. Stop it. Get your processes sorted out. Then maybe think about automation.

If you're under pressure to spend money no matter what (yes, that does happen), park it on a services contract. As this effort grows, you're going to need bodies to help. Maybe next year you can start thinking about buying tools, or you can have the service contractor provide one.

If you want to set up a collaboration site such as SharePoint to manage the operations of the board, by all means do so. But only if the organization is already comfortable with such tools. If not, don't be the innovator during these early days.

A successful PPFMO keeps things moving forward while leaving the overt marks of its activities in the background as much as possible. The focus must be on the governance board with its high-level, organization-wide composition, and not on the administrative activities of the PPFMO.

A tool will distract you, consume your limited resources, and perhaps become the immediate cause of the PPFMO's demise. Once again, no, no and no!

Accountability

It's a natural tendency for people to avoid unnecessary risks to their career, or less dramatically to their self-esteem. In many ways, the introduction of governance processes invokes that risk as initiatives may be delayed or lose funding, and the manager ends up looking bad in front of high-ranking executives. Certainly, there will be a decrease in the previous level of autonomy.

Constrained in so many other ways, that's the aspect of their work that most managers today cite as the number one motivator (and de-motivator). You're invoking powerful forces when you mess with that. Unfortunately, that's exactly what a PPFMO does. Be aware, and try to soften the impact and the perception wherever possible.

All of this makes it important to keep re-emphasizing the benefits of integrated governance, while doing everything possible to minimize the adverse impacts.

Remember that all but the smallest organizations have already tried some or all aspects of PPFMO and governance, and decided those efforts weren't worth continuing.

Entrenched program managers – and project managers beneath them – have every reason to believe that minimal compliance and passive resistance will win again. Some will even seek to test the limits of the board's willingness to exert itself. Where one finds a way, the rest will follow.

Now and again the board will have to establish through forceful action that it's not just an exercise in free assembly, but rather the only legitimate route to investment approvals. Until the organization gains a culture of scrupulous honesty, the board will depend on the PPFMO to keep things honest by maintaining the record of what was agreed to, and presenting the current situation against that baseline.

However, the PPFMO mustn't be made to be seen as the "bad guys," or the flow of information will dry up.

The PPFMO must present the facts as furnished. Effective yet simple presentation of the data, combined with a bit of pump-priming with the board members prior to the meeting to draw attention to certain aspects of the material, will allow the board members to be the ones to draw attention to the conclusions.

The board must have a mechanism for ensuring the information it receives in order to make decisions is as sound and accurate as possible; that the decisions it makes are carried out; and that the allocated resources go only to the purposes for which they were approved.

Don't allow the PPFMO's efforts to clean up incomplete, inconsistent or inaccurate information to get twisted into accusations that the PPFMO has tampered with the material. Ensure that what goes to the board or shows up during a presentation is exactly what the programs delivered.

Then where necessary, make the point by submitting an explanatory note that compares it against other known data or what the program said last month. But don't change what they submitted.

That approach makes clear that there is a collision between the expressed desires of the board members, and the program manager's choice to ignore that guidance. It's up to the board to decide when to make an issue out of it.

Don't expect on-scene fireworks. How a board implements that enforcement will depend on each organization's culture and tools. In many cases, executives register disapproval with nothing more than a raised eyebrow. And more dramatically, by announcing they've heard enough for today and will readdress it another time. Strong messages, if they ever occur, take place in back rooms.

Though fear shouldn't be the dominant feature of an organization, it is the primary factor that spurs a change in behavior. (NOTE: This is widely known in adult-learning circles. For a well-nuanced view of the positive and negative roles of fear in the workplace, see Dan Rockwell's article, *The Real Truth about Fear* – URL in the References annex.)

The lack of enthusiastic endorsement is often enough to spur many lower-level managers into fits of reactionary defensive activity. Equally often, nervous managers inflict it upon themselves out of fear their masterpiece hasn't been well-received.

Sometimes nothing will happen. Remember, the organization is once again trying PPFM because it doesn't have a culture of accountability. It may also have difficulty drawing the line between empowering lower-level managers and allowing them to set up independent principalities.

In that case, the PPFMO director should engage the sponsoring executive to get a better read of the situation. And if necessary, reevaluate the PPFMO's direction and value proposition.

In that organization, people know when a smack-down has occurred regardless of how executives react. In an immature organization, the first time someone does something about a failure to comply will be a newsworthy event, and will generate a gratifying swing of the pendulum.

Likewise, if the first refusal to comply is tolerated without comment, that news will spread as well. If the tiger has no teeth, it will soon enough become a rug.

Next Steps

In this chapter you've seen how to prepare a governance board for its tasks. It's become engaged, and is preparing to take its first steps in applying top-down leadership to the governance process.

In this chapter's exercise, you'll take the steps to getting your own governance board into operation. In Chapter Seven, you'll get the PPFMO working on some constructive tasks so the board will have something to make decisions about.

EXERCISE 6: PPFMO PLAN

This chapter's exercises will require some paperwork. Soon you'll be demanding that every program, project and operations manager must come up with more documentation every year. So if you're groaning about doing this, think about how they'll feel.

The exercises provide very high-level outlines that include all the necessary elements from the PMI Program Management Standard (you can obtain samples and templates in native format from www.Simmer-System.com). Most of them probably apply in some way to your PPFMO initiative, and to any other initiative requiring executive backing and funding.

Develop a Charter for the PPFMO:

Answers are required for each topic, but should be tailored to the size and complexity of the PPFMO's responsibilities. Even if the topic is relevant, the charter doesn't require a long-winded answer:

- Justification (business case)
- Vision: end state
- Strategic fit
- Intended outcomes
- Scope
- Benefits strategy
- Assumptions and constraints
- Program components
- Risks and issues
- Timelines or roadmap
- Resources (people, money, etc.)

Develop an Operating Procedure for the Governance Board

- Summary of Goals:

    o Recap the goals of the organizational segment over which the governance board has jurisdiction.
    o Success Criteria
    o Quality standards

- Structure and composition of the governance board

- Stakeholders' roles and responsibilities (including PPFMO)

- Current program structure, scope, timing and performance measures

- Program decisions

    o Managing existing programs
    o Annual review of programs: current year; progress and performance records; requirements for future years
    o Budget allocations
    o Ratification of planned scope and performance criteria
    o Oversight of ongoing programs (see following sections)
    o Establishing new programs: how scope and performance criteria are determined
    o Closing programs

- Program Oversight Activities

    o Performance Management (assignment and tracking of metrics)
    o Planned Governance Meetings
    o Program Methodologies and Lifecycle Models
    o Event-Based Approaches: Phase-Gate Definitions and Review Processes
    o Time-Based Approaches: Periodic Health Checks
    o Dependency Management
    o Program Reporting and Control
    o Issues Escalation
    o Change Management
    o Meeting Structure

Finished? Great!

Now you can get the wheels turning on your governance board, and start gathering the information you'll need to support it.

Chapter Seven

Seven Things You Need to Know to Get the PPFMO Started

"I've got them on the list, I've got them on the list, and they'll none of them be missed."
~Koko, the Lord High Executioner in
Gilbert and Sullivan's "The Mikado"

In this chapter, you're going to learn how to set the foundation to clarify what's really going on in the organization. Since inconsistencies often emerge, you should resolve them assertively but not aggressively. This will all work out when opposing forces begin to balance one another, as described in the subsequent chapters.

It's Your First Step, So Take it Easy

Don't just do something... stand there!

Most of you reading this book will be accomplished business managers or PPFM professionals or both. You've had the opportunity to observe some aspects of PPFM and governance working in other environments.

You were probably selected for your current challenge, or perhaps you self-selected into it because of that knowledge.

However, this situation is different. Your organization is just beginning the voyage into process-driven management. Or worse, it is reluctantly reattempting a path that previously proved to be unsuccessful. This isn't a matter of clearing off some action items – this a special challenge you'll have to face.

In one engagement, the sponsor asked me, "Why are we wasting time with all these meetings with these people? Half of them don't give a darn anyway. Can't we just go down to Barnes and Noble and get any one of half a dozen books off the shelf and just do it?" (This from the person who lectured me about building and spending political capital.)

I explained that since nobody was complying with current policies now, the important thing was to have the managers make the new process theirs rather than mine. In this case, the PPFMO would ask only for the information that was truly needed, and the managers would be told how the PPFMO intended to use it.

"Unless you want to crack down on these folks to be more open and honest in their planning and reporting," I added. "Of course, I'm all for that and you have the authority to require it. But are you ready to deal with all the whining that will create?"

Apparently not. It would have cost too much political capital.

In any PPFM initiative, one thing that won't work is to start marching through a best practice document. This isn't said to disparage those frameworks, as they're very important in providing an overview of how things will look once everything is sorted out. But it will be a labor of many months or even years to get to that point.

In the meantime, you have to work with people to determine how PPFM can best support their management concerns, specific methods of providing that support in ways that fit well with the organization's culture, and specific actions that are desperately needed or acceptable as a starting point.

Most complications will arise from people-centered challenges (which is common throughout the lifecycle of almost any PPFM initiative, regardless of how mature the organization may be). So don't feel like you're the only one dealing with this.

In all honesty, you'll never be free of it. If you don't like dealing with people issues, a career focused on the governance disciplines might be difficult and frustrating for you.

A process-averse organization presents two additional handicaps:

1. **Subversion**: Since there will be people hoping this effort will fade away into oblivion along with the previous ones, it's important not to over-reach and give them any ammunition early in the game. Get only what you need. There will be other days to dig deeper once you start showing some value.

2. **Fog**: Process-averse organizations are very poor at writing things down. They don't do what they wrote down anyway, so you'll have very little information to begin assessing the situation and any alternatives. And what you do get may be misleading.

> Most data sets exist in fragments. Scattered across multiple locations, they're maintained by different people and often contradict one another. All of that assumes you can find these data caches in the first place, so your first steps will be to start collecting data.

The rest of this chapter discusses the types of data you may need. While it's not an exhaustive list, neither is it a firm prescription. You may not need some of these items, and may find you need other data to address your specific situation.

One caution applies to all forms of data-gathering at this point: Don't collect it in an evaluative manner. Don't express shock that nobody is allowed to see the organization chart, that the last strategic plan was written in 2004, or that the budget consists of a flock of Post-It notes. All you're asking for is the basic orientation to what the organization is about that any newcomer would ask for.

Of course, if you're not a newcomer it might not be possible to appear to be quite so naïve. But you're just gathering the basic information necessary for someone in your new position.

And remember, in many of these cases, the absence of the data is just as meaningful as the information you do get. Those gaps may be your PPFMO's best opportunities to make forward progress.

From having read the earlier chapter on *The Pasta Principle*, you know that eventually all PPFM activities converge into a coherent whole, which includes the ability to assess the progress of the organization's programs and projects. That's why you're collecting data now: to find at least one strand you'll be able to stick your fork into and start twisting.

Meanwhile, the managers know that they've seen PPFM initiatives come and go with no damage to themselves. You're not asking for anything dramatic; in fact, you don't seem to be asking for anything that has any possibility of impacting them.

Whether or not you have top cover, they'll humor your requests as long as they don't seem to be threatening. If you're wasting your time, so much the better for them! Many people will endorse the efforts because they'll be just as interested in finding out the answer as you are.

Ride this wave of good feelings by keeping your initial data-gathering focused on establishing what exists, and steering your efforts away from seeking out information that you or someone else could use to evaluate them (the following discussion helps that to some extent).

But first observe your organization at each step to see what kind of reaction they're giving before you proceed. It's not a race to get this information. Half of it will prove rather useless because it's outdated or wrong. It doesn't matter if you don't know which half it is. You're just getting people used to working with you on innocuous requests. These are occasions where you can do a little bonding before having to do more searching analysis.

Remember that you're beginning with nothing on the table. So getting anything at all will be a big improvement!

Things You Need to Know to Get Started

While some of the data suggested in this book might seem trivial, it might be surprising to learn that many organizations don't have basic information such as a simple organizational chart; others hold them as closely guarded secrets. Either way it's a red flag.

This kind of information isn't shared because:

- They don't know the answer.

- The answer changes so often, it isn't worth the trouble to publish it.

- The people responsible for publishing the answer are incapable of getting it done.

Most of the people in such an organization would appreciate anything that broke through one of those barriers.

Exposing a weakness often generates defensive reactions. Without giving away too much, state why you need this information and what you plan to do with it. The source of these issues may be outside your organizational lane, which can cause the reaction to be even more bitter.

If the initial data set is inaccurate, or missing a good chunk of data, allow transparency to make your point. Once it's revealed as the organization's best data currently available, there will be pressure to clean it up without you having to be the person making an issue out of it.

For that same reason, once the keeper of the data agrees to provide it to you, they'll do a deep data cleansing as they won't want to look unprepared to their colleagues when their data is finally shared.

If your organization has all this data readily available, so much the better. Congratulate yourself on being in an organization that's nowhere near the bottom of the barrel, and collect the data since you'll need it anyway.

When you do locate information, you shouldn't create your own version. That would exacerbate the problem of separate and conflicting stores of information.

You may not be aware when the information changes, so what you'll have in your store will be wrong. It's better to expose the official version to the light of day.

Use tools such as SharePoint to link to the information source. Or just include instructions in your standard operating procedure about where that information can be found, then use it as if it were correct. If it isn't, let the other managers take up that battle.

Where you have to be involved, work with the data-owning office directly without making a fuss over it. Remember, you're trying to build alliances here – not recruit enemies.

Recognizing the proper data owner will build tremendous good will, as they're also struggling with the shadow databases people created instead of using the official data source. By linking to their data instead of copying it, you're emphasizing their ownership role and their responsibility to get it right.

Here's a list of seven things you need to know to get started (in the order of difficulty of attainability; **the first four are discussed in this chapter**):

1. **organizational chart, missions and functions**
2. **strategic plans**
3. **personnel rosters and skill sets**
4. **budgets**
5. **contracts**
6. **priorities**
7. **projects and activities**

The first few items arguably should be part of the orientation for any new manager, regardless of their role. By the time you get to the bottom of the list – the "real meat" – you'll be asking for information that pertains more to the core of the business. People either won't have it, or will be reluctant to share it. You're building trust by not abusing what you collect in the early steps.

1. ORGANIZATIONAL CHART, MISSIONS AND FUNCTIONS

One of the more common symptoms of a process-averse organization is the lack of basic things such as an organizational chart. Without this, there are no defined lines of authority and functional areas of responsibility.

In a highly political organization, that's exactly the way managers like it! In at least three different organizations I can recall, the PPFMO's first steps of recognition as a potentially useful partner came as the result of getting the organizational chart into the open.

Modern management writers like to emphasize that the organizational chart doesn't always show the true lines of decision-making. While that may be true, the organizational chart usually depicts which groups are responsible for what sort of transaction. Remember the supporting processes monster? That's who you have to go through to get things done.

The more ineffective the organization's processes, the more important it is that the PPFMO staff build solid relationships with their counterparts in the administrative groups.

The U.S. Department of Defense uses a "missions and functions" document to describe level-by-level the core missions of each organization and its components, and the business functions for which those components are responsible while carrying out their missions. Similar documents exist in most public and private organizations.

Such a document also identifies the key business support functions, and specifies which group is the proponent for that function wherever it occurs across the organization.

For instance, almost every organizational unit does certain human resources activities. Some may only supervise with almost all other functions reserved for the HR office, while others might hire, pay, discipline and reward using internal HR sections or just highly-empowered line managers.

It might be obvious, but don't forget: processes described on websites, and those embedded in automated solutions, are in fact documented. It may be difficult to make copies of such documentation. But it's actually the best kind because it's usually current and correct.

Why Do You Need It?

The main reason for the chart, and the even more important functions manual, is to become familiar with the organization and how it operates.

You wouldn't think it would be necessary to explain why you need an organizational chart. As bizarre as some of the situations may sound in this book, all of them actually occurred in more than one somewhat reputable organization.

Some may consider a functions manual to be administrative overkill. That's all very well as long as everybody shows up for duty every day and is fully proficient with their work, and that of anyone who might be missing.

But how often does that actually happen? An organization can't be effective if it relies solely on personal knowledge of who the key people are who do particular work. As an example:

- If Julie is the go-to person for getting documents posted to SharePoint, what happens when she's on vacation or on sick leave?

- How does a new person find out that Julie is the person to see?

- How does a customer get in touch with the right person without having to play 20 questions with a chain of people, beginning with whatever name they can scrape off the website? (Thanks to various privacy laws, it's become nearly impossible to get a name from a website.)

Determining the allocation of activities across the organization is a concern for the PPFMO in several areas:

- If this is an IT-centered PPFMO, then the organizational chart exposes the essential business architecture of who does what and why. This is important when designing IT systems so you know about reusable solution elements, and the authoritative source of each element of information.

- Because the same concerns are still highly relevant in non-IT settings, there's no point reinventing a business process that's working, and no value in duplicating solutions and investments across divisional lines.

- If this document is relatively complete, it will identify activities that form part of the daily lights-on operational effort.

Operational efforts are very important. Almost all of the books about PPFM address only the project aspects of organizational activities. As noted earlier, that's usually between 20 and 40% of the organization's total activity and expense.

Very few organizations, let alone those struggling with process maturity, can state what goes into the other 60 to 80% of their activities. All they know is that operational emergencies keep pulling resources away from completing projects on time.

Meanwhile, operational groups note that there wouldn't be so many emergencies if the organization hadn't chartered so many half-baked projects that deliver half-baked products. Until who does what is identified, everyone will do pretty much do whatever they want ... or nothing at all.

What Will You Do With It?

From the PPFMO's point of view, the organizational chart provides the first look at how the organization divides up its work. Even more importantly, it represents how it views itself, particularly from the leadership level downward. Your opinion, however accurate and insightful it may be, as to the most effective way to organize this lot simply doesn't matter. You're just the PPFMO, so you'll need to tailor your processes to match how they're already organized.

Even if there's another "real" organization that's quite different from the one the chart portrays – and even if you're able to accurately plot it out – you won't be able to use that knowledge in any formal statement of the PPFM practices.

However, that is good information to have. Your recommendations will go further if they work with the informal organization, as well as being tolerable within the framework of the formal organization structure.

What will you really do with this information? And where will you begin?

Since all work is done by people, you have to know which people do what work. It's useful to understand which group does what, and what the upline chain is above a particular project or activity as it will be the primary model for setting up the program structure.

It will give you an idea of how many internal people are allocated against various business functions (some organizations also include contract staff on their charts). The functions manual will also help identify unrecognized stakeholders or effective cross-project or cross-group dependencies.

Eventually, you'll be able to use this information to create proper like-to-like efficiency benchmarks to make a solid case for the funding that should be going to operational activities, and the standards of performance they should be meeting.

In the short-term, you'll be identifying many support activities that make up that undefined 60 to 80% of the budget.

Beware: In the process-averse organization, there's little reason to believe that anything you find in the document represents reality. So use it to get ideas for the processes that might be in place, not as validation that the process works as described.

Why Wouldn't People Want to Provide It?

This is another of those areas where it would be a mistake to express surprise that such information doesn't already exist.

The organizational chart is the least sensitive of the internal documents because, at least in theory, it contains information that already exists and is familiar to everyone.

How could this go wrong?

Executives often don't want their contact information released to prevent being bombarded with calls and emails from people seeking to do business with the organization, or with pesky customers wanting to bypass the normal channels to get a response to their needs.

Since 9/11, many organizations have become paranoid about releasing physical addresses in case employees are tracked to or from the workplace.

Charts intended only for internal distribution may include non-work information that would fall under various privacy-related statutes and regulations.

Even if you never publish the chart and it only resides on your computer, if that computer is lost or hacked **you** are responsible for any breach of privacy.

The chart may be out-of-date; might have been prepared for a reorganization still under consideration; or it never happened. Releasing such a chart either internally or externally would create confusion among the staff, and complications with other stakeholders.

In the most process-averse organizations, publishing a chart reduces managers' ability to reassign people and roles. Sad but true, this is usually the real reason.

Since the request is reasonable, there shouldn't be much suspicion about your motives. But you should nevertheless be sensitive to these considerations.

What if You Don't Get It?

You'll need a frame of reference when speaking about who does what within the organization. A key role of the PPFMO is to make sure resources are directed to the right place, and that work flows effectively between the various work groups.

If there isn't an organizational chart, or no one will give you one, you'll have to create one. It may end up being your most popular product! Don't be surprised if the Human Resources office tries to put a stop to it because, after all, it's outside your lane.

Speak to the stakeholders to find out what they do. If someone suggests preparing a document that would in effect be the missions and functions document, find out if someone already has that responsibility and talk to them about their plans.

If they don't have any, propose a collaboration between them and other primary players to develop a clear understanding of roles and responsibilities, then create the chart. Just that single effort could earn you valuable trust and credibility for your efforts.

However, if the organization won't participate and maybe directs you to leave it alone, you'll have to develop a shadow organizational chart on your own.

Draw on your experience. Once you get past the mission and customer-facing activities, all organizations have similar versions of Finance, Purchasing, Human Resources, IT and so on.

Just remember, this exercise isn't to prescribe processes but to identify them. It doesn't matter how you would do things; what matters is how **they** do them.

2. STRATEGIC PLANS

Another document that shouldn't raise many eyebrows is the organization's strategic plan. Don't get picky about the name; all you need is a statement of what the organization is about and where it thinks it's going. Even if nobody takes it seriously, it's good to remember it's the face the organization is showing to the outside world.

Start by first asking for the highest level strategy, and any implementation or tracking plan, as this will give a good sense of the level of process awareness. You'll be constrained by what your PPFMO will be able to do within that decision-making environment.

The subordinate divisions may or may not have developed more detailed plans. Ask how the organization tracks its strategy's accomplishment and go from there. It doesn't matter if lower-level plans don't exist, because at this point all you're doing is establishing a framework.

What Will You Do With It?

Over time, the strategic plan will become the root of a structure you'll use to align the programs, capabilities and resources in a way the organization will understand.

Initially you may find that lower-level managers give this alignment nothing more than lip service. They often see higher level managers not as the proper source of "their" programs, money and people, but rather as interfering with their legitimate roles.

During the early stages as a newcomer, you might want to state that you need to understand the organization's goals and priorities, and the key initiatives to accomplish them. Remember, this is just a single strand of pasta that does connect everything together, no matter whether you or anyone else wants it to.

Once you've gathered whatever strategic documents exist, you can establish a priority framework that models what's contained in the strategy.

If the strategy is only a collection of random ideas, then that's the main thing you need to know. Over time you'll have to devise some ordering concepts so you can make sense of the lower level activities you'll discover in the next few steps.

Why Wouldn't People Want to Provide It?

Usually, the organizational leadership has composed the strategic plan with an eye to external consumption as much as for internal use. It would be hard to misuse it, at least with regard to the primary text. It may be considerably more sensitive if it includes a section containing detailed investments needed to accomplish the strategic goals.

A key word of caution: Many PPFMOs have met with disaster in this area. Professional training in most governance-related disciplines (project management, program management and enterprise architecture among others) emphasizes the notion that everything needs to align with, and flow from, a top-level strategy. If there is none, they instinctively try to help by starting a process of devising one, which is a fatal error.

Earlier, I mentioned that you need to be cautious about treading on other people's turf and their likely reaction if it appears you've exposed a gap in the quality of their work. Here's another great opportunity to fall into that trap.

Whether or not they actually do it, organizational strategy is a primary responsibility of the executive layer. Even if they're not overtly working on it, there's usually some sort of group that keeps that pot boiling. It may be an obscure office within another administrative group, a trusted external consultant, or a formal or ad hoc working group of the executives themselves. It's possible, but unlikely, that nobody is thinking about this at all.

Whoever is working on the strategy (or supposed to be doing that) will resent the interference of someone from two or three layers lower in the hierarchy. They have much closer ties to the executive layer than a fledgling PPFMO does, and the next step will be a scorching message to the executive who chartered the PPFMO effort, which will then be sent into oblivion in the same manner (and possibly for the same reason) as its predecessors.

Now, finding and working with that group is a different matter altogether. The PPFMO can gain great credibility at the highest levels if it's able to relieve some of the burden from the supposedly responsible group, and gain a win-win by helping them get their document published.

It's unlikely that such a group will publicly acknowledge the PPFMO's success in doing their job for them. But the word will get around that these PPFMO folks are useful to work with.

What if You Don't Get It?

At this point, the strategy is just a means of establishing a frame of reference. If it truly doesn't exist, the PPFMO must work with whatever structure the organization is employing in common daily use. Watch what's going on, engage with stakeholders, and form an idea as to how things seem to be working.

Then with the approval of the PPFMO sponsoring executive, set up a workshop (chaired by the executive having responsibility for all areas the PPFMO will support) with the intention of preparing a top-level strategy and roadmap for that part of the organization.

Make clear that it's only for that part of the organization, and that the intention is to link it to similar plans from higher levels. Then invite the higher-level office responsible for such planning to attend the meeting where they'll provide their insight.

3. PERSONNEL ROSTERS AND SKILL SETS

The next information to gather has to do with personnel. You're easing your way into territory where the rest of the organization might start to get nervous about sharing that information. Fortunately, since you already have the organizational chart, it should be easy to provide the next level of detail.

Ideally you would get a complete list of positions on the organizational chart, which should indicate whether they're employee or contract roles, and also their skill sets. Don't worry about getting complete details. At the PMO level you'll be looking at aggregated groups of skills.

What Will You Do With It?

Over time you'll create resource pools of similar skill sets, which you'll use to determine the amount of work the organization can take on.

Eventually, those resources will populate a project management information system where you can do all sorts of tracking and analysis. However, today is not that day. You have only half of the puzzle because you haven't collected the activities the resources are working on. So for now, don't push your luck.

All you're going to do is create a method of putting all the skill sets into a manageable number of groups, which doesn't have to be precise. The main intent is to identify certain key resources. Soon you'll be looking into whether they're available to work on an activity and when.

Why Wouldn't People Want to Provide It?

You shouldn't generate much suspicion as long as you limit your request for information to what you really need (i.e., headcount numbers against defined skill sets). Only when you begin syncing names to this list will people worry about giving you this information, and your PPFMO might (even should) never need to get to that level of detail.

Don't overshare the information. Names, skill sets and organizational assignments aren't privacy-sensitive. In government organizations where pay grade defines the position, the grade isn't a matter of privacy (although the person's specific pay rate within that grade usually is).

If you end up with a recall roster or a full HR dump file that includes home contact information, salary data, and other information, you'd be wise to reduce the data set to the minimum amount of fields you need.

Your PPFMO will suffer a major credibility hit if it's caught possessing unauthorized privacy information, particularly if it's not being used for anything.

What if You Don't Get It?

The early steps into resource management will only be at a very high level, so getting by-position information isn't necessary. Since most organizations tend to structure themselves along functional lines, all you really need is a headcount of each group.

Employee headcounts are usually available at most levels, and intranets have staff directories by organization group. If they don't, you should be able to get headcounts from HR or from each major division without much difficulty.

If that still doesn't work, then make up something reasonable based on a rough estimation of the number of employees in the organization, how much space they seem to take up, the size of their group in all-hands meetings, and any other measures that may occur to you.

You'll be surprised how close your gut estimates prove to be. At the point when you begin using the estimates, the managers will be more than happy to correct them. Let them have their little win since you're getting what you want.

Contract headcounts and skill sets may be harder to come by, especially when the contracts are fixed-price and don't specify resources, or where the resources are set up on an as-needed basis.

However, you're in luck if you're in an immature organization where support contracts are often thinly-disguised staff extension arrangements. In that case, the line managers have a good idea of how many contract resources they have, and the vendor skill sets align with their subgroup's functions.

4. BUDGETS

Now you're at the point where data may be harder to come by.

The allocation of money is the ultimate expression of the organization's intention. The governance process is responsible for making sure the actions reflect the intention. Data is also the source of managerial power, which is why you may have a hard time getting it.

In the example tables provided on *The Simmer System* resource site, the total dollar values are consistent. It takes more effort to make up stuff that's wrong, because you have to remember what you did to get it that way. (This is another example of the Transparency Principle in action. Once you tell people something, you have to be able to produce the same answer again.)

In the real world, it might happen that your data-gathering exercise reveals a massive gap between the stated versus actual costs of the program. Before assuming either incompetence or some nefarious intent, take a look at the labor-related lines.

Government and nonprofit organizations frequently ignore internal labor costs while planning projects and programs. Budget analysts probably don't intend to suggest to millions of people (including themselves) that their work has no value. Because they know these people are going to be on the payroll anyway, they feel there's no point bothering with all that extra bookkeeping.

But there's an opportunity cost, as workers engaged in one effort can't work on other much higher priority activities. Or that activity can't be funded for lack of resources, while the resources have actually been in that building all along.

Counting all the money and people is a great example of the importance of the Zero-Sum principle.

What Will You Do With It?

Over time, the PPFMO will support the executives in allocating funds to different programs and tracking the cost performance of key initiatives. In the short-term, the budget data will show you the final cut on how the organization sees itself. It's very likely the budgetary structure has a lot of history behind it.

Unless you're working at the enterprise level, your organization often doesn't even develop a real budget. Some higher-level organizations simply announce it.

The organization itself has probably been seeking more autonomy and flexibility for many years, so your PPFMO isn't likely to change it now (although nothing is impossible). You would do well to align your programs and initiatives to the way the organization already divides its money.

While it's possible to do complex mappings to handle misalignments, it's wise to align the financials as closely as possible. That's not just for the convenience and elegance of alignment. It avoids confusion and maintains credibility to line up with numbers that everyone recognizes.

Executives have a habit of remembering certain key numbers, such as their top-line budgets. If the PPFMO's numbers don't match the ones the executives are familiar with, the game is over and the PPFMO will instantly lose credibility, even if it's right and regardless of the explanations it may offer.

For the moment all you're going to do with the budget information is to align the financial information for the overall budget process with the budget for the group the PPFMO represents.

If the data permits, you can also validate and/or improve the resource information you just gathered. For instance, if the organization has no idea how many contract support personnel it's using – but you have a top-level number for contracted services – you can get a rough estimate by dividing the contract values by standard rates.

Why Wouldn't People Want to Provide It?

Follow the money.

Once you get hold of the budget data, you're getting close to the heart of the managerial process, which is why managers may be suspicious of why you want it.

As noted many times already, managers derive much of their power from their ability to control resources, with money being the most flexible.

If it's not exactly clear who controls the money, or how much they have, some managers act with more power than they have because nobody is quite sure who has what. Other managers quietly pursue entirely different agendas using pots of money nobody knows they have.

Aside from that cynical viewpoint (which is well-founded in reality), most managers will have a more practical concern. Anyone with the slightest bit of management training knows governance disciplines will eventually result in tracking against baselines.

The truth is nobody likes to be evaluated, even when they know they're doing a good job (and even more so, if that's the case). "A" students sweat examinations just as much as "C" students ("D" students don't worry about being evaluated as much, because they approach the system from an entirely different set of values).

It's not difficult to see why line managers might be leery of inviting this unknown PPFMO into what's already a highly politicized process. There's no point waving the possibility of tracking performance in anyone's face at this point, as it'll generate resistance long before you're ready to combat it.

What do they fear you might do with this data?

- You could try to have it allocated to organizations and initiatives in a way that doesn't reflect the reality of the complexities of the funding situation. Then they'd have to report their progress against constraints the PPFMO established in isolation.

- You could use it to benchmark the organization's unit costs. Organizations often resist benchmarking for fear that they won't measure well against others.

- You could be trying to insert the PPFMO into a process that seems to be working quite well for these components. Change is not in their interest.

Make it clear that you're not seeking to change anything about the organization's financial decision processes. (In later chapters, you'll see the idea is to make sure program managers transparently present the facts.) You're just trying to make sure that anything you do fits in nicely with what's already happening.

Once you establish the right decision framework (the Zero-Sum situation described earlier in the book), you can and must allow the organization to do whatever seems to make sense.

What if You Don't Get It?

Gathering financial information isn't your greatest priority at this point in time. The reality is the organization already has a process for allocating money, and a basic governance process is in place.

How do you know that? Because the money is somehow getting allocated – you just haven't been let in on the secret.

Looking at the long run, a governance initiative that's blind to the financials is a farce. The executive layer has few tools for defining and enforcing its will, except by controlling financial allocations.

If subordinate groups can spend their money any way they want, aggressive shifting of funds can be used to mask failures in delivery and quality.

The subgroups could even decide to ignore the governance board's priorities altogether. Experience suggests there's nothing speculative about this. It's not a matter of they *could*; it's a matter of they *will*.

Later, if the PPFMO is unable to attain some level of cooperation while gathering financial information, the PPFMO head will need to contact the executive sponsor to gain the cooperation of the finance office to get that information.

However, at this point you're not ready to exercise any financial control. Don't panic if you can't get all of the detailed financials – just get what you can.

Somehow your part of the organization is functioning (at least everyone is being paid), so there has to be some sort of financial documentation floating around somewhere.

If you can find it, go with it.

You'll have to eventually do something about it. But you have a few more chapters to go through before you have to fix this problem.

Next Steps

Perhaps you've done enough at one sitting. So review what you've read so far, then you'll pick the action back up in the next chapter.

List to get	Why you need it	What you can do with it	Why they might not give it to you	What if you don't get it?
Organizational chart, missions and functions	Know who does (is supposed to do) what.	Define operational, non-project activities.	Information sensitivity? Or over-controlling managers.	Make your own as you get to know people.
Strategic plans	Expresses things that are most important.	Root of all other structures.	Contains long-range planning information. Or may not really exist.	Develop strategic plan at your level (with sponsor's support).
Personnel rosters and skill sets	Basis for creating resource pools.	Identify high-level capacity to do the work.	Concern over release of pay grade information.	Total group headcount, or best guess estimate based on overall cost.
Budgets	Money allocation is the ultimate expression of intention.	Align governance process with the way the money works.	People don't want to be tracked. Exposing budgets can weaken power.	Don't worry about it. Delivery dates are your first priority.
Contracts	Identifies extended capacity to do work by skill set.	Verify what managers are doing with their money; improve budget quality.	Legitimate concern for conflict of interest or sensitivity.	Wait. The information will emerge when you start looking at work capacity.
Priorities	Understand prior decisions, processes and compliance.	Create integrated priority list, then compare to reality of activities.	Priorities have not been established	Get the current top three priorities, and the sponsor to require a list of objectives.
Projects and Activities	Identify activities that are really going on.	Aggregate the total lists, and start setting up program groups.	Seldom an issue. But it will be an extra chore for disorganized managers.	Use the top three priority lists to get started.

EXERCISE 7: BUILDING DATA TABLES

Most of you have plenty on your plates without self-imposing additional tasks. Whether or not you choose do anything else in this book, this particular exercise will help you in your real job.

Your task is to get the items described below. Use this as an opportunity to make friends in other organizational groups while requesting materials that are usually readily available.

Getting the last three items (described in the next chapter) will require calling on your colleagues to do quite a bit of work. Once you've completed this exercise you'll have:

- an organizational chart, missions and functions
- strategic plans
- personnel rosters and skill sets
- budgets

The Pasta Principle is at work with just with these very introductory lists!

Most organizations typically have their own format for preparing each of these items. The information probably won't be structured in the way you need, gladly accept what they have and shape it to your needs.

You may choose to use wall charts, mind maps or other tools for the first few items on the following lists.

The bonus materials at www.Simmer-System.com include rudimentary spreadsheet templates you can use for gathering and structuring this data. When working with a real organization, your spreadsheets may start out looking like those simple examples, but will quickly grow more complex.

You'll start to see relationships between the sets of data you've assembled, and will begin building more comprehensive spreadsheets in preparation for transition to a proper data tool.

Organizational Table (Exercise A)

An organizational table is a tabular representation of an organizational chart. The chart needs to be turned into a table because it's the foundation for the more elaborate tables you'll build on top of it.

Missions and Functions Table (Exercise B)

With the tabular structure, adding additional information requires adding more columns and rows to handle repeated assignments for the same or multiple organizations. This will work for now. But as it grows more complex, you'll need a database.

Add columns and rows to the organizational table you created above to allocate the missions and functions you've discovered (notice that the business functions and the organizational divisions overlap).

1. Don't dive too deep. The lowest you need to go are the divisions with members on the governance board the PPFMO supports.

2. Don't count situations where a division executes a process another division owns. For instance, every division is involved with hiring and personnel evaluations, but the HR department owns those processes.

3. Highlight the situations where the same function occurs in multiple divisions. If you find yourself getting into topics related to those functions as part of the governance activity, the split responsibility will require more coordination and resolutions than other subjects.

Business Unit	Division	Business Function/s
North	Production	Business Function 111, 112, 113
North	Shipping	Business Function 211, 212, 213
South	Production	Business Function 111, 112, 113
South	Shipping	Business Function 211, 212, 213
East	Production	Business Function 111, 112, 113
East	Shipping	Business Function 211, 212, 213
West	Production	Business Function 111, 112, 113
West	Shipping	Business Function 211, 212, 213
HQ	Marketing & Sales	Business Function 311, 312, 313
HQ	Administration	Business Function 511, 512, 513
HQ	Design	Business Function 411, 412, 413

Congratulations! You've built a business architecture. Now you know how that works.

Don't assume this is all that your enterprise architecture group does, as this is just a very rudimentary view of one aspect of it.

Strategic Plan Assignment (Exercise C)

Add one or more columns to identify which organizational components have been assigned responsibility for the various initiatives listed in the strategic plan. Again, combining this information with the previous table will require repeated rows in the table.

Strategic Goal	Strategic Initiative	Business Unit	Business Function	BU Initiatives
Goal I	Initiative A	North		
			Function 111	Initiative NA
			Function 212	Initiative NB
Goal I	Initiative B	East		
Goal II	Initiative C	South		
Goal II	Initiative D	South		
Goal II	Initiative D	East		
Goal III	Initiative E	North		Missing
Goal III	Initiative E	East		
Goal III	Initiative F	South		
Goal IV	Initiative G	North		
				Initiative NG1
				Initiative NG2
Goal IV	Initiative H	West		
		North		Initiative NW1
		North		Initiative NW2
		North		Initiative NX1
		North		Initiative NZ1

You'll want to highlight rows in which there's either a higher level goal that's not reflected in lower-level activities, or a lower level activity that doesn't trace back to a higher level priority. This needs to be further investigated and cleaned up wherever possible.

This isn't just form-keeping. Organizations are likely to take a hard look at the need for activities that don't do any work that furthers one of the strategic initiatives.

Budget Allocation (Exercise D)

Now record the funds and personnel allocated to the organizational groups:

Business Unit	Division	Current Budget ($M)	Next Year Forecast ($M)
North	Production	8.2	8.4
North	Shipping	7.2	7.7
South	Production	9.1	10.5
South	Shipping	6.5	7.7
East	Production	5.5	6.1
East	Shipping	6.7	7.8
West	Production	8.1	7.6
West	Shipping	6.2	7.5
HQ	Marketing & Sales	3.9	3.4
HQ	Administration	6.5	7.1
HQ	Design	4.1	3.8
	TOTAL	72.0	77.6

Now that you've seen the organizational structure, key initiatives and budget, you're in a position to begin assessing how the money moves around and where the organization is putting its effort (as reflected by its money).

(The workbook provided at www.Simmer-System.com contains additional analysis you may want to undertake at this point.)

Some useful tips regarding the budget:

- At this point, the structure you've drawn up is pure guesswork. So DO NOT try to push it on anyone as the solution.

- Build your concept programmatic structure to conform to the finance division's view of the organization. They're going to dictate how and where the money moves, so you might as well go with their program.

Personnel Capacity (Exercise E)

Collect personnel counts by general skill sets. The ease of doing this will vary, depending on the degree to which the organization tracks personnel skills and assignments.

It may be readily available from personnel and program records. Or you may be able to get a rough estimate from the divisions' managers.

At this point, if contracted labor information is readily available, then go ahead and use it. Otherwise, you'll be coming back to it in Chapter Eight.

Business Unit	Division	Total headcount	Machine operator	Materials mixer	Warehouse	Driver	Sales	HR + Admin	Finance	Engineer
North	Production	32	20	12						
North	Shipping	31			9	22				
South	Production	34	17	17						
South	Shipping	30			10	20				
East	Production	35	25	10						
East	Shipping	25			9	16				
West	Production	30	20	10						
West	Shipping	19			7	12				
HQ	Marketing & Sales	14					14			
HQ	Administration	12						7	5	
HQ	Design	10								10
	TOTAL	272	82	49	35	70	14	7	5	10

You're back already? Great work!

Now, get ready to get busy and proceed to the next chapter.

Chapter Eight

The Meaty Part of the Lists

Getting Down to Work

In Chapter 7, gathering the four sets of information might have felt like repeating your first day orientation. Based on your work in the previous chapter, you now have the following information:

1. organizational chart, missions and functions
2. strategic plans
3. personnel rosters and skill sets
4. budgets

Now you're going to collect the rest of the seven items that may require extensive cooperation with your colleagues (tread gently until you get the lay of the land):

5. contracts
6. priorities
7. projects and activities

Teachers often tell their students the only stupid question is the one that isn't asked. However, once you get into the workplace, people think the definition of a stupid question is one they don't know the answer to.

Managers and technical experts with inflated egos think they know the answer to everything; they'll give you an answer even if it's incorrect. Insecure managers may think someone asking questions is trying to second-guess and undermine their decisions.

Though there's nothing secret about this second half of the list, they're the sort of issues managers don't deal with every day.

You can't change the fact that some will suspect your motives based on the way they act. So expect to encounter delays in getting this information, and the possibility of not getting it at all.

As with the previous chapter, this one provides a general script for what you need, why you need it, and what you'll be doing with it. However, since it's very generic, you'll need to refine it based on the specifics of your organization.

5. CONTRACTS

The next step is to find out what contracts the organization has in place. This is especially important in organizations that extensively outsource their work, as it reveals the capacity to do work and the level of people's skill sets.

It's not of great importance when contracts are largely for the purchase of physical items, although it forms part of your future cost estimation process. This also might be a touchy area: not because people are trying to keep it a secret, but because many line managers treat the contracts office as a witches' coven to be avoided whenever possible. What you don't understand tends to make you nervous.

A caveat is that contracted analysts might have difficulty getting to this data since it exposes the organization's plans for future contract actions.

What Will You Do With It?

Contract information is enormously important as the PPFM process matures, since it's rock-solid evidence of what the project managers required the vendor to deliver. Beyond that, in the new modern economy the organization often performs only core sustainment functions while contractors do the technical work.

In the U.S. federal government, with a few exceptions contractors do almost all of the actual work. Most of your project level data will be created by contractors, then passed through the project managers.

Where this is the case, you don't need to show quite as much tolerance for inadequate information. The contracting companies know how to do PPFM correctly when they have to, unless they can make more money when they don't.

For now, you don't need to address contract performance issues. The people responsible for monitoring the contracts aren't ready for the new kid on the block to suggest they aren't performing their fiduciary duties. As a newbie, you're working on the "win friends and influence people" process. So gather the information, see what it tells you, and keep it to yourself for a few more days.

At this stage, the contracts information will tell you some very useful things:

- **Total budget**. If you had difficulty getting the organization's budget, or thought the information was shaky, you now have a way to get a feel for its accuracy. Since the contracts inventory is a record of everything the organization buys (by definition, it buys everything it doesn't make), then a rough estimation of the organization's total spending is:

    Total spend = burdened employee salaries + total cost of all contracts.

    This is an imprecise estimate, but probably brings you to within 10% of the correct figure. It's a great improvement over having no information, and provides a very rough idea of the data's quality.

- **Total headcount.** If you can find the key services contracts, you can get a good idea of the number of staff augmentation positions by dividing the dollar value of the contract by an average rate appropriate for your industry. This goes towards an improved estimate of the organization's total capacity to do work.

    (Don't include travel costs if those are extensive, as most contracts require separate approvals and accounting for those.)

Your intentions at this point are innocuous as the PPFMO still hasn't addressed any of the organization's programs, portfolios and projects. However, without making enemies, you've gathered an impressive body of information that provides full organizational context for the allocation of resources for the initiatives.

Why Wouldn't People Want to Provide It?

Many organizations closely guard contractual information. Unless the contract documents provide specifications for a highly sensitive product, this secrecy isn't intended to protect the program's content. It stems from the inherent structure of purchasing rules which aim to ensure the organization (and most particularly, the purchasing office) never repeats an earlier mistake:

- **Conflict of interest**. If you're a contracted professional who will be helping an organization establish its PPFM practices, the organization might constrain your access to contract information.

Purchasing managers have long memories of things that go wrong. One area they tend to agree on with line managers is there's no such thing as a "firewall" in private industry. If they provide privileged information, they assume it will get into the wrong hands because they've seen it all too often.

Unfortunately, they don't have any way to know that your company is different. Hopefully they will have made you sign nondisclosure agreements, and included organizational conflict of interest clauses in your contract. But those might not carry much weight for you.

- **Procurement sensitivity.** Contractors aren't the only ones who will slip information to their friends. All too often, "competitive" bids come in within dollars of each other and the organization's own cost estimates.

    Obviously, someone leaked the budget to their friends; in fact, several people have probably done so. But why would they do this? Setting aside personal gain, there may be a vendor who's favored because of solid performance to date, so the program managers want to see them return.

    This concern isn't just about information on future contract actions. Access to the existing contract terms, performance data and staffing levels are often very helpful for someone planning to bid on the replacement contact in two or three years. Either way, until you're better known and trusted, the organization might be reluctant to provide you with information about its contracts.

- **Unit costs for services:** Don't raise this subject at this point. In a later chapter, you'll see how the PPFMO can help move an organization quickly up the maturity curve with the help of simple metrics and comparisons. Interesting discussions can arise from simple arithmetic.

    Divide the total cost of the service by the actual units of the service rendered. For instance, a fixed-price contract of $1 million to service 100 locations means a unit cost of $10,000 per visit. Is that reasonable, given the amount of work required once on-site?

    Strict services contracts are quite clear about unit costs. But the project managers don't always foresee the actual number of units the vendor will eventually deliver, as they often have set up no means of ensuring those deliveries will occur.

Unfortunately, in an immature organization any healthy discussion tends to terrorize managers. Raising these issues implies the manager overseeing this contract was bamboozled when awarding the contract, or is being negligent. Even if those suppositions are true, now is not the time to bring them up.

However, you can ask about service level agreements. Though the organization might have difficulty providing an accurate cost of delivering services, it should be able to explain what you will get if you buy the service.

Make clear you're seeking to understand and perhaps validate the information you're collecting about the organization's portfolio of work. You're right on the edge of being able to start doing some real PPFM work, so this isn't the time to get ejected!

What if You Don't Get It?

Of course, you might not be able to get decent contract information. Everything you can do to cross-validate it will give you a more accurate view of the organizational realities. If you can't get it, don't worry as there is a Plan B.

The PPFMO's first contribution to the organization will likely be the capacity to define ongoing work. For the most part, every line manager should have an idea of the number of supporting contractors. Early in the game, you won't be able to do much about the cost of supplies and products.

Shortly, you'll be asking managers to allocate their headcounts across the work they say they are doing. At that point, at least one version of the total headcount will have to emerge.

6. PRIORITIES

At last! Something that sounds like it belongs with the PPFMO. The next step is to collect statements of priorities in whatever form they may exist.

Places to look might include:

- Strategic plan and implementation memos

- "Top-Ten" lists, and other pronouncements by leaders at each level

- Specific objectives in personal performance plans for managers

Whenever possible, conduct interviews at every level to capture and clarify the information. Then (and only after trying to get the actual priority lists) add one very specific question: "What do you think are the top three things people in your part of the organization should be trying to accomplish?"

Although it may seem evident that managers should provide priorities, all too frequently they don't. In the evolving organizations that are the subject of this book, performance objectives are very rare. When they do occur, employees devise them while filling out the annual appraisal form (often in the last month of the evaluation year), which is why you need to question them about their top three priorities beforehand.

The objective is to get a true sense of what leaders consider to be important today, not what might be recorded on outdated paper documents that may no longer serve any purpose. The result will be to obtain at each level the same type of information found in the strategic plan review:

\multicolumn{5}{c}{**Business Unit: NORTH**}
BU Initiative	**Production**	**Shipping**	**Quality Control**	**Management**
Initiative NA1	x			
Initiative NA2		x	x	x
Initiative NG1		x		
Initiative NG2	x	x	x	
Initiative NW1	x		x	
Initiative NW2		x		x
Initiative NX1	x			x
Initiative NZ1			x	x

Once you've got this at the topmost level, start working down all the way to the lowest work unit.

What Will You Do With It?

At this point you're assembling all of these mandates into a single list. In the following step, you will compare it against what people are actually working on.

Don't try to rank-order these lists, as it will make the problem too difficult and debatable. Begin with whether something is on the list. In my experience, even that created a major step in the right direction and got the processes moving.

But if there is simple lip-service going on, then three or four layers of management will probably generate too many initiatives and priorities to handle them with a simple yes-or-no list. If there are too many to be handled effectively, separate them into high-level priorities, such as:

- Do this year
- Do this year if time permits
- Defer to next year
- Defer to the future

For your own edification, keep track of where the requirement came from as you'll want to be able to provide statistics on the percentage of top priorities that people are working on, which will be different for each manager.

Why Wouldn't People Want to Provide It?

You probably won't get access to the actual performance plans. But if you inquire about what's in them, most managers will share the priorities they issued downwards as well as those they received. They might be more evasive if they haven't assigned objectives to their staff. But they'll usually share the fact that their boss didn't assign them any.

Loyalty seldom travels very far!

Even in small organizations with minimal formal HR processes, managers know they should be providing such guidance. The "top three priorities" question will get them off the hook, so you shouldn't lead with it. It's important to track down whatever guidance exists, if for no other purpose than to make sure it can be cancelled if it's no longer operative.

What if You Don't Get It?

This is the first hard requirement in this list. You might not get access to the performance objectives, which may not even exist. And the strategic plan might not contain specifics. These aren't showstoppers as long as you can get managers to provide the top three priorities.

If the managers can't articulate at least those top three priorities, there is no Plan B. Stop, do not pass GO, and head immediately to the executive sponsor's office to discuss the situation. Essentially, the PPFMO's role is to make sure the organization is accomplishing its most important tasks. If nobody knows what they are, or cares, there's no point in having a PPFMO.

Check your facts before you toss a stink bomb into the sponsor's office. For instance, do the organization's relevant offices (i.e., plans and programs, performance measurement, budget formulation, etc.) have nothing to say in this matter? Use whatever they have before declaring defeat, then turn defeat into victory. If those offices acknowledge they have nothing to give you, offer to collaborate with them on a process to help executives establish priorities top-down throughout the organization.

If you received a robust set of priority statements, or had the opportunity to work with executives and managers to develop those priorities, the next step is to find out if the organization is really doing that work.

7. PROJECTS AND ACTIVITIES

This is where the PPFM rubber meets the road. You've learned how the organization is set up, what components do what, what skill sets reside where, and the volume of work (at least in terms of labor years) the staff can accomplish. You also know the most important things the leadership would like to have done.

This final step is to make a list of the activities those resources are working on. Precision isn't particularly important at this point. In a process-averse organization, establishing what people are working on may be a major step forward.

What Will You Do With It?

You've been gathering information behind the scenes while trying to maintain as low a profile as possible. But now it's time to surface and initiate a two-step process to assess the level of effort people are putting into their work.

You'll begin with the managers at the lowest layer of the organization. At this point you won't share the information you've gathered, as you don't want to influence their assessments of the situation. You'll ask them to provide a list of both the operational "lights-on" activities and project-type work to bring new capabilities online.

You'll also want a rough estimate of the effort needed to complete each activity (i.e., "three people, three months" will suffice). Things can quickly spiral out of control if you give each manager room to make exhaustive lists, especially in the operations area. Make it clear that day-to-day operations are seen as a single activity, so there's no reason to break them down.

If an activity seems to contain 60 to 90% of the group's total, tell them they can state it in terms such as, "60 of my 100 people are full-time for the rest of the year," or "All of my 100 people 80 percent of the time." This isn't the time to judge the reasonableness or wisdom of the response. The Zero-Sum principle will shake that out before too long.

There will be discussions about what constitutes a project rather than a daily task. Some organizations define any work requiring more than 40 hours as a project, primarily for the purposes of making sure managers approve the work before it begins. This could lead to as many as 30 or more activities per person annually, which is far too much detail for even a small organization.

The PPFMO shouldn't deal with daily action items. For even a modest portfolio of perhaps $2 or $3 million, or as small as a dozen people, an appropriate timeframe might be one calendar month or more for a person or team to complete. This doesn't mean you ignore this other work; just make sure it's incorporated into some larger activity.

Once the lower-level teams have compiled their information, aggregate the lists and provide them to the managers at the next level of supervision to review and validate. They will undoubtedly come up with more tasks of their own.

Again, capture a rough estimate of the effort needed to perform the work. Remember, this isn't whether the organization has the capability to do the work; it's the work it needs to accomplish. The managers may also be able to fold a number of smaller activities into a single package if they contribute to the same objective.

The second step is to drop in the top-down priorities. After the managers compile the lists, ask them to identify which activities accomplish the top-down priorities and check them off. The PPFMO will now be able to deliver its first tangible value: the answer to two critical questions:

- **What percentage of management priorities are being addressed?** Priorities that aren't on anyone's activity list won't reach completion this or any year.

- **What percentage of ongoing activities aren't found on anyone's list of priorities?** In any reasonable size organization, there will be localized activities that deal with localized problems.

It's unrealistic to expect that a top-down priority list can cover every possible requirement. But there's a problem if a large proportion of the line personnel and managers' attention is going to non-priority activities. Either top-level managers don't understand the realities on the ground, or the organization is doing whatever it wants. Either way, it's a situation that must be corrected.

When presented with the aggregated list, which typically runs from 150 to 500 items of various sizes, it will quickly become apparent that it can't be centrally managed item-by-item.

The organization must agree to create categories into which many related activities can be assembled to permit management to reduce its scope to a manageable number. Any smaller activity can be left to the care of the manager of that category (of course, the categories become the PPFMO's "programs"). The PPFMO will generally have widespread managerial support for this effort, since it implies that upper management will leave them alone to run their business.

Almost all of these programs will already be in place, and the few categories that don't quite fit the model will usually be organization-wide efforts. The managerial discussion of how to assign responsibility for those efforts often engenders a good feeling for everyone concerned because the lack of definition has been a source of frustration to all managers associated with the effort.

Why Wouldn't People Want to Provide It?

This activity tends to generate enthusiastic participation. If managers feel their workload is under-appreciated, they'll seize any opportunity to push the message to the top. Resistance will occur only if the assessment effort becomes another time-consuming activity that doesn't lead to a useful outcome.

This is why you must keep things moving along, and emphasize that it's important to get the entire picture without wasting time on being precise. You can't afford to have this group view your PPFMO initiative as an imposition rather than a possible solution.

Time away from line personnel's jobs means lost productivity. Consider using parallel inputs at first, followed by online collaboration so managers don't have to travel to and from the meetings. This might not work in your particular situation. But anything will help if it can reduce the perception of the PPFMO adding another series of meetings to an organization that is (as they all are) already overwhelmed with meetings.

What If You Don't Get It?

Fortunately, you have a backup plan.

In the previous step, you collected the top three priority lists. You know you have them in your possession, because you insisted the process be halted if people didn't provide them to you.

If the managers couldn't or wouldn't come up with the lists of things they're working on, compile the top three into a default list of what people are holding themselves accountable to complete, and add any published assignments from higher-up (e.g. through the strategy).

Then peruse the organization's status reports and similar documents to cull things that sound like accountable initiatives, all of which will leave you with a fairly robust list of activities.

Make sure you have an operational activity for each functional component. If you don't, add one. How far down you'll go will depend on the organization's complexity. Less is usually better, and you can always add more detail later.

Now you've got a list of what the organization thinks it's supposed to be working on. It's not the same as a list of what it *is* working on, nor what published guidance says it's supposed to be working on. But you now have something that's quite worthy of discussion.

What to Do With the Lists

If people have been reasonably cooperative, you'll have a sizeable amount of information you can mix and match to provide some revealing assessments of the organization's situation. If you ran into difficulties, at a minimum you should have a list of priorities and a fairly robust list of activities, and some parsing of those activities into organizational groups.

At last you have the makings of a governable situation. You have enough information to start some oversight, and an understanding of the scope of the effort and of the resources that can be allocated to do the work.

You could ask the managers when they'll be finished with their top three priority tasks, and if they're encountering any obstacles so you can get issues taken care of. But for now you won't do that, as the process won't be sustainable if it requires top-down pressure to operate.

As long as people are still willing to work with you, allowing the process to play through means the outcome will be their process and not yours. So start doing something without frightening the herd.

The following chapter describes how the PPFMO can engage with managers to move towards functioning governance. You're not going to ask them to suddenly change everything they're doing. That can scare them off. Instead, you're going to offer to help them resolve challenges they are already facing.

Building on the relationships forged during the one-to-one data collection activities, you're going to find opportunities to join them in a collaborative process between themselves and their peers.

Next Steps

While you've been gathering this data, you've also been undertaking the board preparation actions described in Chapter Six. The board is ready to do something useful.

Now, with the information you've gathered, and the analyses suggested in this chapter and the accompanying exercise, you'll have something for the board to look at.

If everything's going great, then you can tell the board how well everything is aligned and how the strategic priorities are being fulfilled. If not, the board can participate in realigning and reprioritizing.

If that's going to happen, then the intervening mangers will hasten to define programs in order to minimize the level of micromanagement the board needs to do. Your governance process will be off to a highly credible start.

Remember, this is happening because you collected ordinary lists. *The Pasta Principle* is at work!

The bonus materials in the resources website (www.Simmer-System.com) includes a table summarizing the reasoning behind each of the data lists as presented in this chapter.

Now (after doing the exercise of course) let's move into the next chapter to see how your governance board is going to be able to make something useful out of these simple lists of common data.

List to get	Why you need it	What you can do with it	Why they might not give it to you	What if you don't get it?
Organizational chart, missions and functions	Know who does (is supposed to do) what.	Define operational, non-project activities.	Information sensitivity? Or over-controlling managers.	Make your own as you get to know people.
Strategic plans	Expresses things that are most important.	Root of all other structures.	Contains long-range planning information. Or may not really exist.	Develop strategic plan at your level (with sponsor's support).
Personnel rosters and skill sets	Basis for creating resource pools.	Identify high-level capacity to do the work.	Concern over release of pay grade information.	Total group headcount, or best guess estimate based on overall cost.
Budgets	Money allocation is the ultimate expression of intention.	Align governance process with the way the money works.	People don't want to be tracked. Exposing budgets can weaken power.	Don't worry about it. Delivery dates are your first priority.
Contracts	Identifies extended capacity to do work by skill set.	Verify what managers are doing with their money; improve budget quality.	Legitimate concern for conflict of interest or sensitivity.	Wait. The information will emerge when you start looking at work capacity.
Priorities	Understand prior decisions, processes and compliance.	Create integrated priority list, then compare to reality of activities.	Priorities have not been established	Get the current top three priorities, and the sponsor to require a list of objectives.
Projects and Activities	Identify activities that are really going on.	Aggregate the total lists, and start setting up program groups.	Seldom an issue. But it will be an extra chore for disorganized managers.	Use the top three priority lists to get started.

EXERCISE 8: ADVANCED DATA ANALYSIS

The bonus materials at www.Simmer-System.com provide rudimentary Excel templates you can use to get started.

While using these templates, you'll see relationships between the sets of data you've assembled, which will help you build more comprehensive spreadsheets while preparing to transition to a proper data tool.

Analyze the Contracts

Allocate each contract to the program, project or initiative that it supports. If a contract supports several initiatives, that's a sign that they may belong to a single larger program.

If the contracts can't be easily allocated to the programs and the investments within them, make a note to fix that as time goes on.

Contract #	Vendor	Business Unit	Division	Current Year Value ($M)
123-456-789	ABC Corp	North	Production	3
987-65-4321	M&M Bros	North	Shipping	2.1
243-465-876	ABC Corp	South	Production	3.6
453-746-424	JKL Hauling	South	Shipping	1.8
845-930-203	JKL Hauling	East	Shipping	2.4
433-345-987	ABC Corp	West	Production	3.2
524-240-350	JKL	West	Shipping	3.2
302-323-923	Analytics, Inc.	HQ	Marketing & Sales	1.1
753-943-092	Swag Company	HQ	Marketing & Sales	0.3
423-535-237	Exec Assistants	HQ	Administration	2.8
423-424-998	GFD Eng	HQ	Design	2.0
			TOTAL	25.5

Priorities

This should be fun. It's always interesting when managers see for the first time whether their instructions are being carried out at lower levels (without visibility, that isn't happening).

(Again, the workbook at www.Simmer-System.com contains additional exercises to help you analyze the information you obtain.)

A. Enterprise Priorities

1. Map the priority lists from the enterprise level down to the priorities at the next level.

2. Repeat the mapping down to one level below the governance board.

B. Local Activities

1. Map all activities on the consolidated list to the lowest-level priority list.

2. Very few organizational groups do nothing but project work. For each component of the organization, assign at least one operational activity (as opposed to a project) to the priority list.

Chapter Nine

See You in the Boardroom: Governance in Action

Sooner or later your PPFMO initiative's sponsor, and the rest of the organization's executives, will want to know when their investment is going to begin yielding benefits for them. The good news is that it will be much sooner than later.

As noted in the previous chapter, the seven sets of data you collect early on start to allow the governance board some insight into what is going on.

Every inconsistency you dig up and every analysis you create, even with this rudimentary data, adds additional clarity to the picture.

As the decision-makers start to see flashes of light on the horizon of what has until now been a very murky vista, they'll want to know more and more. Here you can rely on *The Pasta Principle* to pull the board's oversight capabilities into the mix as a collateral benefit of your initial efforts.

Let's see how these early efforts lend themselves to showing the governance board what's going on, and allow them to provide meaningful guidance that can be carried out.

The List Phase

Just as a quick reminder, these are the seven items you've been gathering (you did do your homework, right?):

1. organizational chart, missions and functions
2. strategic plans
3. personnel rosters and skill sets
4. budgets
5. contracts
6. priorities
7. projects and activities

Since the board members would generally know the first two items, the PPFMO may not need to include them in the board member training sessions. The training will definitely need to include an overview of the next three items (staffing, budgets, and contracts).

As you'll see, even this rudimentary information starts to expose some topics where a bit of top-down interest might be appropriate. So let's get the board set up to start asking some penetrating questions.

Get a Facilitator

It's critical that the early meetings go well. Members must leave feeling it was a productive use of their time.

It might be so obvious that it doesn't need to be stated, but with a skeptical organization the politics can be pretty weird, so I'll say it anyway.

The number one outcome is that the members must not become enmeshed in personal attacks across organizational lines. Though it may be entertaining in a horror show sort of way, you need to remember that an executive never wants to be put on the spot.

In the end, the PPFMO will get blamed for creating the conditions where this could occur. That will indeed be the end, at least of this round of the governance initiative. It will be put on the shelf alongside the other ones that came before it.

That being the case, there would be value in finding a professional facilitator to run the first few meetings until the board finds its own rhythm.

If you're putting this event together, whether in the PPFMO director role or in some other capacity, then unless you are truly a world-class facilitator, please accept that this isn't the time or place to allow over-confidence to get in the way of progress.

If you're not a very experienced facilitator, please find one for a few months. They don't have to be external paid consultants, nor do they have to have domain expertise in the scope of this particular governance effort.

They just need the skills to keep meetings moving along in a congenial, smooth manner, and help board members frame their thinking processes to reach conclusions as to how they should operate.

However, there is one absolute rule in this regard: If you are a voting member, then you must not be the facilitator. This isn't your show – it's for the other board members. So step out of the limelight for a while. Trust me, the other program managers will give you plenty of opportunities to have the spotlights trained on you in the next few months.

Early Questions

You might be surprised by the degree to which very fundamental information is quite a novelty for your board members. That's just the way it is in a process-averse organization. So you may not have to include discussions of the organization chart or the basic missions and functions of the organization. But then again, you just might have to do it.

Staffing may also be a matter of some interest for the board members. Process-averse organizations often have little idea of what skill sets are required, nor what is on hand. They just muddle through somehow. It will take a very solid presentation to get the board members to understand why staffing is often the number one cause of delivery failures, and what they can do to put an end to this problem.

You'll also be able to provide the board with the overall budget to discuss, so make sure you're clear as to what the purpose of such a meeting is. In the first exposure, the current year's budget is pretty well set. There's no point agitating now over what it might have looked like. The idea is to get the board familiar with how much money is being spent for what. Unless you're extremely fortunate in your timing, formal approval of the budget in advance will usually have to wait until the next budgeting cycle.

Is it Really on the List?

The early lists "are what they are." There may be some questions, as we've just seen. But for the most part, these are organizational realities that can't be adjusted in the short-term. The last few lists, which are more about execution choices, will allow for more substantive inquiry and perhaps some decisions.

The first serious debate will likely be over the top ten items of priority. In an early stage organization, this may be the first time some board members have seen these lists. Even if they thought they'd seen something like it, they may be dismayed to discover their priorities are no longer on the list.

This is where the meeting facilitator will need to keep the discussion looking at improving the future process, rather than letting it bog down in recriminations and finger-pointing.

By the time the lists are complete, you'll be able to observe how the work the organization is doing matches against the published priorities, which usually makes for a lively discussion the first time around.

Case Study 6: The Amazing Disappearing Priorities

An organization I worked with undertook this comparison of plans and actions. The activity listing was supposed to address only project activities, and operational activities were gathered on a separate list.

In any event, their strategic plan only looked at the big changes anticipated for the future. It didn't specifically recognize continuation of current activities, so this discussion includes only project-type activities.

Their enterprise strategy contained 12 initiatives that were assigned to Organization X, which would have resulted in approximately 48 projects. (The numbers have been adjusted to further obscure which organization this might have been.)

However, in the next layer down, Organization X's priority list included only one DIRECTED initiative (i.e., drawn from higher authority) that generated four projects.

Effectively, the enterprise's 11 other initiatives, with 44 associated projects, were *lost*. However, Organization X assembled its own priorities into a top ten list, which actually contained 13 more initiatives and 45 more projects.

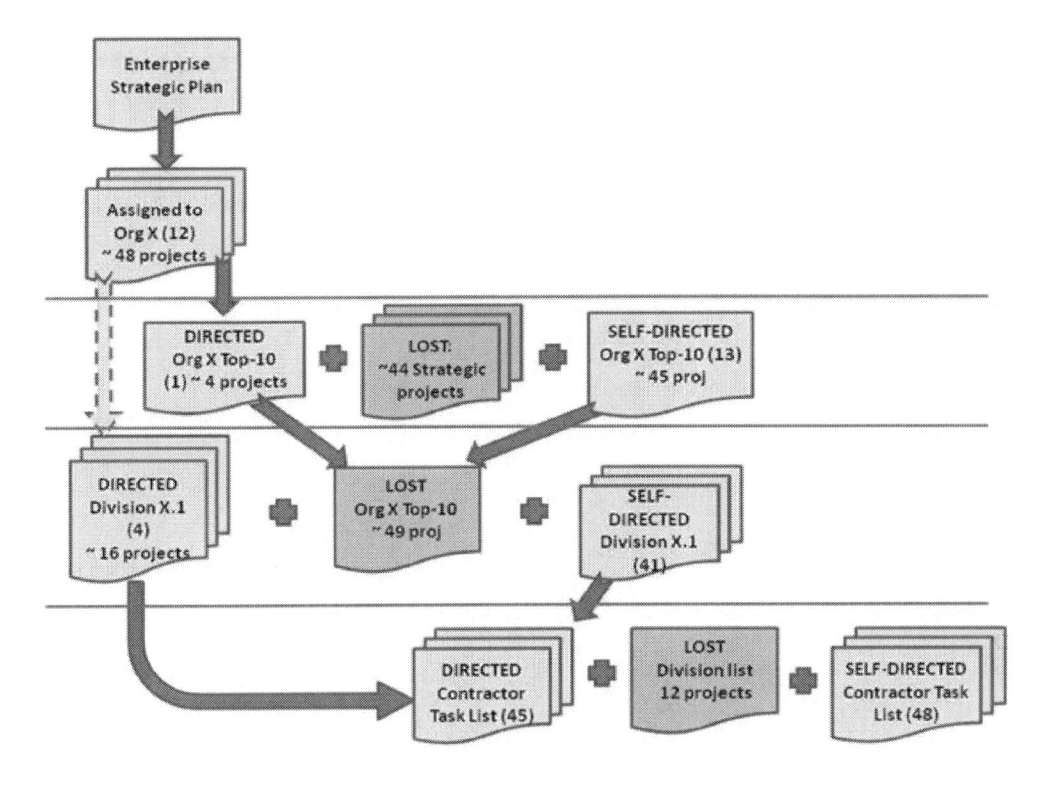

[Flowchart showing hierarchical project flow from Enterprise Strategic Plan down through Org X, Division X.1, and Contractor levels, with DIRECTED, LOST, and SELF-DIRECTED branches at each level.]

How Strategic Goals Wash Away

Ironically, at Organization X what went around came back around. The division heads included precisely zero of Organization X's priorities on their divisional priority lists. All 49 of those projects were *lost*.

Fortunately, whether deliberately or accidentally, the division level heads had started projects that aligned with four of the initiatives from the enterprise strategy, and so those were recaptured. The divisional plans also added 41 projects that didn't trace back to any higher plan. In other words, they met local interests only.

Finally, we discovered the direct support contractor's active task list included only 45 of the 57 projects established at the division level. Surprisingly, the contractor had a total of 93 projects on its own list (meaning they had generated 48 additional projects for themselves, and about half of their effort was going towards those projects). With the remaining portion of their contract effort, at the time of this study they were only addressing about half of the division's priority projects.

Don't over-interpret these results. Much of the local-level work **was** necessary. As you move down the levels, many of the "projects" will be more operational activities.

The point isn't the actual number of projects in play; it's that in the absence of an oversight effort or any tracking capability, few of the priority efforts were being worked on. And a great number of the things that were actually going on didn't trace back to any priority list. Yet everyone was working toward what they thought was in the enterprise's best interest, whether that be with or without guidance or in spite of it.

How does this happen?

In part, this organization was floundering from one hot button to another. So the answers would have changed from week to week, depending on what they were working on that particular week. That sort of churn creates the outcome that you aren't really working on anything.

At the same time, managers at every level had come to view the strategic planning processes and the associated strategic initiatives as irrelevant make-work. Since nobody was checking to see if any of these initiatives were being carried out, perhaps those managers were right. So they submitted slapdash responses, and returned their attention to those activities they believed constituted the real business. When they know nobody is checking, everybody just does whatever they want.

Whether the work was misguided and much of the money was wasted, or the guidance was simply misguided, this shows the power in an early stage organization of something as simple as comparing lists. The governance board might have a lot of work to do just sorting out the priorities, let alone making its own decisions.

Slicing the Pie: Allocating Funds

How Should it Be Sliced?

One of the most important roles for the governance board is the allocation of funds to the various initiatives. Other roles such as ongoing reviews, or developing (but not approving) strategies, could be delegated to the most affected members or a staff office.

What the board must **not** do is to "delegate" by dividing the budget between business units in their traditional proportions, and letting the member from each business unit make the decisions for that portion of the budget without any further explanation. The whole point of the board is that it is intended to balance, not perpetuate, the needs of the different business units.

The idea is to implement the creative tension between the needs of the different business units. When the competitive due diligence has been completed, then all of the representatives have a consensus that the funding is being applied to genuine needs. If the board punts on this issue, it has essentially put itself out of business.

The allocation activity is known as "portfolio management." Though there are many books on that topic, this book was written because most of them are based on highly-flawed understandings: first of how financial advisors allocate assets, and then of how organizations really operate and make decisions.

That may explain why so few organizations have been able to adopt any of the existing portfolio management advice. The entire portfolio management language was borrowed from Wall Street. If you have any investments such as a 401(k), pension funds, brokerage accounts, etc., you've seen it in action.

Picture yourself as the governance board with control over a certain amount of money (like your 401(k)). Your advisor asks you to consider your risk tolerance and time horizons in order to construct a customized allocation model (many mutual fund families already have this, such as a "30-years-off retirement fund") where you allocate portions of your money to stocks, bonds and cash holdings.

Maybe you consider tax consequences of particular classes and subclasses of investment, such as lower interest but tax exempt municipal bonds.

Then your advisor presses a key, and out spits a list of specific investments that will hopefully generate the best return for your money based on your risk preferences.

Most authors of portfolio management books have made the model even more simple and elegant: Rank all the proposed projects based on an expected return on investment; then draw a line when you reach the organization's budget.

All done! Right? Well, no, you're not. That little "improvement" just rendered the model worthless.

Such prescriptions miss the more basic part of the financial advisor's process. Using a strict mathematical system, only one investment has the best return, even while accounting for risk. So in theory, you should go all in for the top-scoring candidate (unless you're Warren Buffett and have money left over after you finish buying it).

Of course, that's not what the system actually does. In the background, using a fairly simplistic splitting process based on your preferences, it's already divided your account into certain classes.

If your risk tolerance is high and you have a long timeframe, the model might allocate the portfolio to 80% stocks, 10% bonds, and 10% real estate. It might also have rules such as no one investment can be over 5% of the total. These rules are based on prior experience. But there's nothing mathematical about them – they're just what the industry considers the wisest.

This Wall Street model has another fundamental difference from organizational realities. In the end, all investments deliver the same outcome – a return on investment in actual dollars – which is easy enough to track.

You just have to know how much you spent on the investment, and how much you receive when you sell it (or since there's an active market, what it would be worth if you sold it today).

You rarely have an emotional attachment to any particular investment, unless it's issued by the company where you work. Or if you're socially conscious, it may be a matter of conscience for you to invest only if the issuer refrains from practices you find unacceptable.

This isn't the case in an organizational setting, as the returns on investment aren't nearly as easy to measure. If all activities are viewed as part of one big grab-bag of money, and multiple activities contribute towards a single goal, how is the credit for the return allocated?

In addition, most organizations will have numerous activities that really don't add any value to the eventual product or service (the legal compliance office sometimes falls into this category). But as a business reality, it has to be funded anyway.

There are no differential equations to solve that challenge, unless you start introducing subjective rules to the process ("give 2% of the money to Legal"). There's also no right or wrong answer. There are answers that work, and ones that don't work as well or not at all.

The governance board largely exists to make the subjective decisions needed to make this not-so-mathematical process work. Sometimes it will try to save time by writing down the rules, or the rules are inherent in the decisions it makes. Obviously there's no right or wrong way to do this.

The point is to gain a consensus across the organization as to what levels of investment it wants to provide to its various objectives and capabilities, which in turn will trickle down to the programs it established to deliver those objectives. That may sound complicated, but all it means is everyone needs to agree on how to slice the budget pie (since we've been talking about Italian food, let's make it a pizza pie).

Some people slice a pizza into equal parts without considering that some guests may want a large piece while others want a small one, and some may not want any at all. If you do that, then somebody will have two slices, someone will have none, while everyone else only gets one. Or perhaps the person who didn't need a slice will have to have one anyway.

In some households, guests cut whatever size they want, which works well as long as there are no teenagers at home, in which case there might not be enough pizza to go around.

Many organizations have been advised they can toss all of their projects into the mix and rank them. Then when the pie runs out, the allocation process is complete. However, it never works out that way as there are several weaknesses with that approach. For example:

- If a midsized organization has 50 or more projects underway, a board can't effectively rank that many, particularly if they're different in nature.

- Even if the board could make such distinctions, there's not enough time for the board to meet, give each project ample attention to evaluate, then rank it.

- The rules-and-ranking approach will always leave out some investments that can't be turned off. So something on the list will have to be eliminated, and the wrangling starts all over again.

It gets worse. Operational activities are left out of the mix in most organizations. Leaving out operational activities asks the governance board to make strategic decisions on 20% to 30% of the total funding, while the other 70 to 80 % percent is treated as a shapeless blob.

Logic might guide you to do it the other way around. Operational emergencies will trump project needs, and managers will siphon money from projects to meet those emergencies. Will they take the resources from the effort that is of the least value to the organization? Possibly and possibly not.

Organizations that *have* tried to integrate operations and projects into a single ranked list run into a simple math problem. The fundamental criteria (risk, return, impact) can't be set to enable one type (projects or operations) to exist on the list without eliminating all investments of the other type.

None of the dozens of organizations I've worked with have been able to devise a mathematical model that accommodated both operations and projects. (If you can come up with such a model, please send it to me. It needs to be publicized!)

As noted in earlier chapters, the solution is to make decisions based on programs (packages of activities designed to yield a capability or outcome over an extended period).

How Many Slices?

Once you accept the need for programs as an organizing concept, the simple answer is one slice per program, but the slices won't be the same size.

You may see large organizations allocating multiple slices of funding to a program based on the "color of money." While you hear that term more in government, which uses different fund appropriations for different purposes, the private sector also considers whether something is an operating or capital expense.

That may be true. But still it's a just an accounting convention, and not a good reason to carry out a completely separate decision-making process.

As you head into the next step (defining needs), decisions will need to be made on the overall scope and direction of the programs. Once you start making decisions in advance of the affected budget cycle, rather than being imprisoned by the current one, funding can be allocated to the correct "color" early on.

Naturally, things will change over a few budget cycles. The board may have to adjust short-term allocations to deal with them, which will occur more easily if it begins with a coherent plan. So one program, one slice. Save the financial razzle-dazzle for a later time when the programs are sophisticated enough to make it worth the trouble.

How Big Does the Slice Need to Be?

This a trick question. It's perfectly valid to ask, but it never gets answered. Typically it would be stated as "This is how much I want," and the response would be "To do what?" For every budget cycle, each program needs to establish the amount of funding it thinks it will need as follows:

- What capabilities it's supposed to deliver.
- How it currently delivers them in terms of method and performance metrics.
- How much it costs to operate (and if possible, how that cost compares to other providers).
- Within the planning horizon, what changes will affect the program; what changes will need to be made to the program's capabilities to deal with it
- How much it would cost to deliver each of the anticipated changes, and the practical consequences of not doing so.

This information allows the board to understand the total value of each program in an absolute rather than competitive way. Program managers will no doubt see it as competitive, which may encourage them to put their best effort into this presentation.

Making the Slices

The preceding list amounts to a program plan. Once all the plans are in, the total needs or wants will exceed the realistic amount available, usually by about 100%. With the analytic support of the PPFMO, the board now determines the level to fund each program within a total overall budget.

This allocation process isn't a simple mathematical solution. If it were, the decision board could be replaced with a calculator.

Sometimes high-ranking people (definitely not leaders) will seek to avoid making difficult decisions by adopting across-the-board solutions, and increase or reduce the prior year's budgets by the same fixed percentage.

That's not leadership, and it doesn't put the organization's money where it's most needed. It kick-starts long-term competition to see who can most grossly overstate their requirements in order to have more left over after the cutbacks.

The board needs to consider the entire budget, then allocate it to various programs it created to accomplish the outcomes it values the most.

Programs need to explain what they're going to do, how they're going to do it, and the resources needed to do it. They should also explain their plans to operate, and the consequences of doing so, under various levels of funding.

As part of that process, it's imperative not to disassociate the operational and innovation costs of each program. Most of the efficiencies and reductions in operating costs can only be accomplished through the associated projects.

A budget that assumes such reductions, while at the same time defunding the necessary projects, is headed for disaster. The board needs to be advised of the feasibility of those cuts, and the consequences of proceeding if they are made. Because if the savings don't materialize, the bills will still have to be paid.

If operating costs are excessive, that program manager and division chief need to be the ones to work out the innovations needed to bring the costs down within the amount the board sees as an appropriate top line budget. If the effort is successful, then the savings should roll back into that program so it can go back to optimizing its accomplishment of organizational objectives within that reasonable cost ceiling.

The board will need to:

- Determine the level of credibility of each program's request, and adjust it accordingly.

- Assess the effectiveness of each program's operational activities. Then determine an appropriate operational funding level going forward, taking into account any productivity improvements implied by the program's project investments.

- Set up a base level of funding for each program to include this revised operational spending, and pulling forward any project funding required to achieve it.

- Review the program manager's assessment of new capability requirements, the approaches to achieve them and the prioritization and timing of those capabilities, and make any appropriate adjustments.

- Based on the overall level of risk these investments imply, set up an enterprise-level reserve fund.

- After program assignments, allocate leftover funding to ongoing operations, operational improvement projects, and the reserve fund.

- Ensure that the final allocation of funding is in proportion to the "must-have" project investments the board agreed upon. Allocate the funding to the program and not to specific projects.

- When the board wants to see a specific project move forward – or has concerns over the execution of a particular project – that project is declared to be of enterprise interest and flagged for more aggressive oversight.

The board now advises the programs of its initial determination, and invites last-chance submittals of requests for reconsideration (often known as a "reclama").

Many of the requests may be quite reasonable, as it's almost impossible to make top-down allocations without forgetting about some aspect of them. Still, the fact is that any fund increase within a fixed amount of money also means a reduction in someone else's funding.

The more open the meeting, the less likely programs will seek funding adjustments without a very strong rationale.

Once the board makes its final decisions, the PPFMO issues a record of the allocations. Procedurally it would be best to do this using a high-level program charter (or updates to the existing charters, if any).

Though this might not be the time to say so, the board has just set its first program-level baselines. If the PPFMO gets this far, celebrate! You're now in the top half of your class!

Next Steps

Thus far, the PPFMO and the governance board have conducted their business in the manner of test flights. There are plenty of safety features, as many time-outs as you need, and not too many observers.

So far, the board is simply handing out money (or at least permitting it to be spent) – an activity in which you can make many friends!

In our next look at the board, you're going to have to ask it to take on a more uncomfortable role: checking to see what happened to all that money.

But first, let's give the board a few more things to learn about through the outcomes of the collaborative activities you'll start undertaking in the next chapter.

EXERCISE 9: DECISION BOARD RECORDS

You did a lot of work in accomplishing the earlier exercises, so just this once you're going to be cut a bit of slack.

Now would be a good time to determine where, when and how to publish the results of board decisions. If the results are to survive, they shouldn't be posted only on a specific website, but anywhere people can find them.

First, set up a board meeting calendar. Depending on the capabilities of your collaboration tools, you'll want to associate materials used for the meeting with that meeting event. Ideally, use hyperlinks to the file locations.

It saves storage space, it can take people to the complete record. And most importantly, it ensures that everyone is looking at the same documents.

But some systems don't permit that. To be more accurate, some of the document storage tools and/or some of the security rules placed around them don't permit it or make it very difficult.

Next, set up your document filing system. You may choose to file documents by program and initiative, in which case you'll need subfolders for the specific review meetings. That way you can look at an exact record of what was presented at each meeting, not a later updated version.

Or you may choose to file by meeting date, in which case you'll need to have a means of reassembling all of the documents that pertain to a specific initiative.

Some of the associations can be handled with descriptive file naming. But that has its limits, especially with the default tool available in most organizational environments (SharePoint) that limits a file name to 200 characters. That includes the names of all the folders in the path to the file name, so it can get used up pretty quickly.

So you're probably going to want to get familiar with the concept of "meta-data" (data *about* data), and how to use document tagging within libraries. This is true whether you use SharePoint or some other tool.

Don't forget the post-meeting documentation (minutes, action items, and follow-up activities), and of course the formal record of decision. All of the other documentation means absolutely nothing if you don't have a record of what the board actually decided!

Now you're ready. You have a place that everybody can access, at least in read-only mode, to find out what is being proposed and what was decided.

At first, this level of transparency might feel uncomfortable to people. In the skeptical organization, board members aren't accustomed to people peering into their deliberations, even at a summary level.

And project managers are often nervous about people looking at their less-than-perfect materials. All of them may be concerned about losing the ability to re-remember events the way they want to remember them, rather than the way they actually happened. But after a few months pass and the sky hasn't fallen, they'll get over it.

Lastly, set up a folder for templates for the various artifacts you may require as an initiative goes through the lifecycle you're going to settle on in Agreement One in the next chapter. If you're going to tell people they have to present certain information, then it's wise to provide them with a template for doing so.

You'll probably have reached Agreement One long before this, so you might be able to start populating some of those folders. If not, you already know one of the first documents that you'll want to include: the charter.

To set the bar at the appropriate level, you should provide an example of what a template looks like when it's properly filled out. If, as recommended, you use the same templates for all initiatives regardless of size and complexity, then you should definitely provide samples of well-done templates for very small and very large initiatives, which will result in better submittals and also helps in the discussions about tailoring.

But make sure those examples are provided as PDFs, scans or other non-writable formats. Otherwise, I can promise you that most of the submittals you get are going to parrot the examples, even when the text is ludicrously inappropriate.

Chapter Ten

Let's Make a Deal: Eight Collaborative Agreements

Project management asks that you should do what you agreed to do by the time you said you would do it. Or at least notify colleagues as soon as you find out you can't.

Is that concept so remarkable? After all, your family members expect at least this amount of courtesy out of each other. So surely the workplace, where they give you money to get things done, deserves as much.

Eventually, yes. But some organizations can be just as dysfunctional or abusive as some families. And the recovery process is at least as complicated and time-consuming. If the organization hasn't been used to this kind of communication, it will take time to get there. Pushing too hard too soon will bring the learning process to a complete halt.

This chapter provides eight commitments to collaborative information sharing that form stepping-stones towards a tolerable level of accountability.

All Managers Become Project Managers

You, and probably most of the managers in your organization, have been trained on management, and project management in particular. You don't have to be a certified project manager to understand that in order to get things done there has to be...

- an objective

- some sort of a plan

- a step-wise approach to the objective

- decisions about what the different members of the team will contribute.

Should you assume that not everybody is going to work on the same parts of the work at the same time? In that case, the most important thing people probably need to keep the work moving forward is to agree on when they'll transfer parts of the work to each other, and the condition of the work when they transfer it.

There's nothing special here for any reasonably competent manager. In fact, the highest level of organizational project management evolution (the accepted maturity models notwithstanding) isn't the situation with the most elaborate PMO procedures. Rather, it's the point where the job title of "project manager" disappears because these skill sets are inherent in all managers' duties.

These expectations are rather mundane, so it should be possible to get a consensus that this minimal level of activity is reasonable. If the managers agree they're accountable for the product they are to deliver, the date when they must deliver it and the cost of completing it, then the iron triangle is alive and well.

And the organization is already operating with the concept of "baselines," no matter what they actually call the commitments.

Your reality will be different at first. If that weren't the case, your organization wouldn't have decided it needed to get started with a PPFMO practice, or get the one it has under control, whatever the case may be.

Stepping Outside the Cubicle

So far, the actions in *The Simmer System*[SM] have required mostly researching things that are probably already in place. Getting the information shouldn't have been too difficult, and hopefully you made friends around the organization while you were becoming oriented.

Now the hard part begins. As discreetly as possible, the PPFMO is going to insert itself into people's work streams, so it's best to be invited in.

Right now the PPFMO doesn't have the credibility to withstand stonewalling. You're going to be asking people to relinquish some of their time to sit in meetings with you and their colleagues just to explain what they're doing.

No matter how well-disposed they might be, they won't see any added value in this until the magic of collaboration begins to be realized.

Because you'll have to start with the parts people can agree upon, you may have to make one or more of the following choices. If these activities and data sets already exist, use them even if they're not as good as they could be.

At this stage of the game, the objective isn't to provide precise data for decision purposes; it's to allow managers the opportunity to identify major gaps in information and processes, and for them to allow you to collect the data while they fix those gaps.

The order isn't hard and fast. Picking arbitrary numbers, if you can get numbers three and five without difficulty, then go ahead and get them first. Otherwise, the list isn't as random as it might appear. It's a sequence that's made it possible to secure consensus in many other cases, with the easiest one being listed first:

1. The elements of work that will need to be transferred from one group to another (dependencies).

2. The expected lead time for work handoff.

3. The date when each initiative will be completed (top-level or milestone schedule).

4. A high-level description of the end product of each initiative (definition of 'done').

5. A category-level understanding of the types of resources that will have to perform the main elements of the work.

6. The expected dates when dependent work will be transferred (internal milestones).

7. The condition of the work when it is transferred.

8. The means of dealing with obstacles and issues.

The quicker you can gain consensus for several of these points, the better. But if you can't, don't press for more than the managers are willing to recognize (meaning, they agree the action is pretty self-evident).

You might be able to convince them of the value of your idea, and they might even try and do it for a while. But as soon as things become difficult, they'll revert back to whatever the culture finds acceptable, and it will take a long time to get them back.

Some of these steps may seem trivial and frustrating to a professional manager. So you'll just have to have a little faith in *The Pasta Principle*.

For a while it may seem like all you're doing is low-level scut work, when you want to get out there and do some real program manager work. Hey, whatever works for you. I can only warn you that if you rush through the implementation of PPFM, you're going to end up getting red sauce on your nice white shirt.

Even the limited commitments at the top of the list have lots of unexpected effects. For instance, managers won't be able to deliver on them without coughing up related information, which the PPFMO will write down.

Once they see the benefit of being on the same page on at least some topics, they'll begin to demand more. And the next thing you know, you'll be struggling to keep up, which is a great place to be!

If managers refuse to undertake a public commitment to **any** of these aspects, the organization is showing signs of anti-maturity. So take a moment to revisit the chapter on Executive Support, and get major issues resolved before your credibility (and sanity) is destroyed by trying to push for something that's just not going to happen.

Assuming you can come to some agreement on some of these points, you have the beginnings of a PPFM practice where managers commit to do something, track whether it was done, and make the status of that commitment public.

Don't call these partial commitments a "baseline." Apart from the fact it will likely frighten the managers who have some PM background, it will weaken the proper baseline you'll edge toward over time. There's no particular reason to give these agreements a name – just live with them!

If you must name them, then "commitments" is a good term because it reminds people they agreed to do this.

An important point to notice has been the deliberate use of the word "initiative." As the organization comes to terms with its work, there will be a see-sawing between claiming the project-type work is impeding the ability to keep up with daily operational responsibilities, and counter-claims that projects are late because nobody could be broken loose from routine or emergency tasks on the operational side.

The structure you create must include both operational and project-type activities, so that all of the organization's efforts are included and tradeoffs can be seen. Because an *initiative* means both operational and project-type work, all work must belong to only one initiative.

The following sections discuss how to capitalize on whatever agreement you are able to achieve.

THE EIGHT COLLABORATIVE AGREEMENTS

Dependencies First

PPFM-immature organizations tend to operate in isolated function-specific groups, sometimes called "silos." The strength of silos contributes to the organization's difficulties in effectively completing its work. But even in the most dysfunctional organization, there's recognition that any complex undertaking requires interaction between some of the organizational groupings.

Despite any adverse attitudes the groups may have toward each other, managers understand that work is going to move from one group to another. If nothing else, each group may be concerned that it will be undermined in important work because "those people" failed to do their part properly and/or on time.

While there are many adverse consequences of such thinking, it does provide the PPFMO with an opening. All parties will agree they have a right to know the condition of the work when they receive it, and when the group in line before them will be handing it off.

If you're trying to build communications, it's best to start with something everyone will agree to. So the management of cross-group dependencies makes a good starting point for the PPFMO to begin building the collaboration and accountability needed to make the organization successful.

Agreement 1: How is the Work Broken Up?

Organizations with strong silos tend to have one of three conditions:

1. Very well-defined processes that all other groups are required to follow stringently, even when they're counter-productive to the current situation.

2. Very well-defined processes nobody follows, because each group ignores the others while resisting efforts to hold themselves accountable.

3. Very poorly-defined processes, because the group isn't really accountable to anyone, including its customers. They're free to make things up as they go along, and reinvent them for each new instance of the same service.

As a result, it can be quite illuminating when managers start defining what their roles are in the overall initiative lifecycle. Everyone will have a general idea of what the other groups do, so at a high level the panel will be able to quickly define the basic pattern.

You only need enough detail to serve the purpose. As long as your sketch shows the major business units, the different types of work they do, and where the hand-offs occur, then it's good enough. More detail may be more accurate, but it won't help people understand the situation any better.

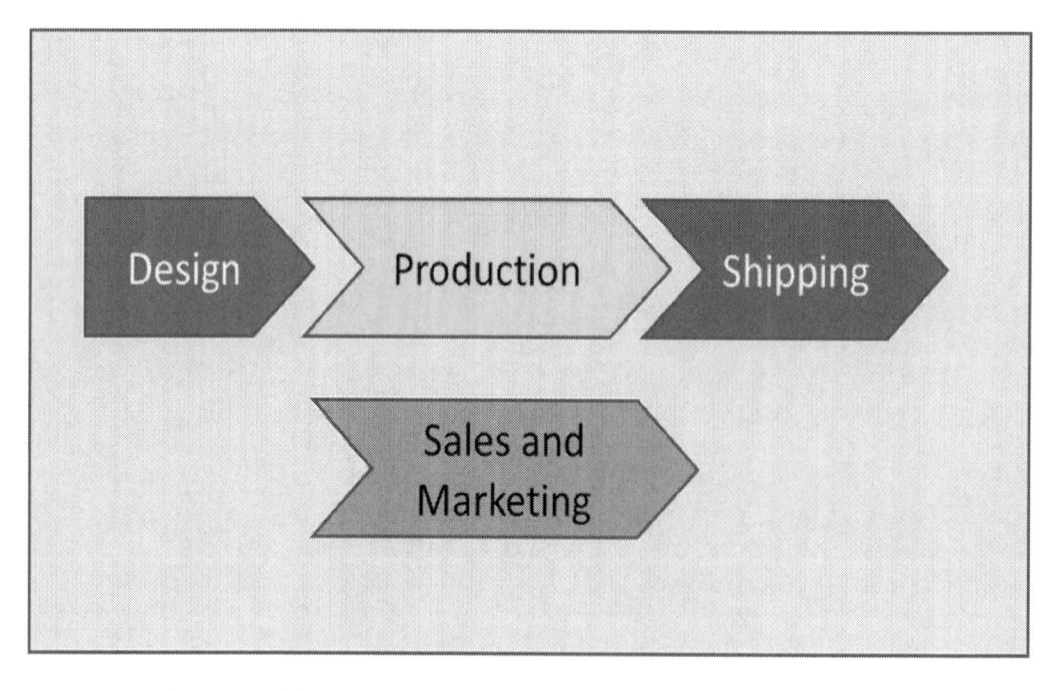

Design → Production → Shipping

Sales and Marketing

It may take considerably longer before the groups resolve what's in those spaces between them: How exactly does the handoff occur? What level of quality is the downstream group entitled to expect?

Don't let those details slow down the process of getting a basic agreement on the overall lifecycle pattern.

This may not seem like much of an accomplishment. But if the organization has never really thought about its work before now, it's a giant step forward.

Being quite uncontroversial, it can form the basis of cross-compartmental collaboration, which in heavily-siloed organizations may not have been seen for some time. It also makes the next agreement possible.

Agreement 2: When is the Next Handoff?

The next question places a little more burden on the managers. Instead of just describing the process, you're now asking for specific commitments, but only for the activities they're currently working on.

Resist the temptation to plan a series of completion dates amounting to a full project schedule based on the overall framework just agreed to. If managers come up with this idea on their own, then of course accommodate it. But don't let it become an excuse for a cycle of extensive analysis that must be completed before any next steps can be taken.

Now that the managers have agreed upon the performing group for each of the initiatives, it will be perfectly natural to ask when that group intends to hand the work to the next group in line.

In many cases this is where the hemming and hawing begins, and why you don't want to bring on that sort of reaction for every lifecycle phase of every initiative all at the same time.

Instead, gently press for an estimated date for the next handoff in each initiative. If the manager is unable or unwilling to commit to a handoff date, then set the initiative aside for the next meeting, which will be a dependency resolution meeting to be held in a few days.

Give the managers time to look into the reasons why a handoff date can't be predicted. Then at the resolution meeting they must either provide a date, or an explanation of the issues impacting the initiative so the organization can come up with ways of alleviating those issues:

Business Unit	BU Initiatives	Design	Production	Shipping
North	[Initiative NA]			
	Initiative NA1	8/31/2015		
	Initiative NA2		10/15/2015	
East	Initiative EB			
South	Initiative SC			11/30/2015
South	Initiative SD	9/30/2015		
East	Initiative ED			
North	Missing			
East	Initiative EE			10/31/2015
South	Initiative SF		11/15/2015	
North	[Initiative NG]			
	Initiative NG1			8/31/2015
	Initiative NG2			
West	Initiative WH	11/30/2015		
North	Initiative NW1			9/30/2015
North	Initiative NW2		9/15/2015	
North	Initiative NX1	7/30/2015		
North	Initiative NZ1			12/31/2015
North	Production Sustainment			
North	Shipping Operations			
South	Production Sustainment			
South	Shipping Operations			
East	Production Sustainment			
East	Shipping Operations			
West	Production Sustainment			
West	Shipping Operations			

At the end of this cycle, the PPFMO will have established the due date for the next milestone in each initiative. It may not sound like much, but it's a lot more than it had the previous month.

More importantly, each manager with work in progress has made a commitment as to when that work is to be completed. Remember, for many of them, this is a completely novel concept. From that little seed mighty oaks will grow much quicker than you might imagine.

Given the understanding of the general workflow and the next handoffs, you've probably already figured out it won't take too much additional information to build something that reasonably looks like a schedule. Just don't press for it yet.

Don't Worry – You're Gonna Love It!

The next area where constraints are usually accepted is the top-level schedule and concept for each initiative.

At this point you may feel you've entered the Twilight Zone. You've just gained agreement on at least one of the internal phases of each initiative where previously there was none. But only one of those phases.

Now you're going to go in the opposite direction. You want the managers to decide on the final delivery schedule without having agreed upon the content or timing of the rest of the work in the lifecycle phases.

You're also going to have the managers establish the initiative scope, rather than having it handed out from the executive sponsors (unless of course that's already been defined).

Your PMBoK is spinning on its spiral bindings.

You mean they started work on the project without knowing what it was? It might seem incredible that managers can agree to put resources to work without any real idea of the intent of their contributions. There are several reasons why this is a frequent occurrence.

In any organization with hundreds or thousands of people, there will be some "budget dust" – activities that middle and lower-level managers cobble together using resources scavenged from the edges of the larger initiatives.

These efforts tend to be poorly defined, because their scope and timing depend on the amount of resources siphoned in their direction at any given moment. And managers are reluctant to expose them as commitments for those same reasons.

Top executives have devised strategic initiatives to achieve things that are important to the organization's future. One would expect the importance and intent of those initiatives would be clear to everyone, whereas that's seldom the case. But people will charge off and start working on them, because that's what the boss' boss wants to hear.

Even in a well-run organization, good leaders learn to set strategies in broad strokes and leave the details to the imagination of the lower-level leaders. Great executives who follow this approach also understand that the important thing is to "trust but verify." In other words, hold people accountable.

They'll demand that their subordinates explain how they're going to carry out vague directional guidance in the strategy. Then they'll make sure those things are done, which is precisely the aim of the governance processes a PPFMO manages. That function has existed for some time in those kinds of organizations.

However, the primary focus of this book is the situation where those attitudes and that governance entity don't exist. In less-functional organizations, executives learn that issuing vague instructions and not following up on them allows everybody to feel they won without the need to fight any battles. Each division interprets the title however it suits their needs, and nobody has to argue about anything until it all starts coming together. That's how an organization can launch an initiative that consists of nothing more than a title.

At this point in *The Simmer System*, the PPFMO isn't ready to demand an integration of all the parts. In this type of organization, push merely leads to shove (in this case, the PPFMO getting shoved out the door once again). Instead, the idea is to have managers develop the top-down guidance that should have been issued.

Agreement 3: Launch Date

The number one complaint among project managers in most organizations is they're forced to accept a fixed delivery date before the project has been properly planned. Yet my recommendation is to do exactly that.

How is it possible that everyone will be in agreement about when a product can launch (or other project-type work can be completed) if no one knows what that product is? Actually, this is quite a common situation. Many events must occur on a certain date, but present a wide range of options as to the actual content. (The Olympic Games is the situation most often cited, but there are many ordinary examples.)

When two people announce they're getting married, it's easy to pin down a timeframe for the wedding (this year or next? fall or spring?).

They might want a specific day for sentimental reasons (the day they met, or the same day Dad and Mom got married). There also may be practical reasons (perhaps it should be before the first child is born).

The same applies in other areas. Large events need to select a venue by a certain date if they want to get a big enough space, even though most of the details of the event remain unknown. The same is true with routine activities in your organization.

The infamous Y2K deadline was well-known, even though many organizations had no idea what the work would be right up until and past the last minute.

Supplies or product changes, or new government regulations, may force the organization to rethink its entire approach and implement a new solution by a certain date.

No matter how well-justified, an arbitrary date may seem useless if the scope of the work hasn't been defined. On the contrary, it's very powerful.

For one thing, unlike the actual scope and cost of the work, it's the one data point that's hard to cover with smoke and mirrors. A calendar doesn't lie.

If everyone agrees on a must-have date, as it approaches, the pressure to achieve the work will ratchet up by itself without the PPFMO having to force things. All you have to do is maintain transparency of the date itself.

So expand your calendar to include this new information.

Strategic Initiative	Business Unit	BU Initiatives	Design	Production	Shipping
Initiative A	North	[Initiative NA]			**3/31/2016**
		Initiative NA1	8/31/2015		3/31/2016
		Initiative NA2		10/15/2015	1/31/2016
Initiative B	East	Initiative EB			7/31/2016
Initiative C	South	Initiative SC			11/30/2015
Initiative D	South	Initiative SD	9/30/2015		5/31/2016
Initiative D	East	Initiative ED			3/31/2017
Initiative E	North	Missing			
Initiative E	East	Initiative EE			10/31/2015
Initiative F	South	Initiative SF		11/15/2015	4/30/2016
Initiative G	North	[Initiative NG]			**8/31/2016**
		Initiative NG1			8/31/2015
		Initiative NG2			7/31/2016
Initiative H	West	Initiative WH	11/30/2015		6/30/2016
	North	Initiative NW1			9/30/2015
	North	Initiative NW2		9/15/2015	1/31/2016
	North	Initiative NX1	7/30/2015		2/28/2016
	North	Initiative NZ1			12/31/2015
	North	Production Sustainment - North			
	North	Shipping Operations - North			
	South	Production Sustainment - South			
	South	Shipping Operations - South			
	East	Production Sustainment - East			
	East	Shipping Operations - East			
	West	Production Sustainment - West			
	West	Shipping Operations - West			

Notice that the operational initiatives don't have end dates. As a matter of practice, they're generally broken into fiscal years since that's how most organizations fund them.

This step should have jolted a project manager into wakefulness. At last, there's something that can be rendered as scope, schedule and cost (assuming you can match the costs to the initiatives, and get a better handle on the scope, which is your next agreement). From the information provided, it should be easy to construct a launch milestone chart:

	1st Quarter	2nd Quarter	3rd Quarter	4th Quarter	1st Quarter	2nd Quarter	3rd Quarter	4th Quarter	1st Quarter	2nd Quarter
Dec	Jan Feb Mar	Apr May Jun	Jul Aug Sep	Oct Nov Dec	Jan Feb Mar	Apr May Jun	Jul Aug Sep	Oct Nov Dec	Jan Feb Mar	Apr May Jun

```
━━━━━━━━━━━━━━━━━━━━━━━━━━━━━━━━━━━ Initiative NA1
                  1/31 ◆ Initiative NA2
                                    7/31 ◆ Initiative EB
            11/30 ◆ Initiative SC
                              5/31 ◆ Initiative SD
                                                              3/31 ◆ Initiative ED
   1/15 ◆ Initiative EE
                  10/31 ◆ Initiative SF
               ━━━━━━━━━━━━━━━━━━━━━━━
        8/31 ◆ Initiative NG1
                                    7/31 ◆ Initiative NG2
                              6/30 ◆ Initiative WH
        9/30 ◆ Initiative NW1
                  1/31 ◆ Initiative NW2
                     2/28 ◆ Initiative NX1
              12/31 ◆ Initiative NZ1
━━━━━━━━━━━━━━━━━━━━━━━━━━━━━━━━━━━━━━━ Production Sustainment - North
━━━━━━━━━━━━━━━━━━━━━━━━━━━━━━━━━━━━━━━ Shipping Operations - North
━━━━━━━━━━━━━━━━━━━━━━━━━━━━━━━━━━━━━━━ Production Sustainment - South
━━━━━━━━━━━━━━━━━━━━━━━━━━━━━━━━━━━━━━━ Shipping Operations - South
━━━━━━━━━━━━━━━━━━━━━━━━━━━━━━━━━━━━━━━ Production Sustainment - East
```

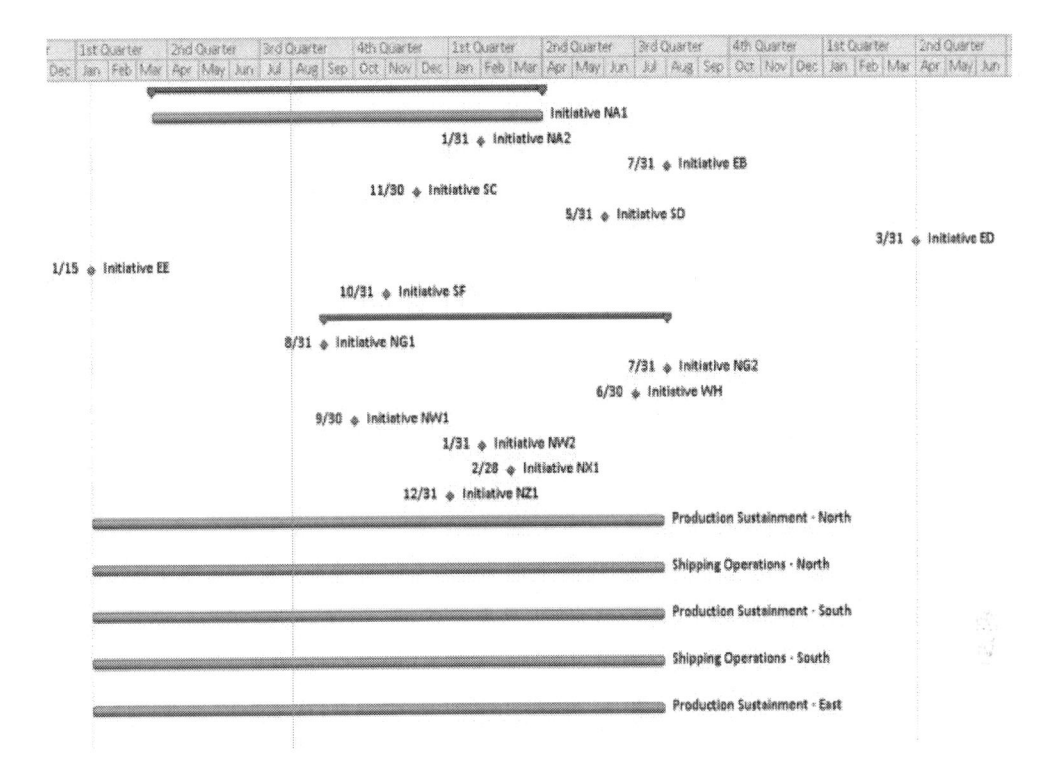

This isn't just something to make PPFM professionals feel more at home. The governance board members, who have been left without much to do until now, will have no difficulty seeing its implications. (I've found that people all across the organization are hungry for information that gives them a view into what's going on.)

Stakeholders will want to discuss delivery date commitments, which will probably require additional information (*The Pasta Principle* in action), which will require an acceleration of the process *The Simmer System* has been suggesting.

As long as the organization is pushing for the PPFMO to do more, things are going really well.

Agreement 4: Watizzit?

Perhaps the greatest symbol of a deliverable that remained undefined even *after* delivery was Izzy, the logo for the 1996 Olympic Games in Atlanta. In contrast to the cute, cuddly mascots that generated millions in sales of plush animals and ancillary products of earlier Olympics – and all later Olympics for good reason – Atlanta elected to go the artsy route and ended up with Izzy.

Its original name was *Watizzit* because nobody could agree on what it was or meant (but it was very artistic, and apparently pleasing to a city sensitive about being thought of as a cultural backwater).

The name was eventually shortened to *Izzy* in an effort to shift the image into a friendlier beastie that could do its job of generating good will and merchandise sales. A rose by any other name ... the name change alone didn't work. The average non-artist person still saw a worm with stars coming out of its butt. *No sale.*

So yes, it's physically possible to roll out a product without any idea of what it is or will be used for. But that's not a very good precedent to follow.

You shouldn't encounter much disagreement with your fellow managers that it's possible to define what each initiative is supposed to accomplish at a high enough level, as long as they're the ones who get to define it. If your collection tool is an Excel sheet or a SharePoint field, it shouldn't feel threatening to others if you ask for details that can fit into a confined space.

What might surprise you will be the amount of lively debate a high-level, concise description creates. Managers will articulate their views of what they thought the initiative was about, and sponsors will press back on any dilution of the scope. Keep taking notes!

As this discussion unfolds, it can cause reevaluation of the work to be done and the availability of the resources, which may be the point where *The Pasta Principle* reveals itself.

Strategic Goal	Strategic Initiative	Business Unit	BU Initiatives	Content
Goal I	Initiative A	North	[Initiative NA]	Lorem ipsum ...
			Initiative NA1	Lorem ipsum ...
			Initiative NA2	Lorem ipsum ...
Goal I	Initiative B	East	Initiative EB	Lorem ipsum ...
Goal II	Initiative C	South	Initiative SC	Lorem ipsum ...
Goal II	Initiative D	South	Initiative SD	Lorem ipsum ...
Goal II	Initiative D	East	Initiative ED	Lorem ipsum ...
Goal III	Initiative E	North	Missing	Lorem ipsum ...
Goal III	Initiative E	East	Initiative EE	Lorem ipsum ...
Goal III	Initiative F	South	Initiative SF	Lorem ipsum ...
Goal IV	Initiative G	North	[Initiative NG]	Lorem ipsum ...
			Initiative NG1	Lorem ipsum ...
			Initiative NG2	Lorem ipsum ...
Goal IV	Initiative H	West	Initiative WH	Lorem ipsum ...
		North	Initiative NW1	Lorem ipsum ...
		North	Initiative NW2	Lorem ipsum ...
		North	Initiative NX1	Lorem ipsum ...
		North	Initiative NZ1	Lorem ipsum ...
		North	Production Sustainment	Lorem ipsum ...
		North	Shipping Operations	Lorem ipsum ...
		South	Production Sustainment	Lorem ipsum ...
		South	Shipping Operations	Lorem ipsum ...
		East	Production Sustainment	Lorem ipsum ...
		East	Shipping Operations	Lorem ipsum ...
		West	Production Sustainment	Lorem ipsum ...
		West	Shipping Operations	Lorem ipsum ...

Make sure the operational activities also define themselves. It may seem trivial, but once you start applying numbers to these initiatives, it will be amazing what washes out of those dark corners.

The Balancing Act Begins

With these two agreements in place, the organization has constructed and accepted high-level constraints on the initiatives. Now, the PPFMO is in a position to provide this information to the manager-level group and the executive sponsors for validation.

This will provide two benefits:

1. Because the managers will have constructed end dates for each of the initiatives, it will become clear that the expected delivery date for many initiatives can't be reconciled with the committed-to delivery date of the current phase.

2. Executives have an opportunity to validate the managers' conclusions. Usually the PM is pushing for reduced scope and delayed deliveries, while the executives, listening to the voice of the customer, are after faster delivery of more scope.

    This is where Zero-Sum comes in. If the PPFMO has already done the data collection on staffing and budgets, it can ensure that these discussions are held within the actual limits on the organization's ability to do work.

    If the board orders more resources to be deployed to one initiative, it must be made very clear which other initiatives will give those resources up and what the consequences will be.

It should be noted that you've moved forward far enough that you now have the makings of an initial PPFM practice. This won't be immediate. The managers must have understood these concepts, and agreed to continue to work towards better coordination before actual PPFM procedures can go into place.

As the primary participants refine their understanding of the work the organization is doing, the PPFMO – which is and must remain a disinterested bystander – will incorporate the results of this assessment into an enterprise-wide portfolio view it constructs quietly in the background.

Getting it Together

By now the organization has agreed upon which groups have responsibility for what kinds of work. They're stating when they'll hand work over to one another, and all of the work is being done to meet a specific timeframe.

There's also **general** agreement as to **roughly** what the initiative is **supposed** to accomplish (how's that for one statement with many caveats?). The surest way to polish those rough edges is to match them to one another as well as to the end customers' point of view, and start making these different perspectives mesh properly.

Agreement 5: The Resource Pool

The vast majority of organizations are structured around functional specialties, meaning that their departments have names like Manufacturing, Sales, Design and so on. Much of your challenge in getting PPFM in place is getting those groups to think less about making things easier for themselves, and more about working together for the good of the overall organization.

Those organizations with product lines may have already grasped the idea of cross-functional teamwork, with the functions working together within their product silos. But despite understanding and practicing the idea of cross-functional teamwork, product silos that are so self-sufficient often have even more difficulty with PPFM when decisions must be made across product lines.

If the operating divisions are large enough (e.g. Dodge trucks and Chrysler cars in the olden days of Detroit), when you look under the hood you discover that below the top level everything has become functional once again.

Almost all organizations are prone to taking on more work they can do, which is mainly for political reasons. Managers hate to tell their bosses "no," even if they have a competent boss. And many bosses can't tolerate hearing "no" even when it's the right answer.

As a result, as soon as you get the cross-group handoff agreements working, the performing group will immediately make excuses as to why its handoffs are beginning to slip. Their excuses are seldom about technical issues. Usually they stem from the fact the group has taken on more work than it can execute.

Here's a simple exercise: Have the functional groups list the key players for each piece of work assigned to them across all initiatives. Then count the number of key people needed to do that work.

If you're a diehard fan of Microsoft Project, Primavera or another full-scale project-charting tool, this is the first point where the tool proves its value. It's not yet essential as the analysis can also be conducted via Excel and SharePoint, but things are starting to get complicated.

In fact, the tools can take you in the wrong direction. They can tempt you to dive into detail just because you can, even though it's not needed at this point.

If the organization is large or complex, by-name resources management using Microsoft Project requires too much data entry and system maintenance.

Despite the impressive ability of these tools to handle massive amounts of details, their more sophisticated capability – and one that many users never master – is the ability to handle things at an aggregate level or using generic resources.

Once you have learned how to do this, project management tools begin to reveal their value.

	Resource Name	Type	Initials	Group	Max.	Std. Rate	Ovt. Rate	Cost/Use	Accrue At	Base Calendar
1	Project Manager	Work	P	Project Manager	1,200%	$0.00/hr	$0.00/hr	$0.00	Prorated	Standard
2	Machine Operator	Work	M	Machine Operator	13,700%	$0.00/hr	$0.00/hr	$0.00	Prorated	Standard
3	Materials Mixer	Work	M	Materials Mixer	9,500%	$0.00/hr	$0.00/hr	$0.00	Prorated	Standard
4	Warehouse	Work	W	Warehouse	3,900%	$0.00/hr	$0.00/hr	$0.00	Prorated	Standard
5	Driver	Work	D	Driver	8,800%	$0.00/hr	$0.00/hr	$0.00	Prorated	Standard
6	Sales	Work	S	Sales	1,400%	$0.00/hr	$0.00/hr	$0.00	Prorated	Standard
7	HR + Admin	Work	H	HR + Admin	2,300%	$0.00/hr	$0.00/hr	$0.00	Prorated	Standard
8	Finance	Work	F	Finance	1,100%	$0.00/hr	$0.00/hr	$0.00	Prorated	Standard
9	Engineer	Work	E	Engineer	2,100%	$0.00/hr	$0.00/hr	$0.00	Prorated	Standard

At this point in the game, all of the resources are generic and no names are needed. For instance, setting the Project Manager at 1200% capacity means there are 12 such people on hand, which is all you need to know. The more details you have, the less the message comes across.

Be careful to note when you take your snapshots of your data, and always refresh them before you print them. Usually, in the first resource sheet you produce, the resources aren't over-committed (in Microsoft Project you can tell that because they're not listed in red).

But a few days later when the project managers apply resources to the work, it turns out they're indeed over-committed.

You'll find the total number of resources needed to do the agreed upon work far exceeds the number actually on hand, which often happens in this type of organization as the same resource has really been assumed to be available to each task independently. The organization is used to getting away with that because people assume that much of what is said won't get done.

Typically, people are reluctant to decline a tasking. Instead, they claim to be doing everything they've have been asked to do, which usually results in only a bit of work done on each item so they can say, "I'm really slammed, but I'm working on it."

When key people are supposed to be playing a role in several initiatives at the same time, at best they can spend only one or two hours per week on any given initiative.

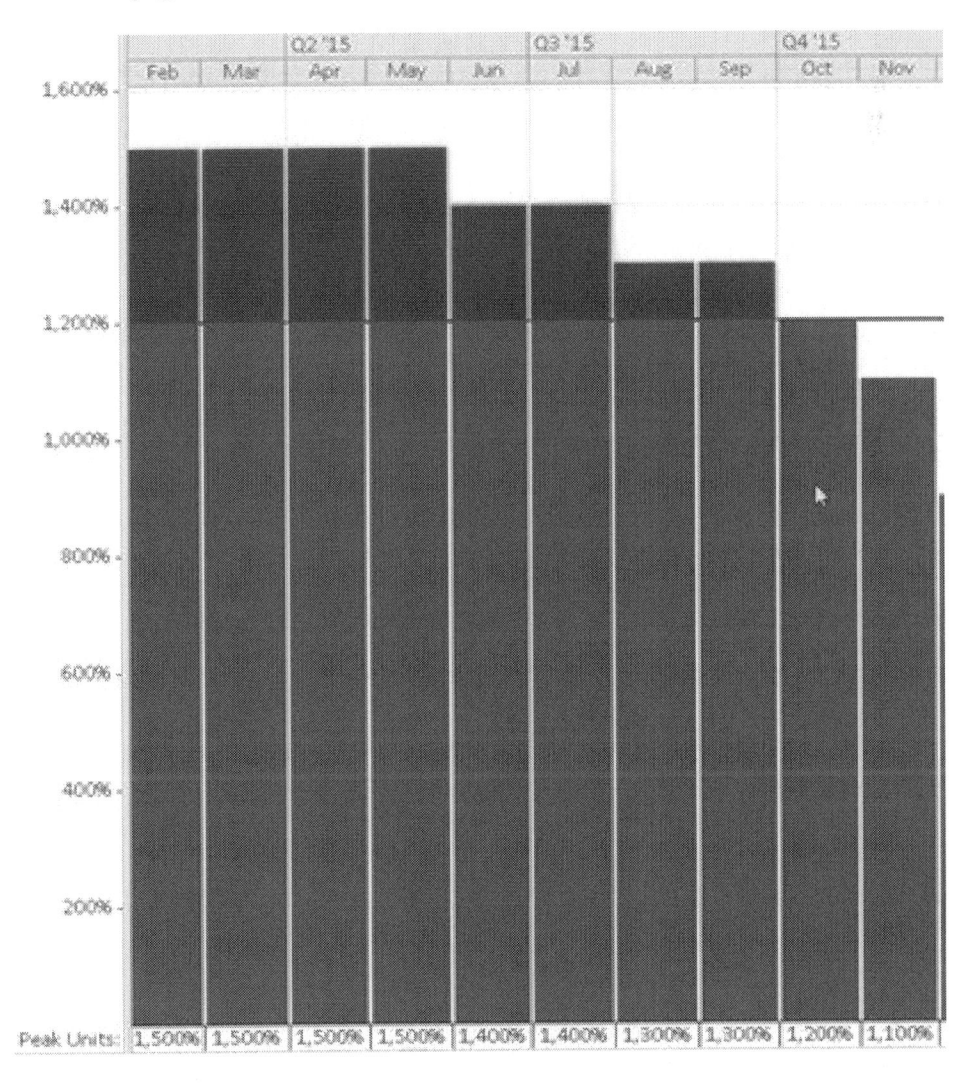

	Q2 '15				Q3 '15				Q4 '15	
	Feb	Mar	Apr	May	Jun	Jul	Aug	Sep	Oct	Nov
Peak Units:	1,500%	1,500%	1,500%	1,500%	1,400%	1,400%	1,300%	1,300%	1,200%	1,100%

You already know the organization isn't well-disciplined, so you know how this is going to play out. In fact, for some time the organization *has* been seeing inadequate involvement of the most qualified resources in the form of delays, incomplete work or shoddy products, with the likely outcome being "all of the above."

You've exposed that several critical elements of the work can't be done at the same time with the available resources. Assuming you're not going to continue trying to switch people's tasks on a twice-daily basis – which is what has been going on with very unsatisfactory results – there's no choice but to prioritize the work.

Because the divisions have already been choosing what work to assign and what to defer, decisions made by the producing group about each element of upstream work has a direct impact on the downstream group (i.e., the customer) with follow-on effects.

Those decisions need to be coordinated in some manner. It's easier to do that coordination one-on-one between the work groups; in fact, they'll start doing it as soon as the issue is revealed. But their priorities might not match the direction of the overall enterprise. That would require a top-down priority schema and coordination process, which may be more authority than the PPFMO has at this point.

Never mind. At least now some things are getting coordinated and moving forward. That's progress.

Program coordination meetings will be discussed in a later chapter. For now, once this step has been reached, the different groups will have started working together to develop delivery schedules and resource priorities. Congratulations! You've moved a long way up the maturity curve (not that it's being counted as a criterion).

But wait ... there's more!

Agreement 6: Are We There Yet? Committing to Handoff Dates

Back in Agreement 2, you got to the point where the business units would at least commit to providing notice of a pending delivery.

That commitment had several benefits. It provided managers a reasonable notice of a shift in their group's workload, and gave them the opportunity to have people wrap up existing work and pick up the incoming work in an orderly manner.

That's a great improvement over the uproar of an organization in turmoil where work arrives and departs in near-random fashion. Still, once you get beyond the individual work unit, it doesn't do much to encourage orderly progress.

You only have a hint of when things might be delivered. A "hint" is a great development compared to "not a clue," but it won't impress customers very much. You took a step towards solving that problem in Agreement 3 when you staked out a launch date. Once that's done, managers tend to shuffle resources around in an effort to meet commitments to external customers (particularly if they're bringing money to the party).

The practice of making those commitments is a critical element of the overall process of growing a sense of accountability. It also goes a long way to restore customers' confidence in the organization.

From the PPFMO's perspective, a commitment to a launch date drives a *Pasta Principle* effect of pulling in a whole range of project management best practices.

Even so, you may have arrived at Agreement 6 feeling the chaos hasn't abated much. With the various internal processes still muddling through, every associated activity has to wait until an unknown date when they can begin their work.

With a final somewhat fixed delivery date, the odds are the steps at the end of the production process will get short shrift. The organization will be running around trying to complete the most urgent tasks needed to meet the next delivery date.

Anything that doesn't get the product in the package and out the door will be skipped. That may well include most of your quality assurance processes. In the long run it isn't much help, as the product will be back for rework and have to be reinserted into the work queues.

Now, in Agreement 6 you get managers to commit to the actual dates when they'll hand off their work, and you'll be able to generate a list or table showing the handoff dates.

As you saw earlier, a typical lifecycle breaks into phases that correspond roughly to a shift in the primary skill sets needed for the next chunk of work

So without asking for a detailed breakout of the overall schedule, if you can get managers to provide the expected handoff dates, the schedule will construct itself.

Viva la Pasta Principle!

BU Initiatives	Planning	Design	Production	Testing	Shipping	Current Estimate	Outbound Dependency	Incoming Dependency
[Initiative NA]	.	.	.	.	3/31/2016	2/2/2016	.	.
Initiative NA1	.	8/31/2015	.	.	3/31/2016	2/2/2016	.	.
Initiative NA2	.	.	10/15/2015	.	1/31/2016	11/4/2015	.	.
Initiative EB	.	.	.	.	7/31/2016	5/18/2016	.	.
Initiative SC	3/25/2015	.	.	.	.	3/25/2015	Planning due to EE start by 3/26	.
	.	5/20/2015	.	.	.	5/20/2015	R&D due to WH R&D by 5/21	.
	.	.	9/9/2015	10/7/2015	11/30/2015	11/4/2015	.	.
Initiative SO	.	9/30/2015	.	.	5/31/2016	6/1/2016	.	.
Initiative ED	.	.	.	.	3/31/2017	3/29/2017	.	.
Initiative EE	.	.	.	.	10/31/2015	7/24/2015	EE finish due to NG1 start by 7/27	Start 3/26 dep SC Planning
Initiative SF	.	.	11/15/2015	.	4/30/2016	10/28/2015	.	.
[Initiative NG]	.	.	.	.	7/31/2016	1/19/2016	.	.
Initiative NG1	.	.	.	.	8/31/2015	2/5/2016	.	Start 7/27 depended on EE completion (not recognized in initial plan)
Initiative NG2	.	.	.	.	7/31/2016	3/9/2016	.	.
Initiative WH	5/21/2015	.	.	.	.	3/25/2015	.	.
	.	11/30/2015	.	.	6/30/2016	12/13/2015	.	R&D 5/21 start dep on SC R&D
Initiative NW1	.	.	.	.	9/30/2015	9/23/2015	.	.
Initiative NW2	.	.	9/15/2015	.	1/31/2016	12/30/2015	.	.
Initiative NX1	.	7/30/2015	.	.	2/28/2016	2/24/2016	.	.
Initiative NZ1	.	.	.	.	12/31/2015	12/30/2015	.	.

At least initially, you're going to get this information by gleaning it. If the managers succeed in delivering against the individual commitments made under Agreement 2, they'll be better positioned to make additional commitments more confidently and accurately.

Of course, you'll still have to make sure they share their updated and refined estimates with each other. The program commonly does this through a periodic dependency management meeting.

As a rule, less meetings are better, so do you really need another one? The programs can supply much of the information the PPFMO needs. Implementing some type of file-sharing for even simple Excel sheets eliminates more meetings and people can input their own data.

Modern technology provides several techniques for doing that (i.e., posting them on a notice board, in a worksheet or on a SharePoint site, etc.), but those tools only offer one-way communications. It takes a lot more courage and provides a lot more accountability if the managers of the various initiatives can look one another in the face and declare their intended handoff date.

So yes, you need a meeting, which I believe is one of the most important aspects in creating and sustaining program-level governance. If you can get this working, it reaches deeply into the overall set of management practices and *The Pasta Principle* will go to work for you.

Agreement 7: Standards of Done

During the phase when you got groups to agree upon when they'll hand work off to others – and when you determined the intent of each initiative – you set aside tight definitions of "done," particularly at levels below the initiative.

If more than a few weeks have gone by since those coordinative actions, disputes may have arisen due to the lack of definition creating misunderstandings between contributing groups.

I'm sure you've worked out by now that the PPFMO's solution isn't to try to make people do things. Let the PPFMO be a solution to a problem for which the managers are demanding a solution.

At one level, each major phase of an initiative's lifecycle is generally the responsibility of one performing group. In fact, that's mainly the reason why defined steps exist in the first place. Multifunctional Agile teams don't exhibit such lifecycles; they fluctuate constantly between design, development, testing and deployment.

Traditionally, the performing group gets to define the processes and procedures by which it plans to operate. To minimize the amount of "enterprise" (or cross-group) documentation, it's better to have the receiving team specify *only* what they need to move forward with their step, and (if appropriate) how the delivery to them needs to be structured.

Once the performing team validates its ability to meet those requirements, the two groups are positioned to hold a businesslike discussion.

Things aren't that different at the enterprise level, as the performing managers develop more detailed descriptions of key elements of the overall initiative requirements to help define what the solution should do.

As always, various groups will have different opinions of the feasibility and utility of any particular requirement. If the sponsor is routinely engaged, the definition and negotiation process can incrementally occur on the fly in some form of Agile process.

If the sponsor is largely disengaged, then the process will look more like a traditional waterfall approach with periodic decision gates.

Agreement 8: Stop Whining and Start Winning – Dealing With Issues

As groups begin engaging with each other, it will be important to emphasize points of collaboration. When the PPFMO was formed, a great part of the organization's problems may be attributed to the fact the groups don't communicate well, if at all.

To a degree, their isolation is a defense mechanism that precludes hostility. Any perceived lack of performance on the part of another group tends to be greeted with, "Well, that's typical of those guys. What else can you expect?" With the effort to collaborate, there will be more instances where groups have to confront the reality that commitments have been made but not met.

Until a consistent track record of slippage is established, it may be best to permit shifting delivery forecasts rather than seeking to browbeat group managers into getting the deliveries back on track. Thus, it's important to have an ongoing dialogue of honest estimates of completion.

You can let the dates slip, but keep a record of them using a register of issues and resolutions. (You'll find an editable template on the resources website, www.Simmer-System.com.)

More importantly, the slippage should be treated as if it were the organization's failure. Therefore, the PPFMO needs to inquire into the causes of the slippage to make sure the organization acts quickly to provide the local manager with necessary relief.

Issue ID	Current Status	Priority	Issue Description	Currently Assigned to	Expected Impact Date	Impact Summary	Actions	First WBS	Date Identified	Issue Owner	Actual Resolution Date	Final Resolution & Rationale
IN-001	Open	Critical	Marketing and legal have not agreed on regulatory status of product	General Counsel	12/01/15	Would have to stop project	COO directed Legal to report to board by 10/30/15	3.1.2	04/01/15	Marketing		
AP-032	Work In Progress	High	Authorized staff have not been brought on board yet.	Dir. HR	ALREADY IMPACTED	Work is taking longer to complete than planned	Dir HR to report on status of all open hires at 7/31 Board meeting	7.2.3	01/01/15	Dir. Design Center		
FV-351	Closed	Medium	Key supplier is being acquired (by non-competitor)	Dir. Logistics	09/30/15	Could impact deliveries. Will require rework of contracts.	Meet with contracts director of new parent company	4.0.0	03/15/15	Dir. Contracts		
		Low										

In my experience, the big momentum shift for a PPFMO implementation occurs when the first initiative to be brave enough to declare the existence of an issue suddenly receives a shower of resources and waivers (accompanied by increased executive attention). The other initiative managers will quickly pick up on this cue!

Make it Worth Doing

People often use "baby steps" to describe the initial effort towards shifting a culture. However, there are two drawbacks to this metaphor:

1. Baby steps often lead to falls

Your intention behind accepting partial progress is to make sure the program *doesn't* fall. As history has proven – maybe even in your own organization – once the PPFMO falls, it can't get back up.

2. Baby steps are somewhat aimless

Your steps may not be as big as you want. But each one you take makes a decisive move towards the final objectives.

To return to the simmering analogy, if you start to get cocky and relax your attention, the contents in the pot could boil over. When that happens, you remove the pot and lower the heat before returning the pot to the burner. What's surprising is even if the pot has cooled, when you put it back on a still-hot burner, it will quickly return to a full boil and the food starts splattering once again.

First reduce the heat to a simmer. That will eliminate boil-overs and splattering, and the food continues to cook. It may take a little longer, but at least you won't have to start over.

If you allow the boil-over situation to go too far, the pot has to be removed from the heat until it becomes cooler. The food isn't likely to catch fire, at least not at first since the pot is full of water. But as the water boils off, the food in it turns into a gooey (or worse, hardened) mess that may be hard to clean off.

Photo credit: www.frikkinawesome.com

Even if the pot isn't permanently ruined (which can happen), it's going to be taken out of service while you can scour it to remove every last blob of the caked-on mess. Until it's ready to be cooked in again, you have to order take-out while you recover your confidence.

It's exactly the same with *The Simmer System*. In other words, where the PPFMO encounters too much resistance, it must slow down its process improvement efforts to a level the organization can tolerate. But it must keep things moving enough that the processes are still in place.

Even if the "pot" isn't permanently ruined, the PPFMO can go out of business and the organization scrubs itself "clean" until every vestige of it disappears. Rattled by the experience, it shies away from any form of governance for a long time.

Please don't think I'm exaggerating the consequences to make a point. This is no overstatement. In one engagement, I joined an organization that had adopted fairly heavy governance processes which were appropriate for the massive projects it was undertaking. The executive in charge of that group had forklifted those processes over from another organization.

By sheer coincidence, I later ended up supporting a PPFMO restart back at the organization the executive and the processes had come from.

Yes, I said "restart."

When I arrived, there was no sign of those processes, nor had they been replaced with any others. We began stepping through *The Simmer System*, which I had formulated by then. It was actually pretty interesting to have a case study come to life in front of my very eyes! We began at step one: locate the organization chart.

You can't make this stuff up.

This is just one of many cases I've seen over the years. Since I had the before-and-after photos in hand, it was clear how fast and how completely the culture had ejected PPFM as soon as the sponsor moved on. Remember too the speed with which the new-old management team disbanded all governance activities in the case study back in Chapter Two.

* * * * * * *

So heed signs of frayed relationships heating up. Keep simmering, and don't let things boil over!

It may take patience to work through the various increments managers will accept.

Rest assured that each time the organization agrees to make certain commitments, and each time a digestible change makes things better without causing much discomfort, the managers will become increasingly willing to accept transparency and accountability.

Next Steps and Summary

So far *The Simmer System* has tried to proceed with very small, deliberate steps to avoid raising people's hackles. Determining whether those steps are big enough to be productive is to see if they're moving you in the right direction.

They can still be quite small steps. Nothing in the previous chapters places much demand on the program managers. But look at how far you have come:

- You've identified the work being done.

- Managers are collaboratively timing the work they're handing to one another.

- You know when products or deliverables are expected to be ready.

- At a high level, you know what the end product will be able to do.

- You have identified the primary types of resources needed to get the job done.

- You've learned how to adjust your work allocation so that resources are available for the most important work.

- You've committed to specific dates where handoffs will occur. You'll have a set of the important milestone events, which amounts to a supportable built-up schedule for all projects in the program.

- You've achieved an agreement on the condition of the work when it's transferred from one group to another.

- You have a means of communicating and removing obstacles to progress.

It may have taken several months to get here, but it's a good place to be for an organization that only a few months earlier was starting below zero on the process maturity scale.

In fact, many organizations give up before getting this far. They can still run in a reasonably organized way if managers would just live up to their commitments (the rest of this book explains how to facilitate them doing just that).

You've been told many times about the need to defuse resistance, and how too much opposition can lead to the termination of the PPFMO. This can led to timidity.

You can get a margin of safety that allows you to push further and faster if you provide the program managers with a means of appealing the need for process, particularly under emergency circumstances.

In the next chapter, we'll see how to implement a waiver system that can provide pressure relief. Meanwhile, in this chapter's exercise, let's take a look at the artifacts the Eight Agreements will generate.

EXERCISE 10: BUILDING THE BASELINES

Now is the time to do the following if you didn't do them earlier:

1. Develop and use a milestone chart.

   a. Use the committed end dates to construct a launch milestone chart.
   b. Obtain the sponsor's permission, and publish the milestone chart.
   c. Hold a governance board meeting to discuss the milestone chart.

2. Add the high-level scope descriptions and definitions of "done" to the list of initiatives. You now have a Work Breakdown Structure (WBS) dictionary to publish. Don't tell too many people the name as it can it sound intimidating.

3. Go back to the division managers. You already have an estimated handoff date for each work package in progress. Now see if you can find out when they started on it. Before long you'll be able to develop general timeframes for each major step in the workflow, and build a very high-level schedule in your organization's preferred tool.

4. Add the important resources (i.e., skill sets, unique skills, operational activities) at the initiative level:

   a. Here's the exciting next step: The resources identified for the work will often exceed the amount of people by multiples of two or three. Hold a meeting with the organization heads where the intent is to negotiate the reduction of the resources needed to actual resources available.

   Remember, the work is supposed to be already ongoing. So it can't be an impossible problem to solve, which is where the Zero-Sum principle comes into play. Let the divisions battle among themselves as to who is doing what – the only rule being the total resources that are needed can't be greater than what's on hand.

   b. In most organizations, the only way to solve the problem is to cut back on initiatives that are on the books but aren't being worked on. The PPFMO now takes the proposed changes to the various decision groups (assuming there is more than one layer), and eventually to the governance board for review and approval or no approval.

5. Hold a meeting of the divisions to identify at a high level, and working downwards only one or two levels, whether the performing division expects to complete its products as scheduled.

   If not, record the new expected completion date. More importantly, determine why timely delivery isn't possible, then use the Issues Log to begin an escalation process.

Chapter Eleven

Waivers — Recognizing the Practical Limits of a Process

This is a short chapter, but the waiver is a very big part of your PPFMO's success. So I didn't want you to miss it.

****

Emergencies happen. Every process needs to have a cut-out mechanism so actions can be approved immediately, as long as those snap judgments are made at an appropriate senior level and documented so everyone else knows what was decided. The PPFMO can make use of the same dynamic.

Aww, Do We Hafta?

One of the best ways to defuse charges of "process Nazism" is to provide a well-publicized and simple means of avoiding the whole process.

*A waiver **is not** a surrender flag. It's still part of the process.*

An emergency is a situation in which a decision must be made before all or a reasonable amount of the facts are available. A response must be taken with the resources available even if they aren't the most appropriate for the task.

Emergencies crop up in all organizations, but far more so in process-averse organizations, if only because they don't have any mechanisms for dealing with abnormal but predictable events.

When the situation doesn't permit decisions to be handled in regular order, a decision authority either makes the decision without the normal reviews, or allows an appropriate individual to make such a decision. In whatever form it takes, the decision authority's action constitutes a "waiver"; that is, the normal process steps are waived.

Notice also that if the proper decision authority isn't consulted, you don't have a waiver – you have an unauthorized action. It may prove to be the right response, but it had better be. If it turns out wrong, then the person who took it not only made the situation worse, but did so in evasion of advice from the proper person.

These waiver decisions aren't secret. The proper governance board must be furnished with a detailed accounting of all waivers issued between board meetings. It can then overrule any of those emergency decisions, assuming that it's still practical to do so.

The existence of a waiver path doesn't provide a basis for being obstinate about coming up with the facts when there's no emergency. If a manager says, "We don't have time to do that" two weeks prior to the governance board meeting, it might be true that the packages can't be assembled within that timeframe.

But there was plenty of time when they were reminded about it ten weeks ago.

It would be fun to watch the board berate the program manager for failing to have this information, although that's probably not going to happen. Or to have the investment held up until the documents can be produced. But if this is something the organization needs to have done now, then it doesn't help to not do something that's really needed in order to resolve internal training problems. So go get a waiver and move on.

It may seem that uncooperative people are being given a free pass to avoid the process. While this can feel frustrating, remember that early in the game the PPFMO isn't in the position to win every battle.

Nor is the infrastructure ready to specify every action needed to support the governance board's decision-making process.

If you won't permit deviations from the process, but you don't have the processes ready to go, the stakeholders have very little choice but to go back to ignoring the PPFMO and getting their work done, which is basically going back to where you first came in.

A subliminal point is being made here. By using the waiver process, these people are in effect accepting the legitimacy of the process. A process waiver doesn't bypass the process; it demonstrates that the process exists, is mandatory for everyone, and has been followed.

Waivers That Work

As soon as the waiver process is in place, people who are impatient with a process in general will avoid having to think about their requirements before demanding resources.

A successful waiver process includes three key features that allow the waiver to bypass the process when needed, or keep a firm lid on it. In fact, they may be even more stringent than if the PPFMO wrote rules for obtaining a waiver:

1. A very high-level approving authority

2. A signature by the approving authority

3. Complete transparency

The Principal's Office

In the principal's office, even when you know that severe discipline isn't on the agenda, there's always a little worry that it might be.

A critical success factor in setting up the waiver process is to make the approving authority someone high enough in the chain of command (and not the PPFMO), that people are reluctant to impose on them too often for fear of looking incompetent.

However, the decision authority – such as the CEO – mustn't be so unreachable to make the process impractical. If that's the case, there will be a demand for the process to be delegated to a more accessible level. But once that starts, the delegation will continue down the totem pole until the approving authority ends up being the same person who wants the waivers.

Having found an appropriate level, the PPFMO director must ensure the decision authority is firmly on board, and knows the waiver approval level can't be re-delegated under any circumstances.

It's also a good practice to have one — and only one — alternate who can sign a waiver in the event that the decision authority is unavailable. That alternate should be someone with the requisite domain knowledge so they're able to assess the risks of any proposed waiver, while being rather unlikely to be seeking (and signing) a waiver for their own division.

Make Them Get a Signature

In large organizations, executives tend to be reluctant to sign anything that's not absolutely necessary, as it could rear its ugly head after everyone has forgotten about it.

Your waiver form needs to be simple and to the point, and needs to convey that the proposed action hasn't undergone any of the usual reviews. The decision-maker is taking it upon himself or herself to ignore the issues and permit the waiver to go forward.

Since it is an emergency, nobody but the program manager can vouch for the technical feasibility, the administrative practicality, or any corollary impacts of the proposed action. And often, they're not too sure either.

That's how emergencies and the PPFMO are. You do your professional best, and you don't get the usual paperwork. However, you should be pleased that you have information on an initiative that in the earlier days would have scooted under the radar, no matter how big or critical it may have been.

To obtain the waiver, the program manager must get the form and complete it (again, keeping a record of the waivers), then take it to the decision authority for their signature.

Weak decision-making authorities seeking to placate powerful program managers will sign a flood of waivers in the beginning. The PPFMO must keep the decision-maker apprised of the count, and, wherever possible, the reasons behind the waiver (which requires a bit of follow-up when things have settled down).

Over time, either because the numbers begin to increase and attract the governance board's attention, or because the executives are being held personally responsible for the consequences of a waiver they signed, the screws on the waivers process will tighten down.

Just let it simmer.....

Before long, the daily parade of waivers will have diminished to an occasional straggler, which is just what the waiver was intended for.

Total Transparency

A transparent process is self-correcting. An excessive amount of waivers will raise questions as to the approving executive's commitment to the corporate process.

So how do you make personalized transactions transparent?

- Make sure there's a way to find out the waiver has been issued. Usually it provides authority to spend money or make a purchase, so that information can be captured as those actions occur.

- Treat each waived action as a regular transaction so that it goes into the log along with everything else.

- Include the proportion of waived transactions by dollar value and percentage in any overall report.

- MOST IMPORTANTLY, furnish the governance board with a copy of all waivers issued since the last meeting.

- If the board thinks the delegated authority isn't taking the process seriously enough, the board probably won't entirely revoke that delegation. That's not how executives work. If the board registers its concerns, a couple of offline discussions with the waiver-approving executive will likely result in a significant change in attitude.

Over time – especially as the PPFMO reports metrics on the proportion of funds approved through a regular process versus those that scooted through under waiver – the waiver-approving authority will ratchet up the standard for granting such waivers. Or the governance board or some other higher-level authority will start tightening the screws from its end.

Assessment of the waiver process isn't just a matter of the number of waivers granted. The PPFMO should generate metrics that track whether the waivered activities are costing more and taking longer than equivalent actions that went through the proper planning and approval process.

In my experience, the personalized grilling from an engaged decision authority who understands the technical domain is far more intensive than the questions received from the governance board which is only generally involved in the solution space.

In all but the direst emergencies, the decision authority's questions require the program manager to go back and perform research before obtaining final permission.

The program manager may find that it's faster and less embarrassing to complete the paperwork to get the proposal approved in normal order at the next governance board meeting than to pursue a waiver.

Next Steps

In this chapter, you learned about the safety valve to permit activity to continue rather than waiting for a decision board meeting. The next chapter describes what should be happening in those meetings to set the organization on the right track and keep it there.

EXERCISE 11: BUILD A WAIVER FORM AND PROCESS

1. Customize the template waiver form for your situation (the native version of the template may be found on www.Simmer-Simmer.com).

2. Get the form approved, if that's a requirement of your organization. One of the reasons organizations become process-averse is the processes they have tend to impede progress rather than propelling it forward.

3. Train the decision authority on what it means and how to use it.

****

REQUEST FOR EMERGENCY WAIVER [TEMPLATE]

Waiver Number: _____ [call PPFMO]
Date Submitted: _____

Program:
_____

Investment:
_____

JUSTIFICATION

Investment's Objective:_____

Reason for Emergency Request:
_____

Why wasn't this foreseeable?
_____

Amount of funding required:
$_____

Source of funding:

Reallocate from within program: $ _____
Reallocate from other program: $ _____

Submitted by:
_____

Program Manager:
_____
_____

AUTHORIZATION

In my capacity as Decision Authority for this request, I have decided this matter needs to move forward without waiting for standard review processes.

I have considered the risks and potential implications of this request. In my professional judgment, the need for speed is more important than the potential risk.

[   ] APPROVED
[   ] APPROVED only to proceed to the following process step:

_____

Decision Authority:
_____

Signature:_____

PPFMO Implementation

    _____ Recorded
    _____ Governance board validation
    _____ Baseline adjusted

Chapter Twelve

Taste Before Serving: Oversight

While there are many good doers and many good planners, few have great insight **and** can effectively execute plans. If all program managers were superstars, your organization probably wouldn't be process-averse, or perhaps it just wouldn't matter.

Many best practice models assume that having skills in PPFM-related undertakings can be codified into a checklist, and that it's just a matter of finding a good recipe and following it. I own one of Italian chef Mario Batali's cookbooks. But I can assure you that unless it's a real fluke that day, you're not going to get any gourmet meal if I'm the one doing the cooking.

Checklists work fairly well in the planning phases where the situation remains firmly planted on the paper. However, once you get into operations, things become a lot more fluid.

Since 1969, adults and children around the world have watched the educational television show, "Sesame Street."

Image credit: www.comicvine.com

Do you remember the Swedish Chef who wore the uniform and had all the kitchen equipment? During his cooking segments, ingredients and utensils would fly everywhere. Things never worked out too well for the well-intentioned chef.

You might have seen that type of scenario at work. Plenty of money is allocated, highly-trained project managers are assigned, and a governance board is in place and actively reviewing business cases.

So how it is possible the Standish Group and the Federal IT Dashboard (to cite a couple of sources) keep showing billions of dollars of failing projects? Corollary to Murphy's Law: when you've planned for every imaginable contingency, the actual event is always much worse than anyone could possibly have imagined.

As a project progresses, normal human interactions including errors, things that go wrong, and even some deliberate resistance are going to occur. The science of project management attempts to develop protective measures that can minimize turbulent events, if not eliminate them altogether. But as the reports continue to show, checklists are no match for Murphy's Law.

The fact is, once the project starts, bringing it safely to completion requires skills far beyond simple manipulation of a Gantt chart. Leadership (usually without much authority) heads the list.

Skills like tact, diplomacy, communication, and interpersonal relationship-building don't lend themselves to international standards, and they certainly can't be simulated with checklists.

Many organizations have elaborate processes for allocating funds and approving work, but nothing beyond that. Work goes from a business case directly to success or failure without coming up for air, unless the program needs more money.

You can have a great recipe, the best ingredients and capable cooks. But that's not enough. You have to check the process as it's cooking. In all too many organizations, once work starts it's never heard from again. *That is, until it fails.*

If the PPFM disciplines are criticized for anything, it's too strong of a focus on detailed status reports and in-progress artifacts (i.e., the processes of execution) without understanding why the work is being done in the first place.

That's somewhat ironic, considering that most of the published standards spend considerably more time talking about how to plan than they spend explaining how to execute. However, this doesn't mean you should also go to the extreme of forgetting about execution.

The Simmer System, with its emphasis on handoffs and in-flight coordination, somewhat redresses that balance. The system has brought you through the "why" phase and the early execution phases where you get things done by collaboration rather than as the result of formalized oversight.

Sample Frequently

Now, you're going to learn how to keep an eye on the pasta to prevent it from overcooking. On Gordon Ramsey's cooking show, "Hell's Kitchen," a terminal error is to fail to taste the dishes as they're being prepared. Sometimes when contestants (amateurs and experienced alike) find a key ingredient isn't available, or a dish isn't turning out right, they use their expertise and intuition to make minor alterations. It's always wise to test the outcome before handing the dish up for delivery to the customers.

When it's not quite right, the contestant may decide the entire thing is a mess and start over completely. Sometimes they produce a stunning replacement dish during the last 15 minutes of their allotted time. Sometimes they don't.

If they checked on it and it's safely edible (i.e., not raw) and reasonably spiced and sauced, they'll get away with it, perhaps even with commendation, despite not being as prettily presented as the other contestants' dishes. After all, it's possible that one of the other contestants committed a much worse sin.

"Did you taste this?" Ramsey questions.

"Now you mention it, it could have used a bit more salt," the contestant weakly answers. A no-brainer as Ramsey thinks seawater needs more salt.

Exasperated, Gordon hisses, "I [bleeping] told you it needed more salt. So one more time, *did you taste this*?"

Shifting their eyes to the floor, the contestant mumbles incoherently.

"If you don't want to taste it, how the [bleep] can you expect your guests will want to eat it? Aww ... [bleep] me!" Ramsey shouts, tossing the plate into the trash, which isn't the worst insult. Sometimes the aspiring chef has to eat their creation. If you don't sample the product from time to time, it should be no surprise if it turns out to "taste" unsatisfactory.

Case in point: Healthcare.gov (hopefully PPFM professionals will never forget it). Though the program reported problems early on, somehow the red stoplights got changed to green go-lights. Allegedly the program manager, who must have been a blithering idiot, was told it wasn't possible to test the system because of the multiple entities and the anticipated heavy loads that characterized this system.

Any IT professional knows that's complete nonsense. Any project professional, even one with no knowledge of IT, would have immediately identified that such a risk statement pointed the way to the very things that most needed to be tested. They just needed to figure out how to do it.

Despite the program being the most important goal in the presidential administration, and despite the impact on millions of American citizens, none of the program managers or politicians bothered to check to see what was going on. The warning signs were visible, but nobody was paying attention to them.

Actually, somebody did, since they took the trouble to change the reports. According to the Integrity principle of *The Simmer System,* that is the one thing a PPFMO can't allow. Is a billion-dollar fiasco, completely avoidable, enough to convince you of that?

Calling the Pass: Reviews and Approvals

If you were running a restaurant, you could hire the greatest chefs in the world. But it would be a complete disaster if you allowed them to cook whatever they wanted whenever they wanted. The customers wouldn't get what they ordered; in fact, it would be difficult to tell them what they could order, and the necessary ingredients wouldn't be on hand anyway.

Your diva program managers have been used to doing just that. You can't have them arguing among themselves about what needs to be done, who should do it, and who screwed it up, especially while the food is still merrily flaming away on an unattended grill. That's exactly what a process-averse organization does, and what brings the teams on Ramsey's shows to their knees.

To make a kitchen's staff work effectively, a manager "calls the pass" by monitoring customer orders, and coordinating timely delivery of dishes. They're the liaison between the executive chef, sous chef, head cook and head station chef. The manager orchestrates the pace to ensure customers have a pleasing experience that makes them want to return.

Approvals

Earlier chapters describe how the governance board organizes, gets trained, and goes into operation, while the program managers build their capability to plan and manage through collaborative efforts.

During the first few months of operation, the board holds meetings to examine priorities and fund allocation. In other words, they provide permission for programs to get started. From a maturity model perspective (even though you're not going there), the organization is steadily moving up the ladder.

> *"Less starts; more finishes."*
> ~**Common (unattributed) saying within the Agile community**

> *"99% of all projects are 99% complete for 99% of their actual duration."*
> ~**Common (unattributed) saying within the Earned Value community**

For all intents and purposes, your work is still on square one if your organization, like many others, suffers from the "starting everything and finishing nothing" syndrome. You've learned how to begin things, but now you need to get to the finish line.

Getting the Governance Board to the Front of the House

The investment approval documents may be the last deliverable anyone sees until the final product is ready to ship (often in whatever form it's in based on demands by the customer or the CFO to close out the effort). Then everyone wonders how things could have gone so wrong.

During the early days of *The Simmer System*^{SM}, lists and cooperative agreements don't specifically establish oversight activities. However, they do begin asking uncomfortable questions such as why are you doing this? Or, when will you finish it?

You read a lot of books and hear a lot of TED talks about the magic of self-guiding teams. Despite their praiseworthy intentions, those exhortations really apply only to the team level; they collapse if they expand too much. Recall Jeff Sutherland's findings from Chapter One: Scrum (the ultimate in self-guiding team methodologies) doesn't really scale very effectively. The reality is you can't guide a midsized or large organization from the rear or up from grassroots.

The governance board must set a direction and standard, and enforce the decisions it makes. Otherwise, once the managers have tested whether the new process will take hold and discovered that nobody is checking, they go back to doing things the way they were before. A murky process that delivers some results is better than a transparent one that just obstructs progress.

During the first year, the governance board should become organized and begin managing the overall delivery picture (as enabled by Agreements 3 and 4). Once the board states that it expects each program will deliver to the proposed schedule so the organization attains the capabilities it needs, the program and project managers will generally strive to achieve that.

Since the Eight Agreements (or as many as the managers come up with) are collaboratively derived, the PPFMO can't rush to mandate any review and reporting process that dictates the pace of adopting those agreements. Cooperation is the name of the game, at least during the first year.

While collecting this information, the PPFMO can compare what's being said now against what was said at an earlier time. In other words, it can create a rudimentary status report without having to require it.

The formation of the governance board is described in Chapter 6, and its activities in Chapter 9. Now you're in the third governance chapter, which is also the last of the substantive content chapters in the book. This is because it will probably take as long to get the governance process in place as it does to get the initial levels of cooperation across line units needed to work through the Agreements.

Milestones and Reviews

In the chapter on setting up the program structure, you also began work on a lifecycle model that provides the high-level phases and milestones for programs and projects. Although it applies in theory to programs, it's normally used for projects because most of the programs are already in an operational stage, and will likely remain there for many years.

Periodic Reviews

Without any pending event-based reviews, programs undergo time-based reviews at a frequency the board can manage. If possible, this should happen once per year in addition to the budget planning process (which means there are two reviews per year).

What should the program review cover? The reviews will be more elaborate if the programs are more complex. The internal content remains the same as for a small program, except the answers are longer.

Chapter Nine described the information the program needed to provide to support the board during the funding allocation decision cycle. The performance reviews would be conducted around four to eight months later, depending on the organization's calendar imperatives. Again, don't try to conduct the review in the middle of the year-end closing effort.

During the mid-year review, the program should be able to discuss the following, which is quite a bit simpler than the budget approval presentation:

- Any changes in the operational delivery metrics for the ongoing part of the program.

- The status of the new initiatives approved for the year, including expected delivery date and capability, and any issues (including cost status, if it is an issue).

This lesser amount of detail is possible because at this point there's nothing to sell and the deal is done. All you'll want to know is whether the program is going to live up to the commitments it made to the board and to the other programs that may depend on it. If that hasn't occurred, you'll need to know this as far in advance as possible so everyone can start adjusting this information accordingly.

Although there's no intent to have it that way, program managers often see the performance review as an opportunity that has little upside. The program managers may have to expose themselves to the executives to explain why they're not making their objectives, and nobody likes having to do that!

Worse, there's usually an implication the program could lose its funding if its numbers are off. But this shouldn't occur very often at the program level.

Because it has multiple initiatives going on, the program should already be shifting funds towards those efforts that offer the best likelihood of delivering the expected results.

The performance review must get away from "finding fault," and instead should be more along the lines of determining what course correction, if any, may be needed to get the program back on track so it won't be subjected to adverse budgetary decisions.

In a government setting, losing funds due to under-spending (not necessarily under-performance!) is sometimes a possibility, especially where funds are appropriated year-to-year.

As with any other program, a manager has the flexibility to allocate money internally between components. The obligation rate question applies whether or not there's a specific program governance board. It's a budget and contracting issue, and the board should avoid appearing to be the enforcer on that matter.

However, the board would have to approve where any reallocated funding should go. In good faith (and to encourage open and honest reporting in the future), the first use of funds should be towards other previously unfunded requirements within the program.

If the entire program is to be scaled back, then the board should direct funding towards its published list of prioritized, unfunded requirements. The key is not to convey the impression that the entire portfolio is up for renegotiation every time any change must be made.

Event-Based Reviews

When setting up the governance board, certain project activities were identified that merited special attention. Here's an opportunity to reinforce the value of an orderly progression through the SDLC, and to avoid overreaching simply because the tools are there.

At this point in the evolution of *The Simmer System,* the board is looking at entire programs in rather limited detail as outlined above. The Internet has a great deal of material on how to plan and guide a project (as opposed to a program).

Just because a template is available doesn't mean you need to use it, so hold your information demands to what you and the governance board really need.

The board doesn't need to conduct every review in the SDLC. The PPFMO should encourage it to delegate the more technical reviews to the organization's experts.

The governance board can then take note of the status of the project while focusing more on the larger performance questions such as when will we get it? What will we get? Do we still need it? What else depends on it?

Point to Success Rather than Pointing Fingers

Finally, whatever the content of the review meetings may be, the PPFMO's job isn't to report problems in the program or project's presentation. True, it has an obligation to the board to do so if the program manager refuses to work with the PPFMO and get significant discrepancies corrected. But wherever possible, cooperate and then give credit.

Program plans and reports are artifacts produced by the programs, not by the PPFMO. If the only reason decision packages are solid is because the PPFMO is writing them, then the organization hasn't progressed as a whole.

If you persist in doing this, then your processes become a somewhat irrelevant sideshow, while the programs are free to merrily keep doing whatever they want knowing you'll paper it over. Real success means sound decision-making based on sound information. If that is happening in your organization, the PPFMO is doing its job.

The PPFMO's larger calling is to work with the program managers to make the reviews successful. After all, the organization doesn't benefit by having its projects and their associated deliverables delayed or shut down over analytical issues any more than if they were caused by contractual or funding issues.

The PPFMO needs to make sure that presentations contain accurate data and appropriate interpretations of that data. And that the manager is well-primed for the types of questions the board members typically ask. That shift in attitude alone can make the difference between the success of your PPFMO, and the failure of the one that went before it.

Some Meat With That Sauce? Meaningful Oversight

"Trust, but verify." ~Ronald Reagan

You started the review board off with discussions of lists because that was all the information you had. It might have been surprising how many energetic discussions arose as a result of exposing the data that was in place but unused all along.

Then you had the board approve the large-scale programmatic structure and allocate funds.

As part of those decisions, the members looked at investment plans explaining all the wonders that could be if the program received money. Of course, those were just sales pitches. Now they want to know when the nice salesman is going to be back with their product. Or has this been just another scam?

You might think program managers would welcome the opportunity to show their investors (the governance board) the great work they've been doing with the money entrusted to them. But you would be wrong.

People hate being evaluated, even when they know they did a good job. There are too many quirks in a process that involve the subjectivity of a half-dozen human beings, so the executive boards seem like a high-risk proposition just because of who the members are.

You seldom see these individuals in person. Maybe you've seen their names on the organization's website. If the review goes well, that's just to be expected. If it doesn't, "you know what" rolls downhill. So wouldn't it be nicer if your work could speak for itself?

Again, you have an opportunity to portray the helpful PPFMO. The more the process is about validating progress, and focusing the board's attention on identifying and alleviating obstacles, the less need there is for the program managers to be disingenuous in their presentations.

If the process brings the program manager into the board meeting surrounded by green flags (no, not literally! I mean a report card – although if your organization is into showmanship, go for it), the presentation can be focused on "Let me show you this great new product we rolled out this year."

If the review is going to be about getting the board's help with resolving a problem, then make it about that.

Let the "report card" provide the metric data, which will speak for itself. Given the limited time available, the PPFMO can help the program manager compile a compelling case for the root cause of the problem, and the relief needed to get it solved.

Program reviews will become more elaborate over the years. During this first year, the PPFMO will have information on the progress of the initiatives within the programs (at least with regard to scope and schedule) as soon as Agreements 3 and 4 are in place.

Once the PPFMO writes down what the program managers have initially agreed to, it's easy enough to compare that information later against what they originally agreed to.

The degree to which the board can track cost performance may depend on the timing of the PPFMO initiative. It may seem odd to a professional project or program manager to discuss reviews without mentioning costs. If it takes until deep in the fiscal year to achieve Agreements 3 and 4 between programs, that may be all that gets done until it's time for the programs to seek funding from the governance board for the first time.

High-Level Tracking

At a minimum, with Agreement 3 in hand you'll be able to offer a rollout map showing the forecasted milestone delivery dates of each initiative. When the moment is right, the PPFMO can add the tracking information to move the process to an entirely new level of maturity.

Yes, it's time for good old Microsoft Project, although I'm not endorsing the use of such tools at this point. But I am saying that if you're more comfortable with a tool to support your thought processes, then at last you've reached the point where the tool would have something to portray.

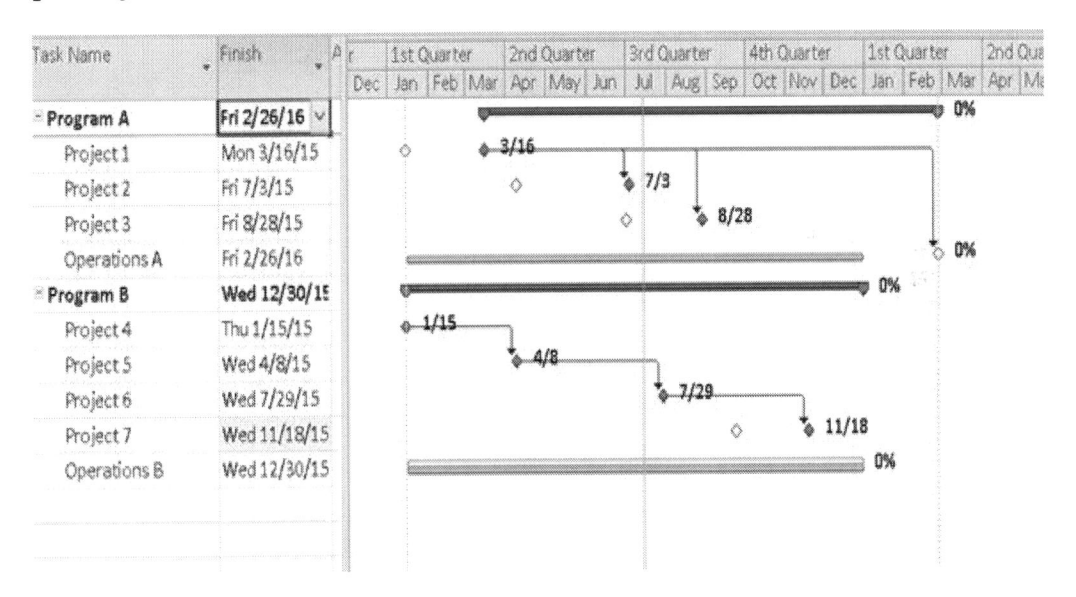

Task Name	Finish
− Program A	Fri 2/26/16
Project 1	Mon 3/16/15
Project 2	Fri 7/3/15
Project 3	Fri 8/28/15
Operations A	Fri 2/26/16
− Program B	Wed 12/30/15
Project 4	Thu 1/15/15
Project 5	Wed 4/8/15
Project 6	Wed 7/29/15
Project 7	Wed 11/18/15
Operations B	Wed 12/30/15

But wait ... there's even more!

Agreement 5 provides for an assessment of the resources required to complete the main sections of the work. From the lists phase, the PPFMO already has an idea of the total capacity available.

This isn't a very precise measure because you don't know when the resources will be used on each project until you've defined all the phases.

However, you can start making allocations of the resources that will work throughout the life of the project. Since these resources tend to be in demand by all projects (e.g. architects, security analysts and project managers), they tend to be over-allocated, so this is worth bringing up early.

What if a project manager is allocated at a 200% level? This is nothing! It's not uncommon to find project managers and other key resources assigned to six or more projects at a time. But just because it happens a lot, that doesn't mean it works. When an organization's key resources become taxed beyond their capacity, it should be no surprise if the projects fall behind.

The board may decide to issue policies to control resource allocation problems (e.g., requiring that key resources are assigned to projects at least 25% up to 100% of the time, depending on the complexity of the project, and aren't assigned over 125%).

Although cooperative agreements occur between the individual project or program managers, only the PPFMO can assemble information across projects, and portray the situation across the enterprise.

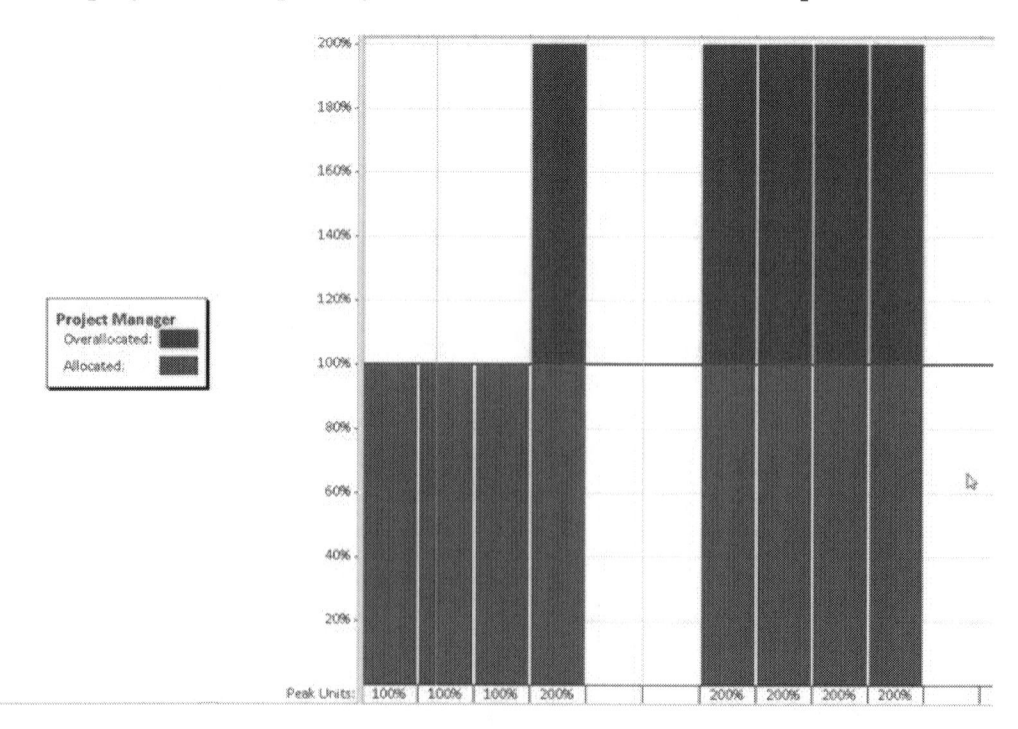

Until Agreement 6 is in place, you won't know when the resource handoffs will occur (Agreement 1 only offered a lead-time warning for the current work step).

Once Agreement 6 goes into effect, you'll know when the internal transfers will take place, and when the key resources will and won't be needed (in other words, when the major phases begin and end).

Now you're able to construct the internal phases that make up each initiative. At the PPFMO level, hold your charts to include only the program and the designated projects. Those internal phase milestones aren't for the governance board.

Even if you have more detail, leave the impression that you aren't looking. But offer the tool to the program managers. It's better if everyone uses the same source of information.

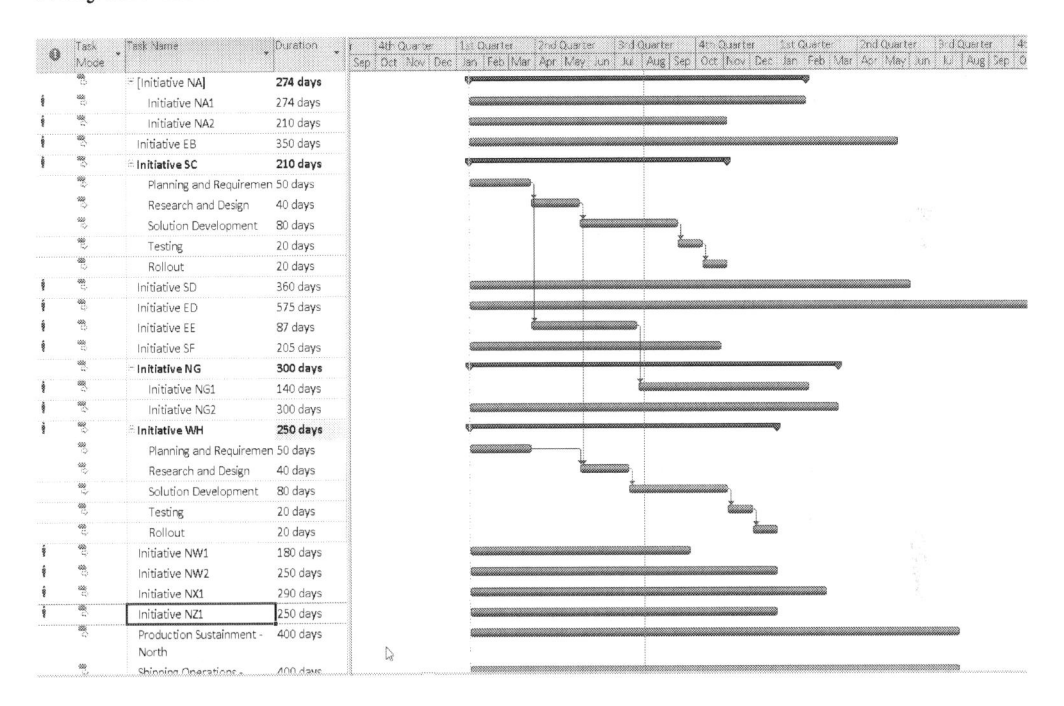

Task Name	Duration
[Initiative NA]	274 days
Initiative NA1	274 days
Initiative NA2	210 days
Initiative EB	350 days
Initiative SC	210 days
Planning and Requiremen	50 days
Research and Design	40 days
Solution Development	80 days
Testing	20 days
Rollout	20 days
Initiative SD	360 days
Initiative ED	575 days
Initiative EE	87 days
Initiative SF	205 days
Initiative NG	300 days
Initiative NG1	140 days
Initiative NG2	300 days
Initiative WH	250 days
Planning and Requiremen	50 days
Research and Design	40 days
Solution Development	80 days
Testing	20 days
Rollout	20 days
Initiative NW1	180 days
Initiative NW2	250 days
Initiative NX1	290 days
Initiative NZ1	250 days
Production Sustainment - North	400 days
Shipping Operations -	400 days

Suddenly, you have a rather sophisticated program schedule, considering that just a few months earlier you didn't know what the organization was working on. You'll also have a detailed understanding of your resource loading.

Dependencies

At any level of a PPFMO hierarchy, one of the core responsibilities is to make sure various groupings' work remains synchronized.

During the Agreements phase, you determined when the programs were going to hand off to one another, and you did further research to place that handoff in context. Now that you have a standard depiction of a lifecycle, you can refine the enterprise schedule.

The resources web site (www.Simmer-System.com) contains a sample of such a program schedule.

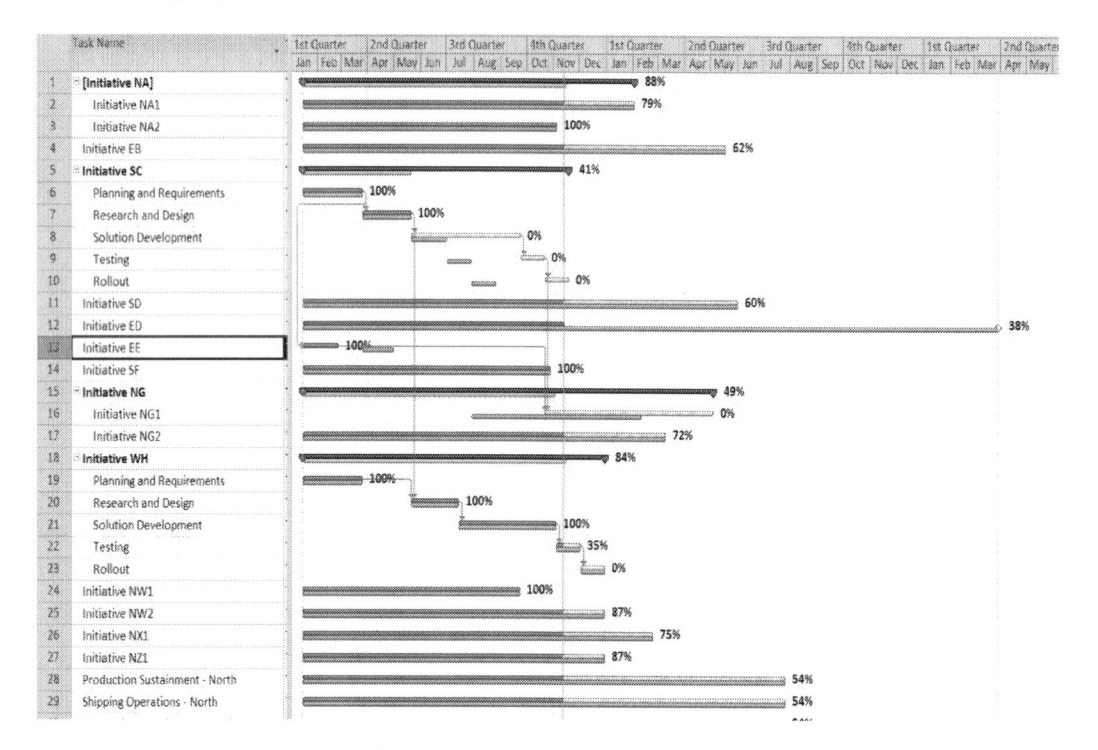

Attention to the dependencies early on can limit delays in initiatives. Perhaps the initiative manager may be lulled into complacency by the completion of its first predecessor three months ahead of schedule.

But another predecessor initiative may be four months overdue, and is taking with it the ability to begin another initiative.

Dependency management allows you to focus on these cross-initiative impacts without getting too deeply involved in the specifics within the individual initiatives.

Now that you've noticed it, you can take some action. Perhaps the potentially-impacted initiative can get started anyway, adjusting its plan so that the real dependency only shows up later in the lifecycle.

Perhaps the governance board can assist in clearing away whatever problem is holding up the floundering initiative, or perhaps it doesn't matter.

In any event, until you had visibility over the dependencies, you weren't in a position to take any corrective action. Now you are.

Red is Good, But Orange is Better

The PPFMO can do even more. Much of this book emphasizes that the governance board and its PPFMO aren't responsible only for the mechanics of project management; their primary role is to optimize the progress towards the organization's goals. The dashboard-style charts provided on the resources website (www.Simmer-System.com) portray only a few items of information to better illustrate the point, and at first that is what you should do too. As time goes on, you'll add many more to suit your board.

Thanks to what you learned in earlier chapters, you should understand the linkages between all elements of the work and the programs and strategic goals those elements support. You've also gathered enough information to provide the governance board with surprisingly comprehensive reports. Keep them simple enough to allow them to speak for themselves.

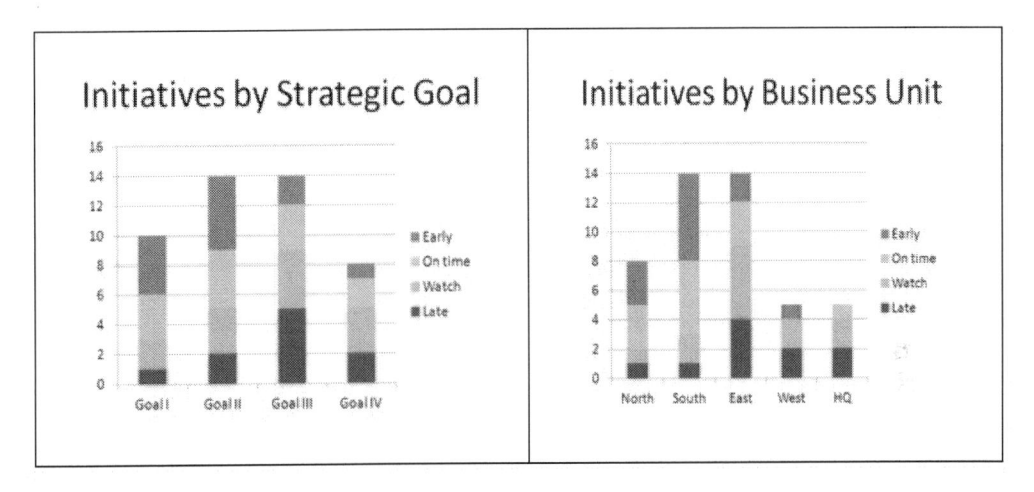

The temperature will rise once you start distributing these reports. **Beware the boil-over!** Even in the best of organizations, program managers don't like having their program called out in front of other people, even if everyone knows they're behind schedule or over-running their budget.

A good proportion of the initiatives having problems are probably guided by the same people giving the PPFMO the hardest time. However, you must resist the temptation to gloat.

Unless the situation's temperature reaches outrage, the organization isn't overtly going to do anything about it. Try not to be judgmental: just publish the facts and let them speak for themselves. The credibility of the complainers will eventually erode.

Raising a fuss can force a confrontation you can't win, and makes people take sides far too early. Payback isn't your problem, so just help the program managers to get the metrics moving the right way. Eventually, the real "problem children" will have their own island of red initiatives amidst a sea of green.

Delays and overruns are not always the program manager's fault. In an early stage organization, there are sure to be institutional deficiencies that create challenges to getting things done in an orderly manner.

It's very likely that the commitment date or project budget decisions didn't take the full range of the estimate into consideration. Quite often, the organization latches on to the most optimistic date as the baseline.

Your peer managers will be knowingly nodding their heads as those counterarguments are brought up – "Yep, that's how it is. Happens to me all the time." – so it's better to focus your effort on resolution of the institutional issues.

To keep the system simmering on a long-term basis, the PPFMO director must emphasize to the board members that the objective is to correct the situation and its root causes, and not to heap blame on the project team.

The reaction to dashboards and charts shouldn't be "Who's running those red initiatives?" It needs to be "Let's look at the issues those initiatives have been raising to see how we can help." Once the right questions are asked, reporting will be more accurate and timely.

Red is good when it gets action. But it isn't good if it's a surprise.

A red condition should have been preceded for weeks or months by an orange or yellow rating, which would have alerted the PPFMO and other programs that there were problems to resolve.

That's the PPFMO's cue to convene coordination meetings to get the matters resolved while the solutions are still fairly simple.

Therefore, if red is good, orange is much better.

Clearing Away the Clutter: Issues Management

"Life is what happens while you are making other plans."
~John Lennon

By their definition, a project implies doing something new, so there will undoubtedly be hiccups along the way.

The PPFMO must provide a means of tracking issues and their resolution to make sure they don't disappear. While many organizations keep issues logs (a template is provided on the resources web site), others never get around to doing anything about them.

The PPFMO must institute an escalation process that moves issues to the attention of people who can resolve them. The failure to do that lies at the heart of many PPFM failures.

If the project teams identify issues, but nobody does anything about them, that's a sign (and rightfully so) that nobody really cares. So why cooperate with the PPFMO and expose yourself to managerial wrath if nothing's going to happen?

Now is when the executives can earn their hefty paychecks by clearing some of these obstacles out of the way. When the vendor's senior management receives a call from senior executives who have a whole bunch of the vendor's contracts and unpaid invoices in their hands, the vendor who's been giving the project manager a limp leg suddenly finds time to meet the deadline and reassign resources.

Or the division chief who constantly reneges on providing his people when they are needed suddenly cooperates before the program manager has time to brief the senior VP that the program is falling behind schedule, and is burning contractor dollars, because that division's staff hasn't been able to hold up their end of the load. And so on.

My experience has been that the PPFMO starts to turn the corner when the first project manager declares a "red" issue and resources suddenly rain on the project.

True, this tends to come with more ongoing executive involvement than usual. Project managers tend to accept that oversight as the price of getting help, and others learn by example. The next thing you know, everybody wants their projects to report "red."

Seeing Red

Red gets action, so red is good. And as you now realize, orange is even better.

The problem with waving a red flag to get attention (and resources) is that by the time you declare the baseline is compromised, it's often too late to do anything that would bring the work back on track. It would be far more useful if the project manager would declare an orange condition in a timely manner; then you could get started resolving the situation much sooner.

It will be far too long before that first "red" report is delivered, even though you can see things aren't as they should be. Recognize that in the past the organization has considered bringing up issues at all to be a highly provocative action. The first person to take that route is only taking that risk because they're desperate, and are probably thinking that turning in that first red status will lead to nothing but martyrdom.

Many organizational cultures suggest that asking for help is whining, throwing colleagues under the bus to blame them for one's own failures, or a demonstration of incompetence. If any of those are the case, that dynamic needs to change.

Executives must emphasize that the cardinal sin – the thing that can get a program manager fired – is failing to deliver without having asked for help along the way.

Can this lead to an overdose of requests for assistance, and cause the project managers to be seen as whiners or alarmists? Yes, it can, although I've seldom seen it happen (at least out in the open).

Another reason why managers might be unwilling to seek help is that any additional resources could change the project's business case, and lead to a decision to cancel the project rather than reinforcing it.

For instance:

- A need to inject additional funds may dilute a reasonable return on investment to a level that's no longer desirable.

- A delay in delivery may cost the period of market advantage that was going to generate the revenues justifying the project. Or it might make it a better idea to skip a technical generation, and wait for the next best thing instead of investing in yesterday's good thing.

Pulling resources from other projects also has both real and opportunity costs (not to mention earning enmity from other program managers). Again, this is best mitigated by focusing on the point of this and all projects in meeting key corporate objectives.

Project managers need to believe they're better served fulfilling those objectives than earning credits for finishing a project that has outlived its usefulness.

A corollary to this kind of thought process is the "cooperate and graduate" syndrome. Usually used by the offending party, the idea is that sooner or later the other party is going to need help. If the offender is ratted out now, that help may not be forthcoming in the future. Of course, this skirts the issue that help was needed but not provided because it wasn't asked for.

Unfortunately, it's an unavoidable reality that the project managers (and to some extent the program managers) have too much of their personal career prospects beholden to the continuation of the project.

Managers who will be laid off along with their teams are likely to put the project and their personal tenures ahead of the organization's priorities.

Reporting Tools: Dashboards or Yellow Pads?

When it comes to reporting, do whatever works.

Less is usually more. Identify and collect useful information, then get on with it. However rudimentary, common acceptance of a process is the starting point for continued improvement.

Don't fall into the trap of allowing a committee (many of whom would rather see the whole matter go away) to spend time coming to a consensus on what needs to be reported (an area where starting from the top is both quick and sensible).

As you learned back in the chapter on the case studies, your strongest argument is that something is required by law or your friendly regulator. If that's not the case, if information is required by the executive board, then set that up as the foundation for your data-gathering efforts. Until you see what does and doesn't work, avoid asking for more than is needed to keep the process evolving in the right direction.

There are no rules on style. If it works, do it. If it doesn't work, then stop. Each organization will find a comfort level in different ways. Some love the flash-and-glitz of automated dashboard systems, and only worry later about whether they're saying anything useful.

Some executive groups would rather hear a story, hopefully one supported by a thin layer of facts and figures. Inflicting one method of conveying information upon an organization that can only communicate in another medium is a complete waste of time.

Now for a very strong caution for those of you coming from organizations with somewhat established program and project management disciplines: Tools that professional project managers have been used to working with are probably going to be as much of a hindrance as help in this early stage of implementation.

Integrated master schedules and other tools can lead a board down the path of trying to manage the details of the projects within the programs. They also provide the illusion of accuracy down to a detailed level, when in reality the plans are completely conjectural.

If you have bad information, an automated system can help you get bad data faster. There's nothing wrong with project managers having elaborate tools, and effectively managing their piece of the work even within a situation of organizational disarray. The purpose of the governance board isn't to manage each of the initiatives, but to manage them as a whole.

In support of that, the PPFMO needs to be able to look across all programs. Not to make sure each one is on track, but to ensure they're on track with each other. Seldom needing a 10,000-line Gantt chart, the board will more likely need "artsy" displays that tell a story that they and everyone else in the organization can understand.

The fact is PPFM is about a philosophy and not about a mechanical process. Almost any communications media and format can be used if it conveys the right messages, and results in the appropriate actions. Some have reached success with powerful portfolio management support tools and Internet-based collaboration systems. Others have been equally effective with nothing more than index cards, hand-drawn posters, and registers written on legal paper pads.

That isn't to say the PPFMO doesn't need automation support. At this early stage of the game, you can organize data on Excel spreadsheets for a large number of projects, and use Excel-based displays as rollout calendars (think of them as ultra-high-level Gantt charts).

This approach has worked for portfolios of up to 150 initiatives costing over $100 million annually, so it should work for your organization as well.

With the advent of Microsoft 365, a small organization can afford SharePoint or any other equivalent Web publishing tools that can add richness to the mix. However, keep in mind you're in the early adoption stage. The fact that a tool can store information doesn't mean you need to use that information, or even collect it.

Focus on asking programs only for information that's needed to address a particular oversight use case that's clearly within the PPFMO's responsibility to support the governance board. Then allow the program managers to instigate the demands to add more detail to the process and systems.

As long as you adhere to the principle that no data is presented to the board unless it conforms to what's already been collected and verified in accordance with the agreed process, program managers will insist on the need for additional data to support their funding plans.

Next Steps

Congratulations! You've made it to the end of *The Simmer System*, and should be in a great place.

The exercises should have proven that you've established a reasonably robust PPFM operation. You've done it on soil that was thought to be infertile, and with a minimum of infighting and bad feelings. Your PPFMO is viewed as helpful and contributing towards the smooth execution of organizational priorities.

Look back and see how far you've come! Don't forget to congratulate yourself and your team, and your peer managers who did most of the work.

When this process started, the organization was floundering. Work groups were at best throwing stuff over the wall to each other, if not being suspicious or even downright hostile. Now you're ready for several new opportunities:

Solidify processes: The processes that are coming together aren't going to be the end-state for your organization (that's not news for many of you). Even the giant systems integrators don't use the full set of known best practices, so you'll always be tinkering and improving them.

In addition, not everybody is using these processes. So you'll have a lot of work to do in spreading them across just your part of the organization.

Qualify the staff: If the organization is just getting started in PPFM, much of the content might be new to many staff members. Even though it's mostly common sense, they need to be shown what to do.

The biggest problem will be the people who know something else. They might not be practicing what they learned elsewhere, but they'll be more than happy to tell you that what you're doing isn't measuring up to the way it was done at XYZ. Either way, there will be lots of training or coaching required.

A word of advice: Now that something is working, don't send anyone to a course to learn how to do it another way. Besides, the PPFMO staff gains extra credibility by serving as the instructors, so teach people what's working and what to do now. Later on they can get generic training for professional development.

Bring on the consultants: Until now, money spent on consultants would be largely wasted. They can't do all the internal peer level discussions needed to get the corporate culture turned around. Nor can they undertake the negotiations and concessions that will occur to keep things simmering (still cooking without boiling over). You'll just be paying for their time while they wait for the organization to settle on things. By the end of *The Simmer System*, the organization has learned to tolerate a little process and seen the benefit of it. Now you can afford a raft of people to help make the processes more robust and start moving *slowly* towards best practices.

Bring on the tool: You saw in this chapter that you're reaching the point of overwhelming the PPFMO's capability to produce useful artifacts from common Microsoft Office products. So you'll need a scheduling tool that can handle the number of initiatives the PPFMO must track. If your organization has a collaboration platform, that and the scheduling tool would be sufficient for any organization that's only a year or so into this sort of process, especially if they can integrate with each other.

Well, you've reviewed where you've been and where you can go next. I hope you've enjoyed the ride! If you did, please hop on over to the website where you bought the book and leave a positive review, as it helps people decide whether or not to purchase the book.

In addition, more reviews help the book show up in Internet searches, so other people can find it. A review on Amazon is always welcome!

There's only so much that can be included in one book, and every situation brings its own nuances and twists.

The Conclusion (you didn't really want a book with 13 chapters, did you?) provides you with leads to additional free material and a source of periodic updates. It's a very short section, so do this easy exercise and then come on back to the next section.

EXERCISE 12: MEASURING YOUR PROGRESS

Hooray! This is the last exercise. Once you've completed it your organization will have implemented the entire *Simmer System*. (Remember, you can find editable templates and examples at www.Simmer-System.com.)

Throughout the chapters you've seen examples of information the PPFMO has the ability to create with the information gathered thus far. If you haven't done so already, create the following for your organization:

- **WBS Dictionary** listing all programs and initiatives, including their intended outcomes and scopes.

- **Program Baseline** showing the current approved performance requirements, delivery dates, and budgets for all programs and initiatives.

- **Master Schedule** showing all programs and initiatives within the programs.

- **Budget** showing allocations of funds to all programs for the coming year, and planned or proposed allocations out to as many years as the organization builds its financial plans.

- **Resource Capacity Chart** showing the needs and availability of key resource types, at least for the coming fiscal period. This view may need to be longer if the organization takes a long time to hire (yes, government, we're looking at you – especially where clearances are involved). Your window should be at least four times as long as it takes to bring someone on board, from the time the need is identified to the time they're ready to participate.

- **Dependency Log** (may be created with the scheduling tool), **Issues Log**, **Change Control Log**

- **Governance Board Operating Procedure**, including:

  o procedures for programs to submit annual proposed budgets and initiatives;
  o a Development Lifecycle model that establishes event-driven review requirements;
  o templates for decision packages to support approval, milestone and periodic reviews;

- operating calendar showing meetings and the topics to be addressed (i.e., there are points in the year when the agenda must be the upcoming budget, or end-of-year financials). The board may want to block other times for designated activities, the point of which is to achieve the proper balance of board workload and delegation;
- Periodic status report procedure and format.

If you think I forgot anything, please add it to your list. See how much progress you've made?

Though I said you weren't going to worry about maturity models, now is the time to congratulate yourself.

If you're in the private sector, see if your company has a Gartner subscription. If they do, get their PPM maturity model (Gartner's competitor organizations such as Forrester and the Corporate Executive Board probably have similar offerings).

If you're in the public sector, take a look at the Government Accountability Office (GAO) maturity model, current publication 04-394G. It periodically changes, so go to their website to get the latest version at www.gao.gov.

Then look to see how many of the program and portfolio activities your organization is now doing. On the maturity models, you may find that you're deep into Level 3. But you can't score above Level 2 because you haven't published standard practices for managing projects within programs.

You may be surprised to learn the organization already has fairly solid project management practices that are widely available skills (after all, the data is somehow coming up to the PPFMO).

Now that the PPFM structure has fallen into place, that dormant expertise may be flourishing again. If not, then you have a focus for the coming year.

Finally, I'd like to suggest redoing the exercises in Chapters 1 and 2 because I think you'll see a dramatic change in your attitude towards your workplace and colleagues, and your contributions. That alone should be well worth the journey.

Conclusion

This section is a quick recap of *The Simmer System*^{SM}, and provides you with access to resources. *The Simmer System* will:

- Help you get project, portfolio and program management (PPFM) working in your organization.
- Greatly reduce the pain and conflict typically involved in trying to induce major behavioral change.
- Get results quicker than you imagined possible.
- Ensure that the results will stick once you've worked through this process.

It relies on four core principles:

1. **The Pasta Principle:** Everything is connected to everything else. The strategic plan, budget, staff resources, project reports and governance board all fit together. Start wherever you can stick a fork into the "noodles," and the rest will follow soon enough. Just keep moving forward.

2. **Zero-Sum:** Set up the governance processes to include all money, people and effort. There are no secret pots. That way, the organization has to make the tradeoffs explicit.

3. **Integrity:** The PPFMO may compromise on many things, but not its integrity. It must never shade the truth to avoid a conflict, because as soon as it does the exercise is over.

4. **Purposeful Humility:** Take on the tasks nobody else wants, as long as they help you achieve your goals.

Before the PPFMO has gotten underway, you can make significant advances by gathering and understanding the information the organization already has:

- organizational chart, missions and functions
- strategic plans
- personnel rosters and skill sets
- budgets
- contracts
- priorities
- projects and activities

Once you understand how the organization actually functions, you can serve as an honest broker to the line managers by helping them form cooperative agreements that increase the overall process maturity from the ground up:

- What elements of work will need to be transferred from one group to another (dependencies)?

- The expected lead time for element handoff.

- The date when each initiative will be completed (top-level or milestone schedule).

- A high-level description of the end product of each initiative (definition of done).

- A category-level understanding of the types of resources that will perform the main elements of the work.

- The expected dates when dependent work will be transferred (internal milestones).

- The condition of the work when it's transferred.

- The methods by which you'll remove obstacles by escalating and resolving issues.

If you can gain consensus for several of these points all at once, so much the better.

The Simmer System also covered how to gain top-level support, and how to set up and operate the governance board that must orchestrate this work.

In addition, I'd like to welcome you to a community of *Simmer System* graduates. So please join them at www.Simmer-System.com.

If you need help or advice on how to keep things moving, pick up the phone or send an email (for the latest contact information, please check the website). It's the least I can do to thank you for having made it to the end of the book.

As I think of additional things, they'll be made available to you on the website.

Since I didn't get your contact information when you purchased *Let It Simmer*, you'll need to come to the website for materials and resources, and to opt-in to get alerts for the updates and freebies.

Please don't be shy about submitting your comments as I (and other professionals as well) would be very interested in hearing your spins and experiences on this topic.

So come on down!

Douglas M. Brown

Resources

I owe great thanks to many luminaries in the professional authorship field who derive substantial revenues for providing their hard-won advice, but have been kind enough to provide me and many other early-stage authors with more information than anyone could possibly absorb at little or no cost.

Vouching for their authenticity, I encourage you to turn to them if you need guidance in the business of producing a book, and I have provided links to their businesses.

Every one of these resources proved to be inspirational and incredibly useful:

Alex Mandossian (twitter: @AlexMandossian), creator of the Virtual Book Tour concept, whom I found on a Google Hangout. He steered me to the many other generous people who helped me get on the road to publishing *Let It Simmer*.
www.alexmandossian.com

Chandler Bolt, who assembled a superb group of luminaries for his Self-Publishing School series.
www.self-publishingschool.com

Christine Kloser, who assembled a stellar cast for the Transformation Authors Experience in 2015. I'm still drawing on her valuable resources from that remarkable week.
www.christinekloser.com

John Eggen, whose very pragmatic view of writing in a focused way was critical in getting this book off the "someday" list.
www.missionpublishing.net

Vic Johnson, whose very specific tips in his book, *How to Write a Book in a Weekend* (although this book took a great deal longer than that!) and in a stream of perfectly-targeted follow-up resources allowed me to wrap up the project.
www.vicjohnson.com

Rob Kosberg, who provided a series of highly informative webinars of his own, and pointed the way to many other top-notch resources, which convinced me that writing, then publishing, this book was not only feasible but the only sensible thing to do.
www.BestSellerPublishing.com

References

The references section is available in PDF form with clickable links on the resources website (www.Simmer-System.com).

Definition of Cynefin
https://en.wikipedia.org/wiki/Cynefin

Lavalle, Ricardo Guido (22 August, 2015): *Cypher's Syndrome*. Mind the Gap blog.
http://blog.gap-baseddelivery.com/2015/08/cyphers-syndrome.html

Rockwell, Dan (28 July, 2015: *7 Responses to Reasoned Resistance*. Leadership Freak blog.
https://leadershipfreak.wordpress.com/2015/07/28/7-responses-to-reasoned-resistance/

Rockwell, Dan (14 July, 2015): *The Real Truth about Fear*. Leadership Freak blog.
https://leadershipfreak.wordpress.com/2015/07/14/the-real-truth-about-fear/

Suster, Mark (26 July, 2015). *What You Can Learn from a Scorpion*. "Both Sides of the Table" blog.
http://www.bothsidesofthetable.com/2015/07/26/what-you-can-learn-from-a-scorpion/

Sutherland, Jeff (5 June, 2015: *Scrum as a Teenager: A Retrospective from Jeff Sutherland*. Business and IT Decisions.
http://governancehelp.blogspot.com/2015/06/scrum-as-teenager-retrospective-from.html

Your Motivational Speaker – Grant Baldwin (13 May, 2014).
https://www.youtube.com/watch?v=P_dYkNeNwTk

About the Author

Douglas Brown envisions a world where people have the right resources at the right time so they can use their creativity and expertise to achieve remarkable things in their businesses and organizations. With a Ph.D., and several professional certifications in program and project management and information technology (IT), he is well-versed in best practices.

Douglas has written two books, Let It Simmer which addresses program and project managers, and the forthcoming *Simmer Until Done* for any individual or organization.

His *Simmer System*[SM] (www.Simmer-System.com) provides steps for getting the initial situation under control, then moving to a point where complex undertakings such as best practices can become realistic objectives.

Douglas gained the experience to develop his system during his more than 20 years as an internal manager and a consultant working with private sector and government organizations to install, restart or repair business processes.

Some of his more memorable experiences and results include:

- Found ways to conduct training when Army units had almost no funding, including flying them to international exercises in exotic locations.

- Built solid relations and support with officials in towns and counties across Germany during a time when the Soviet Empire, in its last gasps, was stirring up anti-US rallies.

- Found private sector alternatives for providing decent, affordable housing for military families in high cost urban areas, and for government employees (e.g. Park Rangers) in extremely remote areas.

- Built the financial model for the military base closures process.

- Built a revised environmental model that eventually replaced the ineffective Superfund program approach with a faster and far cheaper results-based method.

- Built cost models and associated management practices and data systems to effectively manage NOAA-operated fisheries facilities.

- Performed economic and policy analyses to help large organizations decide on strategies to approach the confusion of deregulated electricity markets.

- Developed the plan to clean a nuclear waste facility, then convert it into a wildlife refuge in a major metropolitan area.

- Developed pollution control and waste management practices for U.S. facilities in foreign countries.

- Helped a major financial services company transition to new products and markets.

- Built process and configuration management processes in a company building a laser-based alternative to compression mammograms.

- Helped a major IT company plan the construction of a global infrastructure.

- Helped a major telecommunication company plan and manage the build-out of a global fiber network.

- Helped a biotechnology firm set up a PPFMO based on critical chain to allow it to outperform much larger competitors by being much faster to market.

- Built one of the most competitive products in the electronic voting market.

- Helped set up PPFM functions in the newly-created Department of Homeland Security.

- Built a full-featured PPFMO at the Securities and Exchange Commission.

- Built a PPFMO that also included Enterprise Architecture at the Defense Threat Reduction Agency.

- Developed strategies and implementation approaches for mobile computing, enterprise architecture and program management in the Department of Agriculture, Department of Energy, Federal Aviation Administration, a commercial insurance company, and a truck manufacturing company – all at more or less at the same time.

- Helped build a program budgeting process and an enterprise architecture practice at the Defense Acquisition University.

- Helped build the Defense Department's cloud services architecture and cost models.

- Managed a project to build a consolidated testing platform for the Census Bureau.

- Built a PPFMO to manage petroleum storage tanks at the Federal Emergency Management Agency.

- Built a PFMO to manage the business of IT at an agency within the Department of Justice.

During the course of those engagements, and several years as a federal manager, his business analyses saved millions of dollars by bringing runaway projects and contracts under control. Notable contributions included designing the economic model for military base closures, and modeling a revision of the Superfund process that resulted in toxic waste sites getting cleaned up many times faster.

Douglas is currently the Managing Member of Decision Integration LLC (www.decisionintegration.com), a personal consultancy offering short-term workshops to get initiatives planned and moving.

The son of an international businessman and diplomat, he lived in and visited many places around the world. As he loves to travel, he was fortunate that his assignments as an Army officer included Panama and Germany (where he learned Spanish and German) as well as Asian and Central American countries. Douglas lives with his wife Lynn in Alexandria, Virginia, where they enjoy good cuisine and the Washington cultural amenities, especially live theater. Other than working, when not walking their dogs or preparing more books, articles and presentations, he spends too much money and not enough time on his boat, Bugbear.

Printed in Great Britain
by Amazon